THE THERAPEUTIC
PLAY GROUP

THE THERAPEUTIC
PLAY GROUP

MORTIMER SCHIFFER

LONDON
GEORGE ALLEN & UNWIN LTD
RUSKIN HOUSE   MUSEUM STREET

First published in Great Britain in 1971

© George Allen & Unwin Ltd., 1971

ISBN 0 04 361013 7

Printed in Great Britain
by Compton Printing Ltd
London and Aylesbury

to
My family

Contents

Improving the quality of referrals. Consultations in groups and individually. Evaluations of records. "Emergency" referrals. Direct observation. Premature identification. Timing the parent interview. Some special features of play groups within schools. The playroom in an elementary school. Timing of group meetings. Movement to and from the playroom. Perception of the group worker outside the playroom. Meetings held outside the playroom.

6. ANALYSIS OF A THERAPEUTIC PLAY GROUP IN AN ELEMENTARY SCHOOL, 142

This chapter contains the record and analysis of a play group which was conducted for three years in an elementary school in a disadvantaged area of a city. The record is focused on the behavior and the developmental changes which took place in three of the members of the group in particular. The dynamic evolution of the play group is followed from its inception to termination, after 93 group meetings.

7. A SEMINAR IN CHILD PSYCHOLOGY FOR TEACHERS, 187

Formal education influences child development. Teachers' responsibility: fostering growth experiences. Continuing seminar—longitudinal study of one play group. Goals. Composition of the seminar group. Participation of administrators—values and hazards. Starting a seminar, frequency of meetings. The beginning seminar, selective use of content. The "climate" of the seminar. Easing the process of communication. Origins of defensiveness. Fostering objectivity. Interaction within the seminar group. The unconscious "participates." Intervention—when indicated. Aggressive leadership inhibits dynamic evolution of the seminar. Neurotic determinants in interaction. Ethics—responsibility of the seminar leader. The "traditionalist" teacher in the seminar. Manifestations of anxiety. Impulsive personal disclosures. Rivalry between seminar members. The over-dependent participant. Readiness for self-evaluation.

Preface

The practice of group psychotherapy with emotionally disturbed children originated at the Child Guidance Institute of the Jewish Board of Guardians in New York City in 1934. This method of treatment was devised by S. R. Slavson, a pioneer in the field of group psychotherapy. Slavson's early experimentation and his continuing contributions during the next three decades significantly influenced group treatment practices with children, adolescents, and adults. Today, group psychotherapy is considered to be one of the essential clinical methods for treating many emotional disorders.

The first treatment groups were designed for pre-pubertal children. These were activity groups, in which children were enabled to express conflicted feelings through a sustaining relationship with a permissive therapist, over an extended period of time—as long as three or four years. Activity group therapy—as the practice was named—is an ego level form of treatment, based on principles of dynamic psychology but departing radically from traditional methods of analytic psychotherapy. Interpretations of behavior are avoided in activity group therapy; resistance and other defense mechanisms are not explored. The therapeutic outcomes evolve from a long-term supportive and rehabilitative experience in a transference relationship.* †

Activity group therapy has been used with much success in treating many emotional disorders of children who are in the upper latency period of development, between nine years of age and puberty.

I was fortunate in having had the opportunity to work with Slavson in the group treatment department of the Child Guidance Institute for many years, and subsequently when I established the first private practice using activity group therapy with children. At that time I became interested in determining whether the activity method could be used effectively in treating even younger children.

In 1950 I was in a position to experiment with group methods with children in early latency, between the approximate ages of six and nine. I discovered

* "An Introduction To Group Therapy," S. R. Slavson, International Universities Press, 1943.

† "Activity Group Therapy," a 16 mm. motion picture film of an actual treatment group which was filmed over a period of two years. S. R. Slavson and the author produced this film, which is distributed by Yeshiva University, New York City.

xi

rather quickly that some elements of activity group therapy—as I had known and practiced it earlier—were critically important as they applied to groups with younger children. The momentum of interaction in permissive groups with young children proved to be much greater than in groups containing children who were only a few years older. With young children, the psychological balance of a treatment group could change precipitously as the result of rapid modifications in the original presenting problems. The children could easily become catalyzed into acting out behavior of a manic type. Moreover, the therapist could not remain as peripheral to the interaction in the group, as is characteristic in activity group therapy; in the groups with young children it was necessary for the therapist to be more involved.

Modifications had to be made in the techniques of activity group practice, particularly with respect to the degree of permissiveness which could be safely used with younger children and also in the methods of intervention. At the same time, these changes in practice had to be accomplished without sacrificing the essential permissive quality of group treatment practice. More than usual attention had to be given to the composition of the *therapeutic play group*—as I later termed this practice—to insure that constructive interaction could be maintained at a level tolerable to the children.

The management difficulties which were encountered in the permissive therapeutic play group with young latency children were not without reward. Most of the children improved.

About the same time I began to use activity methods with young children in private practice, in 1950, I also had an unusual opportunity to experiment with therapeutic play groups in several public elementary schools, in an urban slum section. I have always believed that schools are in a position of unique vantage with respect to the implementation of programs in secondary prevention with emotionally disturbed children. This holds true for schools in most communities, and it is particularly important in urban sections with economically and socially deprived populations. The clinical resources in such communities have failed to meet the needs of more than a small percentage of those with emotional problems.

Children spend more time in schools than in any other place except for the home. For better or worse, the school represents a large part of their daily lives. The school is not only advantageously situated with respect to the identification of developmental problems in young children, but it also has great potential for carrying on both preventive and rehabilitative programs. No other community resource—including the mental health agencies—can match the potential of school-based special programs for countering the mal-experience in the lives of children.*

* Tnis applies in no less measure to the adolescent population within secondary schools.

The use of special therapeutic group practices within schools, by clinical and para-clinical personnel,* is recommended for both psychological and practical considerations. The children are in a position to experience the effects of corrective measures in the very setting which, in most cases, was instrumental in exposing their personality disabilities. When children find gratifications from participation in special therapeutic programs within schools, both their ideation of school and their attitudes toward it change. If, on the other hand, children remain handicapped by emotional disabilities, failure and frustration fuse into a continuing debilitating experience, with the result that the school itself becomes the symbol of failure. When schools do not succeed in satisfying the special needs of exceptional children, and they eventually move into the larger "group"—society— they are unprepared to cope with the more complex demands which are placed upon them. When formal schooling is over for such children, society begins to reap a harvest of hostility and frustration, displaced from home to school to community.

It was not without a degree of trepidation that I embarked on this experiment with permissive group treatment methods in the elementary school setting. I was aware of obstructive elements which are quite unique to the school, despite my conviction about the school's rehabilitative potential. The concept of the school as a setting for treating emotionally disturbed children was somewhat alien at the time I began to experiment. Even today, there are clinicians who question the feasibility of such procedures.

I have devoted several chapters of this book to clinical practices in schools because I consider the subject most important. Chapter 5 deals with concepts and problems related to clinical practice in school settings and, more specifically, with the use of the therapeutic play group. Chapter 6 is applied in its entirety to a presentation and analysis of the record of a therapeutic play group which was conducted in a public elementary school. This group is described from its beginning to termination, after more than three years of meetings. This was done to give the reader an opportunity to study the psychodynamics of a therapeutic play group, and also, to convey some appreciation of the school environment as it affects therapeutic play group practice.

Chapter 7 deals with a special group technique for fostering communication between teachers and specialists who work in the same school. There are more than a few reasons to explain why much clinical experimentation within schools has either foundered or has fallen short of its goals. Perhaps the most formidable obstacle to success is the absence of objective communication between the different disciplines. When specialists and teachers cannot utilize

---

* Guidance counselors and teachers with special training in working with maladjusted children are in this category.

their professional skills cooperatively and planfully in the interests of needy children, rehabilitative programs are doomed to failure. The continuing seminar for teachers, which is described in Chapter 7, is, in my experience, one of the more effective methods for promoting meaningful communication between educators and child guidance specialists.

From 1950 until the present time, more than one hundred therapeutic play groups have been conducted in many elementary schools of the Board of Education of the City of New York. This program is one of the services of the Bureau of Educational and Vocational Guidance, in which Bureau I serve as consultant in special group processes.

Almost all of the therapeutic play groups have been conducted by guidance counselors who were given intensive pretraining in permissive group practice before being permitted to conduct play groups. They were supervised regularly after a play group was started. The use of guidance counselors should not be interpreted as an attempt to supplant clinicians from their special fields. The need for special services for troubled children is too great and too urgent to be vitiated by unproductive debate over the relative merits of guidance counselors as practitioners with play groups. They have proved to be very effective. Moreover, the therapeutic play group is not intended as a panacea for necessary but all too often absent clinical services; nor is it offered as a single substitute for a comprehensive clinical program of psychotherapy. The minimal requirements of any program of aid for emotionally disturbed children are specialized knowledge and trained personnel. The therapeutic play group is one practice which has proved to be particularly valuable when used in schools, under suitable controls.

The reality of present needs for mental health services has been forcefully stated in the monographs of the Joint Commission for Mental Illness And Health, established by the Congress of the United States.* Unfortunate circumstances which exist in large cities with large numbers of economically and socially deprived families and with many maladjusted children, press urgently for special services. The gap between the needs of such children and the available resources will not be closed in the immediate future. This is one reality which will tolerate no futile discourse between members of different child-helping professional disciplines. Troubled children continue to remain problems to themselves and to others.

Many persons have assisted me in exploring new methods for helping maladjusted children in schools. I wish to express my gratitude to the teachers, clinicians, school administrators, and particularly to those guidance counselors who have worked laboriously in the interests of children. The large

*The Commission's monographs have been published by Basic Books, New York, (distributed by Trans-Atlantic Book Service Educational, London).

number of children who have benefited from their zealous endeavors could speak more eloquently than I in appreciation.

There are some persons to whom I am especially indebted: Mrs. Jeannette Busch, who, as a coordinator of guidance for the Board of Education in 1950, helped introduce the first experimental therapeutic play groups to schools and made easier the early tribulations associated with this innovative practice; Miss Antoinette Riordon, Assistant Superintendent of schools, retired, who supported and encouraged our early work; the late Dr. Frances Wilson, Director of the Bureau of Educational and Vocational Guidance and Dr. Morris Krugman, Associate Superintendent, retired, who made possible the extension of therapeutic play groups within the Bureau; and finally, Mrs. Daisy Shaw, present Director of the Bureau, for her continuing encouragement and—what is even more important in a large educational establishment—for maintaining the administrative flexibility which is so necessary for efficient performance.

Note: The names of all persons appearing in the records have been changed, and the content has been otherwise modified to conceal the true identities. This has been done without sacrificing the accuracy of presented material.

M. S.

1 Principles and Processes of the Therapeutic Play Group

A SYNOPSIS OF THE PLAY GROUP TREATMENT PROCESS

The therapeutic play group is a specialized group practice which is used with emotionally disturbed young children who are in the early and middle latency period of development, approximately six to nine years of age. The practice is predicated on the premise that many problems can be completely or partially resolved in the play group through a sustained, rehabilitative experience with an adult who functions as an optimal parent surrogate in relationships with the children. The therapeutic outcome derives from a process of undoing within the family analog—the play group—some of the psychological trauma which occurred during earlier development.

The process is experiential or, more accurately, reexperiential, since the children "relive" earlier periods of development, during which debilitating forces affected ego development. The therapeutic experience with the group *worker** (psychological parent), and with group members (psychological siblings), is a substitutive experience, opposing and neutralizing the destructive influences which caused distortions in ego function.

Interpretations of behavior are not made by the worker, but he must be cognizant of all communication in the group, verbal and nonverbal, in order to understand both the manifest and latent meanings of the interaction.

In practice, a play group composed of a maximum of six children, meets with a group worker once a week for about one hour, in a play room which is planfully furnished and equipped with toys, games, construction materials, and other items. The worker is permissive; behavior which would be considered unacceptable elsewhere is tolerated in the play group. For the most part the worker remains peripheral to activities in the group, but he is readily accessible to any child in need.

Acting out children soon learn that the worker is neither restrictive nor judgmental; recessive children, on the other hand, discover that they are free

* The term group "leader" is avoided because it has the connotation of active leadership by the adult. Also, play group worker should not be confused with the social group worker who is trained in working primarily with normal individuals in guided group experiences.

1

to withdraw into isolation. The worker intervenes only when the frustration tolerance of any child, or of the group itself, is being overly threatened, or to protect children from injury.

After a sustained experience in the therapeutic play group, lasting several years in most cases, children slowly develop self-confidence, skills, and increased capacities for sublimation. This is effected through complex inter-action processes in which all members of the group become involved. With egos strengthened the children eventually become more responsive to re-direction and when they have demonstrated the ability to cope effectively with the demands of normal group activities the play group is terminated.

EVOLUTIONARY PHASES OF THE THERAPEUTIC PLAY GROUP

There is always a possibility of oversimplification when a psychodynamic group process is separated into its elements and is described historically, from inception to conclusion. Because it is important to an understanding of the evolution of the therapeutic group to recognize fundamental processes and their interdependence, and to be mindful of the effects of the "timing" of experience, it is necessary to describe interrelated concepts as if they were separate for the purpose of elucidation. It must be emphasized in advance that the order of therapeutic evolution follows an elastic "timetable."

The therapeutic process in the play group is set in motion through the purposeful use of permissiveness by the group worker. The ensuing effects during the following years may be grouped into phases, each one transitional and related in some degree to experiences in prior phases. The terminal out-come is based on a psychological continuum of interaction between the children with the worker and with each other.

Preparatory Phase

Introduction to the play group and the children's initial reactions to permissiveness
Testing the reality of the new experience
Discovery and relaxation

Therapeutic Phase

This is the phase of longest duration. Its primary elements are:
Development of transference on multiple levels—toward the worker and the other children
Regression
Aggression
Abatement of anxiety and guilt
Catharsis

Reeducational Phase: Integrative, Maturational

Increased frustration tolerance and capacity for delaying gratifications
Development of personal skills; expansion of interest areas
Improved self-image
Sublimation
Success in intragroup participation; recognition from the group
Group controls become more efficient; responsiveness of the individual to the group increases
Interaction resembles that of normal groups
Transference becomes diluted; identifications move closer to reality

Termination

Temporary regression in behavior resulting from separation anxiety
Acceptance and conclusion

PERMISSIVENESS: DIFFERENTIAL USE IN GROUPS

The degree of permissiveness used in various group practices is determined in each instance by the type of group and the aims of the process. A clinician is permissive with patients in order to induce relaxation and to promote communication. An efficient teacher must also be concerned with permissiveness in determining the extent to which she can permit independent exploration on the part of children to help them learn and grow, without jeopardizing the controls necessary for integrity of the class group. On the other hand, recreational groups and even spontaneously organized sand lot teams show little tolerance for the acting out behavior of individuals. Such groups are more definitively goal directed and they must necessarily control behavior for the sake of efficiency and self-protection.

Permissiveness in the Play Group: Purpose and Effects

In highly specialized group practices, such as the therapeutic play group, permissiveness is not a *laissez-faire* attitude on the part of the worker. It is one of the technics in a planned process and its use is critically controlled by specific psychological determinants.

The basic purpose of permissiveness is to enable children to express thoughts and emotions without anxiety. Because the therapeutic process leans heavily on the role of a tolerant, understanding group worker, it is important to examine in detail the implementation of the permissive experience, differential levels of permissiveness, and the effects of permissiveness on children in play groups.

The playroom, its equipment, and the minimal use of controls by the worker have almost immediate influence on the children. As they learn that they need not fear reprisals from the adult, they become free to express attitudes and emotions which were formerly blocked or deviously expressed. When they observe that the worker is not made anxious by acting out behavior their own anxieties and guilt feelings become lessened. The children learn that the worker's tolerance and helpfulness are not predicated on the way they behave. Familiar components of adult behavior—punishment, denial, threats, inconsistency and rejection—are not evidenced by the play group worker.

The initial "discovery" of the group worker's permissiveness takes place when he fails to act in situations which usually evoke reactions from adults. The situation might be one in which children yell or argue; when paint is accidentally spilled; in any number of different ways. The immediate result of this is that the children become more aware of the responses of the worker or *the absence* of response. Because this experience is altogether unique, they begin to react with increased sensitivity to everything that goes on in the play room.

Some children become suspicious and guarded as they note the absence of controls by the worker and his failure to become angry or even mildly ir-ritated by acting out behavior. They are beginning to perceive a "new" kind of adult and their earlier ideation about authority figures is being challenged. A period of confusion follows; concepts which have already been fairly well integrated into the life experiences of the children are thrown into imbalance by entirely novel experiences in the permissive group.

The Need to Test the Reality of Permissiveness

The setting of the play room and the role of the worker are realistic imple-mentations of psychological theory, but, to the child, the highly permissive setting has an initial aspect of unreality. A parallel to this phenomenon would be the shock effect to perception which takes place in a person who steps into an experimental room in a psychological laboratory; one in which the relative sizes and positions of furniture, doors, windows and walls have been deliber-ately distorted to create a perceptual imbalance in the viewer. The viewer automatically undergoes a process of relearning in attempting to restore the equilibrium of past perception and cognition.

In like manner, the "optimal" behavior of the permissive play group worker makes a child anxious for awhile, and he attempts unconsciously to restore the equilibrium of earlier experience.

Young children tend to react to stress situations motorically, unlike adults, who have more advanced powers of reflection. It is this quality of behavior which leads children in a play group to confirm the reality of the therapeutic adult by empirical methods. This is done first through active tests, to deter-mine whether the worker's attitudes and behavior will remain consistent.

Such tests are conscious and often carefully contrived. Paint may be spat-tered "accidentally" on an easel or on the floor; a tall building of blocks may collapse with an ear-shattering crash; two or more children may convert a mild chase into more aggressive activity, such as shoving and wrestling.

Aggressive children test for the reality of the therapeutic adult by acting out and then demanding help from him; dependent children make enormous bids for attention; fearful children withdraw to the perimeter of group activity, avoiding contact with others, and then they carefully observe to see whether this defensive withdrawal, which is so important to them, will be respected by the worker. Such children test the worker vicariously, by observing his responses to others. At times it may appear as if the group as a whole is planfully testing the reality of permissiveness. This is actually not so: each child uses the group as a vehicle for his own need to explore the meaning of the new experience.

Each child is free to learn in his own way and at his own pace. The worker avoids introducing or initiating activities and does not interfere in the experiential flow of test behavior unless it becomes necessary. Intervention is determined by the requirements of special situations. Limits, if used, should be in the service of a child or the group, and they should be gentle and unobtrusive. When limits are necessary it is a good practice for the worker to initiate other activities which children find gratifying. This not only offers satisfaction but it also deflects behavior which may become excessively threatening to one or more children.

Thus, the early testing by children is a consequence of a state of tension—the imbalance created by the worker's permissive attitude. Each child attempts to find out whether the worker will become restrictive and punitive and thus confirm the accuracy of his prior ideation about authority. The worker, by continuing to be permissive in the face of acting out, creates further doubt, confusion, and sometimes anxiety. Tension increases within the group and the amount of testing also increases. If the play group has good balance in its aggressive-passive components this accelerated period of testing will be kept within the respective tolerances of the children and the worker. Occasionally it becomes necessary for the worker to deflect or limit excessive acting out by one child or by the group, when the self-limiting controls are inefficient. This must be done with care lest the basic therapeutic role be jeopardized.

During this introductory period in the play group the worker is most vulnerable. Children will "forgive" occasional errors if they are not repetitive or antithetical to the worker's essential role. However, should he prove to be inconsistent, the children's anxieties will ebb and flow and the worker then becomes another symbol of a frustrating, adult world.

Adolescents, even adults, might respond to comparable degrees of frustration with angry verbalizations, but young children, with some exceptions, find release through motor activity. Under the impetus of continuing frustration caused by poor management of the worker's role, acting out behavior will gain momentum in the play group as one child catalyzes another, and it might become necessary to end a group meeting prematurely or even to terminate the group.

After approximately six meetings of a play group—a period of time which varies somewhat with the ages of the children and the nature of their presenting problems—there is a decided lessening of test behavior. This occurs when children finally become assured of the reality of the therapeutic adult. Such an adult, although he may be entirely unique in contrast to other adults whom they have known, is no longer a threat to the integrity of prior experience. In the language of children he is "for real."

As testing abates, a short period of relaxation follows during which behavior becomes modulated. The duration of this period varies from one group to another but it is a time of much satisfaction for children. They now make contact with the worker without suspicion and they engage in more constructive work and play. Activities are more purposeful; materials are used constructively, and there is more cooperation between the children. The play room has become invested with a new quality: it is a happier place— a safe place. However, this is deceptive because it is only an interim phase, and the modulated behavior, which gives the play group an aspect of therapeutic completion, is short-lived. It is an hiatus between the period of discovery of the therapeutic adult and an extended period of therapeutic reexperience which is to follow, and which will last for *several years*.

TRANSFERENCE

Interaction Becomes More Responsive to Transference

After the children have confirmed the reality of the play group, and following a short period of relaxation, their behavior becomes more spontaneous and is influenced now by forces which are less concious. During this therapeutic phase the interaction which occurs in the group can be more readily understood if examined in the perspective of the relationship of a child to parent (worker), and child to siblings (group members). A play group becomes, for a time, the psychological parallel of the primary group, the family.

Aggression, hostility, withdrawal, rivalry, jealousy, competitiveness, attempts to monopolize the worker, and other expressive needs of disturbed children are repetitively enacted by them in the group and accepted by the worker without question. Through permissiveness the worker has relaxed some of the more severe superego controls. Because the children no longer need to test him they become more responsive to the transference. At various regressive levels they live through the experiences which earlier, in relationships with their parents, were denied, aborted or insufficiently or improperly experienced.

In the complex of transferences in the play group, in which the components of the group become interacting libidinal members who are psychologically similar to those within the actual family, there is one important difference: the worker does not duplicate the failures and errors of the parents which were primarily responsible for the genesis of emotional problems in the children. Because of this, within the play group, the children are now able to release feelings which were completely suppressed or inappropriately manifested in the form of atypical behavior or symptoms. The freedom to do this in the transference relationship, in an accepting atmosphere, brings about a reduction in guilt feelings and abatement of anxiety, both of which were consequences of hostile thoughts and negative behavior associated with real parents and siblings.*

Momentum of Development of Transference, Its Relationship to Group Size

Transference is more readily established in therapeutic practices with young children than with older ones, or with adolescents and adults. This is so because children of five and six are more dependent and, at this age, dependence becomes readily transferrable to other adults who are psychologically *in loco parentis*. Older children of eight and nine, because they are becoming less dependent and because they are more conscious of reality differences, require longer periods of time to develop transference. Their ego defenses are more firmly established.

It has been determined empirically, through experience with many groups, that six is generally the maximum number of children for a play group. When there are less than six the transference becomes intensified and interaction is more complex as a consequence. Further, when the number exceeds six the worker cannot meet the children's needs sufficiently. Other things being equal, transference tends to be deeper when groups are small because they resemble more closely the family group. If a play group is excessively large, transferences become diluted and the potential of the group as a therapeutic tool is reduced.

Permissiveness promotes the identity of the worker as an idealized parent figure. However, if a group worker cannot maintain the therapeutic role with relative consistency, the transference will vacillate between positive and negative polarity. A child may then become confused in his ideation of the worker

---

* An experiential therapeutic process such as the play group does not become involved with factors such as interpretation and insight formation, which depend on intellectualization, among other things. However, when there are sharply delineated symptoms, and severe malfunction, as in psychoneuroses, insight must be developed before there can be a resolution of problems. Therefore, such children should be treated in individual psychotherapy. It is altogether likely that an ego-level form of therapy like the therapeutic play group is helpful in preparing young children for more intensive therapy, or as a supplement to individual therapy.

and the therapeutic potential of the relationship is lost. The worker then merges with the child's earlier conceptualization of adults as being inconsistent and disappointing.

Transference Intensifies Interaction

During the therapeutic phase of development in the play group there is intensification of behavior in various areas.

Rivalry between the children (siblings) is manifested through competition, arguments, wrestling (no actual fighting is permitted), destruction of the work of others, monopolizing the worker; in other ways.

Hostility towards the worker becomes more apparent, but it is rarely acted out directly. It may be expressed against the worker through the setting by the destruction of supplies; by using tools and materials in ways other than those for which they were intended; by painting an easel instead of the paper. Dependence is manifested through excessive demands for attention, whining, arguments over the sharing of food (served as part of each meeting), refusal to eat food, sloppy personal habits, and other negative patterns.

The therapeutic phase is the longest and the most important phase in a play group's development. It is during this time that the worker's permissive and helpful attitudes, which are, in effect, forms of unconditional love,* fulfill their purpose—to provide an extended opportunity for catharsis in the therapeutic transference.† The worker's patience and skill undergo their greatest trials during this time. Consistency and emotional equanimity must be maintained lest the children again become confused and anxious. The optimal management of the worker's role is an ultimate demonstration of "love," the force which enables children to develop security.

REGRESSION: MANIFESTATIONS AND MEANINGS

Permissiveness in the play group leads first to partial relaxation of ego defenses and in turn to alleviation of excessive guilt and anxiety. Regression takes place as a consequence. Regression is important in the therapeutic process because without it a child has no opportunity for corrective experience at levels of earlier development in which trauma originally took place. Without some degree of regression during psychotherapy there can be no significant modification in personality and behavior. The emotionally disturbed

---

* Slavson, S. R.: An Introduction to Group Therapy. New York, International Universities Press, 1943.

† In the play group, catharsis is experienced actively in the transference relationships children have with each other and with the worker. It is not exposed by the worker for objective investigation, so it remains relatively independent of ideational content. This is different from catharsis and insight formation as they occur in the psychoanalytic treatment of psychoneuroses.

child must be able to express in safety some of the feelings which were repressed or blocked during earlier developmental periods. For example, a child who may have been prevented from expressing hostility toward an actual sibling, finds an outlet for his emotion through psychological siblings in the play group. The same opportunity exists for ventilation against the libidinal object who is the psychological representative of the parent or parents—the group worker. Through such "reenactment" in the therapeutic setting, feelings which were blocked by anxiety become discharged, partially or completely.

The amount of regression which occurs with each child is determined in a play group by factors such as: the age of the child, the nature of earlier life experiences, the reactions of other group members, the quality and quantity of permissiveness, and the degree of transference between a child and the worker.

Young children of five and six years of age are emotionally labile, and the worker must be alert to the amount of regressive behavior that such children, *or the interacting group*, can sustain without engendering excessive anxiety. Children cannot cope with primitive, impulsive behavior which may be set in motion prematurely through the uncritical use of permissiveness. Under such circumstances a play group of young children can become quickly catalyzed by the regressive behavior of one child, and as a result, the group as a whole may become massively activated and destructive.

The regressive behavior which takes place in permissive, therapeutic group practice with children *is a phase in psychotherapy; it is not a therapeutic outcome*.* It is a time in which faults or lacunas in development can be remedied. Because this is a part of a dynamic continuum—since a child may be in a play group for several years—there can be an actual working through of conflict areas which are central to a child's problem. Eventually, through the impact of other, integrative forces in the play group, regressive behavior diminishes and is replaced by socially acceptable behavior.

AGGRESSION: ORIGIN AND MANIFESTATIONS

There are differing views about the nature of aggression and the individual's adaptations to it, but it is generally accepted that aggression is an essential part of man's genetically determined inheritance. Its expressive pathways in each individual are determined by developmental experiences starting at birth.

* The author feels this warrants reiteration. He has observed permissive group practices in which the acting out which is typical of regressive behavior is interpreted by some practitioners as a sign of "freedom," a desirable *outcome*. While it is true that such behavior is an indication that a child feels free to express himself, it must not be considered an end in itself. To do so leads to technical errors in the use of permissiveness and intervention.

From a psychobiologic viewpoint, tension which accompanies feelings of aggression can be partially or completely neutralized through motor activity. An infant gives full expression to frustration through screaming, thrashing about, and even biting. A tantrum in an older child is an unbridled form of behavior in which much aggression is discharged. As the child grows, various forces—family, school, society—bring about alterations in the more dramatic manifestations of aggression. The child must learn to control impulsive behavior or to modify it lest it evoke retaliation from adults. Primitive forms of aggression must be altogether repressed because they would be too disabling if released. Thus, as a result of prohibiting and modifying influences on the child, aggression begins to assume multiple guises as it finds discharge through direct and indirect pathways.

In sublimated forms, some of a child's aggression becomes useful in helping him cope successfully with his expanding world. He discovers many socially acceptable outlets for the direct release of aggression. Among these are active and competitive games and sports. Vicarious experiences are provided overabundantly through television, moving pictures, and comic books.* Aggression in phantasy becomes the least direct level of experience but, within limits, it also serves a useful purpose for the child.

Reactions of Parents to the Aggression of Children

Tolerant and understanding parents can accept the existence of aggressive drives in their children, even tolerate its occasional focus on themselves, and still give assurance to the child that he is loved. It is only when a child becomes blocked from ventilating aggression by parents who prohibit it in any manifestation, or who over-react in response to it, that the child is faced with the need to suppress it. Since he may not always be able to make effective com-

* Unfortunately these communicative media are constantly exposing the viewers to the enactment of all types of aggression, with violence as a common feature. Assaultive, homicidal behavior has become as much an attribute of the "good guy" in the defense of justice, as it has historically been the privilege of the "bad guy." The fact that this has modified the aggressive play of young children has been testified to by teachers in early childhood education, who describe how children four and five years old mimic the assaultive behavior of such television characters as "Batman" and "The Green Hornet." Within the community serious aggressive acts by adolescents have been occurring with increasing frequency. These are in the nature of violent acts, committed by adolescent gangs against property and individuals, with severe injuries and homicides as a not uncommon consequence. *The alarming feature is that much of this is being perpetrated by maladjusted but nonpsychotic personalities.* In this context, this phenomenon represents a form of social pathology. The repetitive flooding of perception by pictorialized violence in television and moving pictures, has had the effect of blurring values and beliefs which were—and still are— necessary to the evolution of healthy ego defenses in the young. The unhappy result is that the "social superego" has been weakened, and aggression of a primary process type is more easily invoked.

promises, one result may be that aggression becomes internalized. This leads to excessive phantasy, symptom formation and possibly, pathological consequences.

There are some children who will continue to act aggressively in the home despite punishment. Others find it "safer" when aggression is displaced from home to school and the community.

The child who acts out severely has been exposed to much deprivation and inconsistent management by parents. When parental behavior is inconsistent, variability in the responses of a child is understandable. From his frame of reference, even a tantrum is a rational form of behavior. After all, why should he suffer deprivation in one instance when the same needs were gratified in prior situations?

Latent Meanings of Aggression

While aggression and other kinds of acting out behavior may be a result of continuing stress in parent-child relationships, the forms they take are not accidental. They are meaningfully related to the psychodynamic interplay between parents and the child. Lying, stealing, fighting, planful manipulation by the child, negativism, and other permutations of acting out behavior, are responses to specific constellatory forces within the family.*

Children are not equipped to manage aggressive feelings with the degree of restraint which adults unrealistically demand of them. Affect control and sublimation are products of maturation. The average six year old child may have learned to control much impulsive and primitive behavior in response to prohibiting forces in the family and elsewhere, but, because he is highly motoric his inner tensions must still find outlets, through physical activity to a great extent. This quality is characteristic of normal and maladjusted children.

S. R. Slavson has described the acting out behavior of children in the therapeutic process as a primary form of communication.† Such behavior is part of the "language" of childhood and it must be learned by adults who hope to work effectively with children in any professional capacity, particularly in psychotherapy.

It follows then that acting out behavior must be examined for underlying meanings within the relationships of children with each other and with adults, if its content is to be comprehended.

---

* One young child, who persistently got into difficulties in school by lying, fighting and stealing, had "learned" in some subtle way that this behavior was particularly disabling to his mother, who was an executive officer of the Parents' Association and a vocal person in community affairs.

† Slavson, S. R.: Child Psychotherapy. New York, Columbia University Press, p. 181.

Aggression in the Play Group

In the permissive play group the latent meanings of children's aggression must be learned by the worker as soon as possible because they determine, and are also influenced by, the interaction between members of the group.

Aggression of itself *serves no purpose* in the therapeutic process when its latent meanings remain unrecognizable to the worker and when its effects become intolerable, either to a child or to the group. The concept of therapeutic group practice with children as a process in which acting out behavior induced by permissiveness is of itself an end product of therapy is grossly inaccurate.

Aggression has etiology, purposiveness, and focus, despite its apparent lack of these qualities at times. In the play group, aggression may be expressed by:

    one child against another
    one child against the group
    the group against a child
    a child against the worker
    the group against the worker
    child or group against the setting (worker)
    the worker against a child or the group (counter-transference)

Aggression Against the Worker: Through the Setting and More Directly

The momentary focus of a child's aggression may be another child or the group, but the group worker is implicitly incorporated in the pattern because it is taking place within the dynamic field he has created. This is best illustrated in the astronomical type of diagram shown in Figure 1.

The umbra and penumbra represent aggression within the permissive group setting, which is actually *a psychological extension (symbol) of the worker*. Because the worker is permissive, aggression becomes safe for the

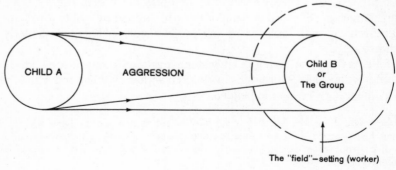

FIG. 1

child, even though the worker is within its "field." The child has become aware that the worker tolerates negative behavior without *sanctioning* or approving it.* However, as a result of earlier experiences with parents and others, he is also consciously aware of what constitutes acceptable or unacceptable behavior. Thus, when a child acts out in the play group, implicit in the context of his behavior is aggression (defiance) against the worker.

Despite the uniqueness of the therapeutic setting the worker is still a symbol of adult authority (superego), albeit a benign one. This is the factor which helps establish the transference through which the therapeutic process evolves.

At times aggression becomes more explicitly directed against the group worker. A child may express displeasure and even anger because the worker cannot supply a special toy or some other item at a given moment; he may complain because other children have taken more than a fair share of food; he may defy limits when the worker uses them.

Aggression against the person of the worker is rarely seen in play groups and if it does occur it must be stopped directly. A direct assault, as mild as it may be, may represent an enactment of an aggressive impulse with unconscious, primitive overtones. Therefore, an aggressive act on the person of the worker can lead to much anxiety in the child who performs it.

Frequently there is aggressive acting out through the setting. A child may hammer at a closet, spill paint, tear paper, throw clay at the walls, even ask the worker's assistance with a project and then deliberately destroy it. Despite its devious expression, such ventilation is important because it represents a discharge of blocked aggression (catharsis). Such symbolic attacks against the group worker are therapeutic because they afford partial release, through pathways tolerable to the child, of aggressive feelings which were originally directed toward the parents but which had to be repressed. For a period of time, in the interaction processes which take place within the play group, the worker becomes a fused symbol of a psychological parent who demonstrates complete understanding of a troubled child and his need to reexperience in the therapeutic transference, and the real parent who caused the child's difficulties.

Aggression and the Withdrawn Child

When children are inordinately fearful, aggression becomes internalized, and the consequences of this psychologically corrosive process are distortions in ego functioning, symptoms, or both. Far from being able to act out, such children "act in." In a play group some fearful children defend themselves against aggression by withdrawing temporarily whenever the interaction

* Schiffer, M.: Permissiveness versus sanction in activity group therapy. Int. J. Group Psychother. 2:255, 1952.

becomes threatening in the slightest degree. Others protect themselves even more completely through persistent, self-imposed isolation.

Blocking of aggression may stem from a child's fear of consequences to himself if his aggression becomes expressed; or a fear of its effect on others. It is primarily the latter which leads a child to isolate himself from contact so that he runs less risk of being catalyzed by the behavior of other children in the group.

The withdrawn child is a passive group member, but he is always a surreptitious and careful observer. For self-protection he must be alert to all stimuli in his immediate evironment. Because he is incapable of testing the reality of the permissive group worker, he becomes dependent on others to do so for him. For him, the initial "discovery" of the permissive play group is a vicarious one, made by observing the worker's responses, or absence of response, to acting out behavior.

When the withdrawn child finally beccmes assured that aggression can be safe, he may be ready to move out from protective encapsulation. The length of time for this to occur will depend on the degree of anxiety originally associated with his feelings of aggression. Such a child's first ventures into contact with others may not be manifestly agressive to the casual observer, but when compared with prior behavior it is definitely so. When voluntary contact is made with the group worker for the first time, it represents a considerable mobilization of aggression since the child's initial responsiveness to adults (authority) was altogether constricted.

The withdrawn child is still hypersensitive to the reactions of others when he begins to move outward and he is quick to withdraw again should he become threatened. The worker should be aware of such reactions and *avoid* being over-solicitous. The child easily misinterprets the intention of the adult who is too zealous in his interest, and he may react to it as if it were a threat. The worker may "reach" for relationship only to the extent that the withdrawn child can tolerate it. Relationship is *built* by the child—*awaited* by the worker.

If the extent of withdrawal is not pathological, as is the case in autism associated with psychosis, aggression will become manifest and it will eventually become similar to that of the other children. During this development, the child's aggression will first be expressed mildly and diffusely, without focus on individuals. A tolerance for aggression must be established before it can be exercised against other group members or the worker—the symbols of siblings and parents.

The Play Group's Reactions to the Withdrawn Child

A play group is unusually tolerant of the defensive isolation of a frightened child. Aggression in the group will flow around an isolate and rarely include him in its sphere of operation. The group will often protect an isolate if he is threatened by one of its members. However, when he is strengthened to the point where he begins to move centripetally within the play group, he becomes "fair game," and the children start to include him in the give and take of aggressive interaction. By this time, provocation and aggression have become expressive pathways for such a child, so that he can tolerate such behavior, both in himself and others. Even more time must pass before the group worker can be included in the field of such a child's aggression.

There are no technical "short cuts" available to a play group worker to mobilize the aggression of withdrawn children or to give it momentum when it finally becomes evidenced. The quality of spontaneity in the discharge of emotions which were severely blocked requires much time to evolve. The worker must be patiently aware of the reasons for ego-defensive withdrawal.

INTERVENTION

Indications for Intervention

In all therapeutic practices the question of intervention arises whenever the behavior of a patient becomes inimical to the therapeutic process and thus potentially harmful to the patient. The decision of the therapist to intervene is clinically justified only if it operates in the interest of the patient.

In group therapy practices, the use of intervention is complicated by a factor not present in individual psychotherapy. The therapist must be concerned at one time with the separate needs of individuals and with those of the group, and the opposition of such needs from time to time. He must make rapid assessments of episodes in a group's interaction in which unusual degrees of tension, anxiety and fear begin to appear, to decide whether intervention is necessary. The difficulties inherent in problems of decision are complicated even further by the fact that excessive intervention deprives a group of opportunities for problem solving, and also interferes with therapeutic outcomes.

Autonomous Functioning in the Play Group: The System of Psychological Controls

In a play group, intervention on behalf of a child or of the group is necessary whenever the psychodynamic controls on which the group process depends for self-regulation become temporarily inoperable. Such situations become manifest when children exhibit intolerable degrees of frustration and anxiety.

A play group's potential for working out its distress situations is determined by two factors: the selection of children with types of problems for which the play group process is indicated; the degree of psychological balance created through a proper grouping of these children. Discordancies in grouping inevitably lead to excessive intervention by the group worker.

The controls which a play group depends on in order to maintain itself as a constructive entity, capable of autonomous problem solving, are vested in the following:

> each child—as determined by intrinsic forces such as guilt, and anxiety, age, and level of maturation
>
> the group—which influences its component members
>
> the worker—through intervention which is determined by therapeutic considerations

These forces act singly and in combination.

Controls by the Child

With the exception of severely disturbed ones, most children are aware of the negative implications of their acting out behavior and they react with varying degrees of guilt, sometimes anxiety. These feelings act as modifiers of behavior. As time passes, membership in the play group becomes increasingly important to a child, and he becomes more aware of elements of his behavior which might jeopardize his status. Fear of rejection by the group is one of the forces which eventually leads to more conscious control of behavior.

Controls from the Play Group

The play group attempts to limit the behavior of a child when he continues to disrupt the equilibrium of the group, thus interfering with the gratifications of others; or, if his behavior threatens the role of the group worker. The group must act to protect not only its own integrity but also to preserve the psychological image of the worker, since both are necessary for the continuation of the therapeutic experience.

Controls by the Group Worker

If the interaction in a play group continues to be destructive in effect because individual controls and group controls are inadequate for the purpose of neutralizing a destructive trend, the worker must intervene. Intervention by the worker, which limits or deflects some aspects of acting out behavior, *is not a denial* of the permissive role. It is a therapeutically indicated maneuver for blocking destructive interaction and restoring the group to a condition of therapeutic homeostasis. The worker bears responsibility for doing for the group that which it cannot temporarily manage itself. Unless this is done in situations which require it, frustration and aggression increase in the group, acting out becomes diffuse, and manic-like behavior may eventuate.

Permissiveness within the play group provides motivity for "safe" ventilation of aggression and other emotions by individual children. At the same time, the worker's noninterference maximizes the "natural" group controls which modify behavior. The result of several influences—each child's need to find discharge for blocked and disabling emotions; the need to perpetuate the transference relationship with the worker; the need to guarantee status in the play group by being responsive to its demands—is a regulating factor which opposes the persistence of destructive interaction.

Intervention with Young Children

The self-regulating process within a play group is less efficient with young children of five and six years of age. The group worker must be alert to the special needs of these children, and he should be prepared to use intervention more frequently than with older children. Young children are much involved with learning to inhibit impulsive behavior, integrating controls, and substituting more mature behavior for primitive drives. Such developmental problems are common to all young children, but the troubled child, handicapped by distortions in development, finds the "demands" of reality much more trying. Because of this, the worker must be particularly alert to his special needs. An uncritical use of permissiveness—without regard for its varying impacts on children of different ages and with different problems—can undermine the efficiency of the ego's controls and expose it to strains which exceed its resilience.

The worker must be permissive in all play groups, but with young children he should be more participative and closer to the interaction which takes place. Acting out should not be allowed to gain excessive momentum. Because the frustration tolerance of such children is limited and their defenses fragile, the worker must be prepared to support them more actively *when it becomes necessary* to do so.

Regressive behavior is tolerated but it must be sensitively controlled. Hostility, rivalry, group play, the use of materials—all the elements of individual and group behavior—should be evaluated constantly to determine whether intervention is necessary. The worker must keep his finger on the "pulse" of the group and be prepared to deflect, limit, or redirect behavior whenever the play group requires it.*

Intervention with Children Who Are Excessively Immature

Immature children have little motivation for changing their behavior, despite pressures from parents, teachers, and others. Immaturity has a self-feeding, perpetuating quality, and children who are so constituted seek continuing gratification regardless of their age. In the play group they tend to use both the group and the worker as agents through whom they satisfy their

* Because of the unusual demands made on workers by young children, inexperienced group workers should start with play groups composed of older children, eight and nine years of age.

infantile needs. They are minimally, if at all, concerned with the needs of others.

The group worker's attempts to respond to all the children during the early phase of a play group is interpreted by an immature child as indulgence, and he soon attempts to satiate himself. This invariably stimulates rivalry, and the play group becomes sensitized to the inordinate demands being made by one of its members. An immediate effect of competitive rivalry is to deny the over-demanding child ready access to the person of the worker. The group may also expose his immature behavior to ridicule, and at times it may ostracize the offending child. In these ways the group interferes with the repetitive, habituating behavior patterns of an immature child.

Approval or disapproval from the group is a force which eventually exerts itself against all children, with rare exceptions. The group is actually more powerful as a modifying influence on immaturity than the worker. It is also the group which takes from the worker the responsibility for inhibiting an immature child; which would undoubtedly become necessary in the absence of the group's influence.

In a play group, immature behavior begins to change when there is assurance that its sacrifice will gain something of greater value. When *membership in the group* (social recognition) becomes important to an immature child, he has begun to demonstrate a capacity for reciprocation in social behavior.

During this time of "trial" in the play group, an immature child is supported by the worker, who continues to tolerate regressive behavior while still responding to requests for assistance and gratification of other needs. It is the gratification experienced through this nurturance from the worker which maintains the child's motivation to continue in the play group despite the stresses imposed on him by the group from time to time.

It does not follow that all immature children will improve in behavior through the play group. If narcissism is pervasive, it has characterological structure which is generally unremitting in its effects on behavior. Such children sometimes attempt to propitiate a group when they are blocked from achieving immediate goals. This is conscious manipulation. If such maneuvers fail, the fragile quality of their frustration tolerance becomes exposed; they then act out in angry, impulsive ways.

Narcissistic children who remain unresponsive to maturational forces in a play group should be removed from the group as soon as possible and treated individually. The permissive process will only serve to solidify, and possibly extend their pathology.

Excessive Intervention

If there are repetitive interaction crises in a play group, tension persists and the worker is placed in a position of having to intervene excessively.

His role is then subject to distortion; it becomes authoritative and restrictive. The therapeutic qualities which are mandatory to the group process—permissiveness, tolerance, neutrality, supportiveness, helpfulness, are supplanted by a more practical consideration—a need to protect children from undue stress. Under such circumstances, both the performance of the group and its composition must be reevaluated.

When there is no amelioration of abrasive interaction in a play group, following a determination of the causes of persistent crises, and after the implementation of corrective procedures, the possibility of therapeutic outcomes is negated. In the absence of a therapeutic "climate" there is little opportunity for rehabilitative experience.

Such a condition may develop in a play group from one or more influences, the following being the most common:

Permissiveness is being used in an undifferentiated, *laissez-faire* manner. This induces acting out behavior which gains exceptional momentum. Unless this is checked, the children can become intractable and manic.

The play group is in poor balance: it contains too many children with impulsive patterns of behavior.

There are circumstances under which a play group may behave in a highly activated manner without it necessarily being an indication that the group's composition is defective, or that the worker is committing a technical error. At times all play groups will become involved in types of interaction in which are inherent exceptional degrees of frustration, excitement, or other forms of emotional stimulation: competition over the sharing of food, for example. At such times it is as if the coping ability of the group is in need of "first aid." The critical factor which distinguishes such a condition of temporary hinderance from a destructive condition of persistent stress, is that a psychologically viable group can be restored to a productive level of interaction with a little aid from the worker.

SYMBOLISM IN THE PLAY GROUP: OF THE WORKER, OF "THINGS"

The "mal-experience" of an emotionally disturbed child's earlier years becomes attenuated, in whole or in part, through therapeutic reexperience in a play group. Before distortions in personality which are caused by parental mismanagement can be alleviated, a child must have extended opportunity for emotional catharsis in relationship with an adult who is psychologically *in loco parentis*. In the play group this occurs through the transference relationship with the worker, who is a symbol of an idealized parent.

During early phases in the play group, young children react to both the group worker and the setting as maternal symbols. The worker's permissiveness, understanding, tolerance of devious behavior, helpfulness, and praise, are essential components of a "feeding" process. They represent love on an oral level of gratification, especially during the beginning and middle phases of the therapeutic process. The enormous amount of rivalry which takes place between children during this time is competition for such gratification. The children may draw upon each other for many important experiences, but the worker is a primary source of gratification.

This behavior is well illustrated by the children's struggle for privileged positions in relationship to the worker, their need for tangible symbols of love—the material objects supplied in the play group setting, and the aggressive competition for possession of such objects.

The serving of food at every play group meeting is designed to satisfy oral needs and also to foster the symbolism of the worker as the source of gratification. Initially, children respond to the food at two levels: they express gratification because of the "treat," and they use food as part of their regressive behavior. What might, in the beginning, be considered acceptable eating habits, quickly change into infantile forms, such as eating with fingers instead of cutlery, spilling, smearing, and grabbing. At times more food is wasted in the process of regressive acting out than is consumed. Parenthetically, this is also true of the eating habits of infants.

Workers are beset during this stage of group development. One reported: "Sometimes I feel torn apart. It's as if I needed four eyes to see everything that goes on, and six hands to meet all the demands they make of me!"

Some children seem to require satiation through concrete "things" before they can respond in the global context of transference relationship to the libidinal object itself (worker). These children express this need symbolically, by making extraordinary numbers of requests for materials and special items which are not part of the regular play room equipment. They ask permission to keep or "borrow" games and toys; they may request unusual types of foods. Security and "love" are equated with receiving material gifts.

At times items are stolen from the play room. This is usually done by children who have suffered severe deprivation in infancy and early childhood, and who have a limited ability to share with other children. Stealing from the play room (worker) may also have etiology of a sexualized nature.

MAXIMIZATION OF THE GROUP AS A MODIFYING INFLUENCE

Conflict situations which arise through rivalry between children eventually begin to act as normalizing pressures for mature behavior. Demands for individual gratification from the worker become inhibited by the group. Because it is a group, it is impossible for the worker to meet all needs; nor would it be advisable even if it were possible. Therapeutic considerations require that the children expand their sublimative abilities, develop increasing capacities for tolerating frustration, learn to accept alternatives in place of object gratification, and to share.

Dependence needs vary; children who have been exposed to extensive deprivation during early development require sustained nurturance in the play group before they can become amenable to maturational forces from within the group. Children of this type must be placed in carefully balanced play groups—perhaps one such child in a group. Others in the group must be able to find satisfaction for themselves, and not become catalyzed into excessive rivalry because a group has too many children who make inordinate demands.

When a child has an extraordinary need to be dependent, the use of therapeutic group processes may be contraindicated. Children of this type sometimes seem to respond to pressures from the group. This is not a maturational outcome necessarily, but rather, a temporary, tactical withdrawal of narcissistic self-indulgence.

The worker's inability to do all things for all children at all times, and the group's reaction to its own excessive demands, lead to mild frustration. However, because the *quantum* of gratification in the total experience far outweighs the frustration, and because the children really know that the worker's failure to respond to instant demand *is not a denial* of attention (love), they do not experience it as rejection. Whatever frustration they may feel episodically is countered by their larger perception of the worker as a person who meets the needs of all children without exhibiting preference. It is this overriding quality which sustains the effects of his therapeutic role, even when the needs of individuals are not immediately or completely gratified.

THE EVOLVING PLAY GROUP

The children begin to respond to the therapeutic leverage of the group through the support of the worker, who has maintained the functional image of an optimal parent over a period of considerable time (perhaps two or three years). His fulfillment of their emotional needs, and the growing security each child gains from status in the group (social achievement), are the forces which foster ego maturation. One of the first evidences of this change in the group is a decrease in the frequency of individual demands on the worker.

The changes which take place in the children, and the modifications in the patterns of interaction in the group, are correlative phenomena. As individualism becomes increasingly subordinate to the claims which a play group makes on its component members, the influence of the group as a modifying force becomes aggrandized; its potential for inducing change within individuals increases. As this occurs, a therapeutic play group assumes the aspect and influence of a social, peer group. Prior to this development, it was a specialized therapeutic "tool,"—an exceptional group.

The emotional growth in individuals is continuously reflected in the performance of the group. Behavior within the group becomes distinguished by social maturity, through an accretion of the strengths of individuals. Perhaps for the first time the specialized group exists as a social entity.* Maturation now finds fulfillment through interaction between children as peers; less as psychological siblings.

Modification of Transference: Changing Role of the Worker

Transference with the worker also becomes diluted. A reversal process is in effect with respect to the children's ideation of the worker. They now respond to him more in terms of his real identity, and less as a person invested with the qualities of a significant, libidinal object. This is a parallel process to that in which the children's perceptions of each other change. In both cases it is a consequence of dissolution of therapeutic transference. The play group and the worker move closer to the configuration of normal groups in other settings.

In this developmental phase there is a realignment of the elements of interaction; forces serving the interests of sublimation and maturation are supplanting regressive forces. New experiences, with new social learnings, are taking place, and they prepare the children for productive participation in groups elsewhere.

This process is meaningfully facilitated by the worker through purposeful changes in his role, with the sensitive introduction of new experiences. The children are now able to tolerate limits which are realistically determined, because of the extensive gratification they have experienced in the relationship with the worker.

The children relax as tensions within individuals, and between individuals, are reduced. Energies can be mobilized and used in more creative ways as the efficiency of ego function improves. At such a time there is a renewal of interest in crafts work and other creative activities. There is more participation in group games, cooperative projects, and in group discussions and decisions arrived at democratically.

* An interesting manifestation of this is seen if a new child is introduced to a play group which has reached this advanced phase. The children may sense the need of the new member to experience as they did in the permissive setting, but they are, nevertheless, intolerant of the new child, and they literally deny him freedom to act out. This is because they identify with him, and as a result, must limit him because he is reminiscent of their own past immaturity. It is not good practice to add children to play groups after the early meetings; children's groups should be closed groups.

Expanding the Therapeutic Milieu: Meetings Held Outside the Playroom

As a play group becomes more self-regulating, it becomes necessary to extend its operational field beyond the therapeutic setting into the community, in order to provide new growth experiences. To accomplish this, the worker takes a play group on occasional excursions to playgrounds, parks, museums, and to other places of interest to children.* These excursions are also opportunities for reality testing by the children, made less frustrating by the presence of the worker, who still acts supportively in situations which require it. The worker also uses the new experience to observe the children's capacities for adjusting to the more demanding requirements of the community.

When a play group begins to move from the relative safety of the play room, the forces which have been modifying the interaction within the group are accelerated. Dilution of the transference relationship to the worker, which has been going on for some time in the group, becomes even more pronounced. The worker cannot be unrealistically permissive as he moves into the larger community with the children. His principal role during excursions is protection through responsible supervision. This does not represent a sudden change in his attitude, because modifications have been made in the permissive climate of the play group prior to this.

A play group may oscillate between the play room and the "outer world" as gratifications and frustrations compete. Occasional failures by a play group or by several of its members to cope adequately with the reality demands of the community should not be construed as a lack of readiness for the transitional experience.

This process of group movement into the community, in conjunction with other changes taking place in a play group, eventually alters the perception of the play room as a unique, protected setting and brings it into closer approximation with reality.

TERMINATION OF THE PLAY GROUP

Temporary Separation Anxiety: Resolution

When the behavioral patterns within a play group are similar to those found in normal, social groups, the group may be considered ready for termination. An opportunity to announce the impending termination of a play group is arrived at through questions raised by children about "next year" or, "after the summer." Such queries occur periodically in communication between children and with the worker. The actual announcement of

* Schiffer, M. Trips as a treatment tool in activity group therapy. Int. J. Group Psychother. 2:139, 1952.

termination should be made about a month prior to the date set in order to give the children sufficient time to adjust to it.

The knowledge of termination evokes expressions of disappointment and at times impulsive demands for continuation of the group. On nonverbal levels other evidences of anxiety and insecurity are manifested. Termination is experienced in the context of a loss, desertion or rejection. There is a re-crudescence of mild hostility toward the worker who now symbolizes, temporarily, the rejecting, parent figure. This affective discharge is tolerated and the children are reassured of their readiness for termination.

One common reaction on the part of children to the announcement of termination is to act out in ways reminiscent of earlier patterns of behavior in the group. This is almost a conscious attempt to "prove" that the worker has erred—that they still need the special group.

Increased verbalization also accompanies such behavior as the children hark back to earlier episodes which took place during important phases of group development. Such recall is a sign of perceptive awareness on their part of changes which have taken place. In a play group, this actually represents the closest approximation to psychological insight on an intellectual plane.

Often there is good natured mimicry or "kidding around" as children "remember when" in their conversations. In the space of a few meetings it is not unusual for a worker to detect a highly condensed "scenario" of a play group's development, which may actually have taken place over a span of two to four years.

If the decision to terminate was justified, in that there has been a significant remission of the presenting problems for which the children were originally placed in the therapeutic play group, and if there has been an adequate resolution of the transference relationship with the worker, the children will cope with feelings of separation without complications.

It would be altogether unusual to find all members of a play group equally prepared for the separation experience. A child may demonstrate continuing need for help after termination has occurred. The fact that one child may still require further help should not alter a decision to terminate a play group. The needs of the other children override the need of the individual, for whom other plans can be made.

2 Therapeutic Play Group Practice

Psychological Balance of the Play Group

A therapeutically effective play group is one whose composition permits dynamic interaction to take place. If such interaction leads progressively toward a resolution of intra-group conflicts, despite episodes which may temporarily interfere with this forward movement, there will eventually be improvement in the members of the group. On the other hand, if a play group is unable to cope with problems generated by its own interaction, tensions will persist and the effects on the children will be negative.

If a play group is to have therapeutic influence on children, frustration, tension, hostility, anxiety, and destructiveness must not be persistent. Should acting out behavior remain unabated, conflict dominates all other experience and there can be no therapeutic outcomes, only destructive ones. The "composite" frustration tolerance of a play group should not be exceeded repetitively if the group is to continue.

A play group's potential for dynamic interaction, and its capacity for self-restoration following episodes of disequilibrium, are both determined by the psychological balance created through a proper grouping of problem types.

It is not sufficient to select relatively equal numbers of aggressive and withdrawn children to create a psychologically balanced group. Qualitative differences in the nature of passive and aggressive personalities respectively, *plus the modifications which evolve in each as a result of interaction in the group*, determine whether the balance of the group is optimal at its inception and will continue to be so. In setting up the play group, personalities and problem types must be blended in such a way that they will affect each other *through eventual neutralization of inappropriate behavior patterns, and not through intensification of problem behavior*.

The efficiency of the therapeutic play group process is also influenced by the degree of consistency with which the worker maintains his permissive role. This, too, will be subject to the psychological "checks and balances" which are built into the play group through the selection process. The extent to which the worker can remain permissive and neutral will be dependent on the self-regulating potential of the group.

THE SELECTION PROCESS

Preplacement Group Meetings: An Empirical Method

In actual practice, selective grouping requires the following procedures:

An evaluation of each child's presenting problem to determine whether the therapeutic play group is the indicated choice of treatment.

A preliminary grouping of children who appear to represent good psychological balance. This is done by what might be termed "pre-visualization" of the activating, deactivating, neutral, and static components of the group, and the probable interaction which will take place between them.

Empirical testing of the tentative grouping.

Determining the final selection.

The adequacy of the preliminary grouping of children can be tested through a series of short meetings, each lasting about one half an hour, conducted during a period of several weeks. The composition of the group may be kept fluid during this time, to permit substitutions of children. During these preplacement meetings the worker can learn more about the strengths and weaknesses of each child as they become manifested in a group.

Young children can tolerate changes in the composition of a play group if they are made during the early stages of a group's experience. Later, at a time when transference has become established between the members of a group, changes in the group's composition cause anxiety.

The amount of information which can be obtained from exploratory meetings is limited only by the skill of the observer. When children are assembled for the first time in a play room and given minimal directions—to the extent of being told that they may play with the toys and other materials—much can be learned about their individual adaptive capacities, or the lack of them. These observations, added to information from all other sources, enable the worker to make a final determination of the group's composition with greater efficiency than would be possible without such preplacement meetings. Thus, from approximately ten children who have been considered as good candidates for a play group, a properly balanced group of five or six children may be set up.*

Examples of Preplacement Group Meetings: Content and Evaluation

The following are partial transcripts of actual preplacement group meetings:

The children are six or seven years of age. This is the first time they are meeting as a group.

* It is important that all children who have participated in preplacement group meetings eventually be placed in groups, or helped through other treatment procedures, if so indicated.

Anthony: He is restless, aggressive and provocative. He often sucks his thumb. He destroys the work of other children. Still, some children seem to like him, and Anthony does want to participate in groups.

Michael: He is hyperactive and a problem in school. He talks excessively; is quite intelligent; at times he makes particularly mature observations. Yet, at other times he is fearful and he withdraws when children are aggressive.

Daniel: Referred because he is "too quiet" and unassertive. He seems to like school and would like to have friends, but he does not know how to respond to other children. He is particularly shy with adults.

Victor: He is a frightened child. The only place he seems secure is at home. Victor has not spoken a word to his teacher during an entire year. It is questionable whether he speaks with children. He talks to his parents and siblings. He avoids all contact with his teacher and with other adults.

Harold: He seeks attention excessively and is overactive. Harold is friendly and responsive with adults, but he is quick to tears. Other children like him and tolerate some of his demands good-naturedly. In school he is not learning; he becomes easily frustrated.

The five children arrived at the playroom almost simultaneously. The play group worker walked towards them and closed the door to the play room. The children stood quietly and appeared to be awaiting directions from her. The worker said, "I thought you would like to play here awhile." Pointing toward the materials and toys which were exposed on shelves she added: "You may use any of these things." Following this she turned, walked across the room, sat near one of the small tables and busied herself with pictures which she was preparing as wall decorations. Ostensibly she was preoccupied with this, but she was so situated that she could observe the children unobtrusively.

After listening to the brief instruction given to them by the worker, the children remained grouped near the door, momentarily indecisive. But only for a moment, because Anthony and Harold quickly ran toward the shelves and began to examine the contents. They took out many of the toys until they decided to use the hand puppets. Anthony used the crocodile puppet and laughingly made it bite the human puppet which Harold had on his hand. Harold responded by pushing the crocodile with his puppet. Both boys laughed aloud and occasionally tussled as they moved freely about the room. Michael, on the other hand, was attracted to the easel which stood near the window, poster color paint, brushes and paper all ready for use. He called across to the worker, "Can I paint?" She nodded and he went to the easel eagerly, put on the smock which was hanging there and quickly became engrossed in his work. He often turned from the easel to call the worker's attention to his painting, as if he needed her approval. The worker responded each time, with a nod or a smile. During the next fifteen minutes Michael painted, on several sheets of paper. As he finished each one, the worker removed it from the easel and placed it somewhere to dry.

Daniel and Victor remained near the door, even after Harold, Anthony, and Michael became involved in their respective activities. Victor, in particular, seemed to be studying the behavior of the other boys intently and he sometimes threw furtive and quizzical glances toward the worker. Daniel finally began to move about the room, occasionally looking toward the worker while concentrating on the setting, the equipment and the other boys and their activities. At one point he stood near the easel, silently watching Michael. Michael looked up and said challengingly, "I'm painting." It was as if he thought Daniel wished to take his place. Daniel was momentarily taken aback by this mild aggression and continued to walk about the room in slow, deliberate fashion.

Victor alone remained as if he were rooted to the spot. He had moved a few feet from his original position but beyond that he seemed to be protecting himself from the "unknown." His eyes darted from right to left; he missed nothing. Once, when he momentarily caught the eye of the worker, he dropped his head, almost in embarrassment. Finally, almost imperceptibly, he proceeded on a slow course about the playroom, always peripheral to the group, and avoiding in particular the more aggressive play in which Anthony and Harold were now engaged. At all times he maintained a considerable distance between himself and the worker, who, at no time, spoke to him.

Daniel located the two cartons full of blocks, sat on the floor and quietly began to build. Victor observed this and squatted close to him without saying a word. Daniel was aware of his proximity and once turned toward him, inviting him with a gesture. Victor tentatively touched a block and pushed it toward Daniel, who then used it in his construction. A wan smile now supplanted the masklike expression on Victor's face.

About fifteen minutes had passed since the children entered the playroom. Anthony and Harold were now openly angry with each other. Anthony was more aggressive and he yelled at Harold, snatching items from his hand. Harold whined and complained but could not defend himself more adequately. Michael yelled at both of them when their movements momentarily threatened the security of his easel. On the other hand, Victor and Daniel were quite puzzled by the behavior of the boys and they looked toward the worker from time to time, obviously bewildered by her failure to intervene.

Harold evidently had enough of Anthony and he went over to the area where Daniel was building, with Victor giving occasional assistance. Harold asked whether he could join them but his question was more rhetorical than anything else, because he immediately took over the project, converting it to his liking. Daniel, with grudging expression, passively permitted himself to be relegated to a secondary role. Victor continued to squat nearby but now he no longer participated. Meanwhile, Michael announced brightly, to all and sundry, "Well, I'm finished. What else can I do?" He spotted the others near the blocks and joined them.

Anthony seemed fretful. He walked to the table where the worker was seated and draped himself across it to watch her. Once or twice he touched the stapler and papers but he had no real interest in using them. The worker acknowledged his proximity with her eyes and a smile. Anthony complained, "There's nothing to do." He denied this in his very next motion, which brought him helter-skelter to the block building. Harold and Michael were now loudly bickering about the construction. Daniel had withdrawn and he joined Victor as a passive, disgruntled observer. Anthony joined the activity like a prima donna making an initial entrance on stage. First Harold, then Michael, then both, tried to push Anthony away. Not succeeding in this, they tried to defend the block structure from him. Anthony threw a block against it, toppling it with a loud crash. Angrily he kicked at the few blocks which had remained standing. He, Michael, and Harold seemed unconcerned over the noise, whereas Daniel and Victor looked apprehensively toward the worker. Harold was almost tearful in his frustration and tried to push Anthony away, encouraged by Michael. Anthony laughed at him and pushed back. Harold walked to the worker and said, "Look what he did! He broke my building. He's always fighting." The worker looked but made no comment. However, a moment later she did rise and began to pick up games and other supplies, replacing them on the shelves.

Some of the children followed her but Victor and Daniel remained aloof, following only with their eyes. The worker did not touch the blocks which had been scattered on the floor.

About a half hour had passed. The worker addressed herself to the children, "I'm glad you could visit today. Perhaps you will come back another day to play." She walked toward the door followed by the group. Outside the play room she gave them over to their escorts. Anthony tried to remain behind but the worker explained that there was no more time and repeated that he would come again.

Evaluation: Before evaluating the content of this first preplacement meeting, it should be stated that much of the behavior of each child was predictable on the basis of available information. However, it is not always possible to predict how the quality and intensity of individual behavior become influenced by other children. The interaction which took place in this meeting was complex, and the meanings to be derived, even tentatively, could expand this present writing much beyond its present purpose which is, to illustrate how preplacement meetings are used in making a final selection of children for a play group.

A coarse rating scale could be used to compare the behavior of these children in significant areas:

Response to the minimal direction given by the worker; capacity for self-initiated activity. This is a quality of aggressiveness. The plus and minus signs indicate relative weights: minus representing a *manifest* lack of aggression:

Anthony	+ + +
Harold	+ + +
Michael	+ (?)
Daniel	−
Victor	− − −

Ability to initiate contact with peers and to respond to contact. This is also an aspect of agressiveness:

Anthony	+ + +
Harold	+ + +
Michael	+ + (?)
Daniel	+
Victor	− −

Ability to initiate contact voluntarily with the worker (authority):

Anthony	+ + +
Harold	+ + +
Michael	+ + +
Daniel	− − −
Victor	− − −

Amount of acting out behavior:

Anthony	+ + +
Harold	+ + +
Michael	+ (?)
Daniel	− − −
Victor	− − −

Impulsivity:

Anthony	+ + +
Harold	+ +
Michael	+ +
Daniel	− −
Victor	− − −

Awareness of the environment; sensitivity to stimuli. This is more a defensive, self-protective pattern:

Victor	+ + +
Daniel	+ +
Michael	+
Harold	+
Anthony	+

Capacity to withstand the agression of others:

Anthony	+ + +
Harold	+ +
Michael	+ (?)
Daniel	− − −
Victor	− − −

Provocative behavior:

Anthony	+ + +
Harold	+ +
Michael	+
Daniel	− − −
Victor	− − −

Summary impressions: There are strong impulsive elements in the behavior of Anthony, Harold and Michael. Anthony, in particular, is too aggressive for this group. While it is conceivable that a group could eventually develop the strength to withstand his provocation, it is not advisable to include him in this group because it has enough activation through Harold, and possibly Michael.

Daniel seems shy but he is responsive to the others. He becomes annoyed when they interfere with his play but cannot defend himself against it.

Victor makes contact with some children with effort but his avoidance and suspiciousness of the worker are pronounced. His failure to speak gives the impression of hostility—a refusal to communicate.

Michael easily becomes preoccupied with his work but he responds quickly to others. His actual capacity for aggressiveness is only hinted at in his behavior.

The summary impression of this group finds it overweighted in the direction of acting out behavior. It was decided to try another child at the next preplacement meeting instead of Anthony.

Francisco was selected. He was a handsome child but exceedingly shy. He was more than a year older than the others.

The absence of Anthony during the next meeting produced immediate differences in the behavior of the others. Daniel and Victor were still quiet but they seemed less tense, as they once again played silently with the blocks. Michael again went to the easel and painted most of the time. Harold was even more active than he had been during the prior meeting. He bounced from one part of the room to the other. Occasionally he annoyed Michael, who quickly and easily fended him off. Francisco wandered about, occasionally smiling in a diffident manner. He watched the others; said nothing; did not participate. Several times Harold tried to take over the block building but Daniel did not seem concerned about this. Victor was also able to manage without distress. Harold persistently made contact with the worker. Once he asked, "Where's that kid?" (Anthony) The absence of the "other kid," and the substitution of Francisco seemed to make the children less tense.

This group was continued intact. Within three months Victor began to talk. He also became provocative of the others and less suspicious of the worker, with whom he began to make contact. Harold became more aggressive, demanding and whining, but the boys were able to cope with him, either singly or cooperatively.

As for Anthony, the foregoing material illustrated only that *this* particular grouping was unsuitable for him. On the basis of other information it was decided that he could fit into a differently constituted play group.

Observations made during preplacement meetings also help determine whether the play group process is contraindicated for some children.

Andrew is nine years old. He has the physique of a six year old child. He had been referred because of markedly infantile behavior, poor speech, and poor school adjustment. The school counselor, who had detected the problem, felt that a modified group experience might help him. Andrew's parents were unresponsive to invitations to come to school but the father finally visited. He was defensive during the interview and only a paltry amount of information was obtained about Andrew's behavior outside of school. He did say that Andrew was demanding at times but he denied that this represented a problem. He did not object to having Andrew participate in a special group, if it was thought necessary.

Information entered on record cards by four prior teachers confirmed the observations of the counselor. It was decided to observe Andrew in preplacement meetings:

Andrew was seen with four other boys who were also being considered for a play group. After the children were given a simple direction that they could play with the materials on the shelves and tables, the group worker withdrew to the side of the room. All the children except Andrew made contact with each other and began to play quietly. Andrew, on the other hand, acted as if he were "shot from a cannon." He moved about like a miniature whirlwind—annoying, teasing, snatching things from the others. For awhile the children withstood this behavior with amused tolerance, but then they began to react more vigorously, defending their possessions from him and even threatening him. Andrew reacted to this with shrill laughter, jeering and even greater mobility. *At no time* did he appear to be concerned with the effects of his behavior on the other children, nor did he seem concerned about the adult, whom he barely looked at. At one point, to determine the effect of proximity, the worker moved across the playroom, passing quite close to Andrew. Andrew became aware of her, glanced up with an expression of irritation and defiance and resumed his teasing. At the termination of the meeting he resisted leaving the room when the others did and ran about, kicking over blocks and other objects which lay on the floor.

Summary impressions: Andrew's behavior was impulsive and markedly immature. This was his immediate response to the worker's directions to the group. In a first meeting, such directions merely suggest that there is more freedom for independent action in the playroom than there is in the classroom. Andrew's capacity for self-limitation and the guilt responses to his own acting out were altogether minimal. Were he to remain in the play group as constituted, the other children would quickly begin to punish him. The worker's essential role of noninterference could not have been maintained because she would have had to protect him from the group. Andrew was contraindicated for the permissive play group. His narcissistic needs must first be reduced in individual therapy before he could benefit from interaction in a group.

Typical Problems in Grouping

A sequence of two or three preplacement meetings with children who have tentatively been accepted for a play group may reveal selection problems of these types:

A group which is without sufficient activation. The children have minimal contact with each other; there may be no verbal communication; there is excessive insulation. These qualities can undoubtedly be modified in time through the interaction processes but such a group can use at least one child with more expressive behavior to add momentum to the therapeutic process.

An aggressive child who is also more mature physically than his age group. He may be considered for a play group with older children.

A child who is excessively frightened by his peer group. He should be placed with children who are younger. This maximizes his adjustment potential because he will be less threatened.

A group which is excessively mobile and aggressive because of a preponderance of acting out children. Such a group denies itself periods of relaxation which are necessary for the reduction of tensions.

Size of the Group, Homogeneity

Six children is the maximum number for a play group. This is an empirical finding, based on experience with many groups. When a group has more than six children it becomes difficult for the worker to be a critical observer and to respond to the demands for attention or assistance. This is particularly true in play groups with young children, five to seven years of age. Because the children are more fragile and more dependent than others who are just a few years older, and because interaction processes with young children are characteristically spontaneous, fluid, often unpredictable, the demands on the worker are more pronounced.

Play groups should be homogeneous as to age and sex. Heterogeneous groups are not necessarily contraindicated for children of six and seven years of age, but they are inadvisable. Children usually remain in play groups for several years, and they soon reach an age when interaction between boys and girls drops off.

The author has experimented with several heterogeneous groups, using a worker team—a man and a woman. These were special play groups for children who had experienced trauma early in life due to the loss of one or more parents.

Closed Versus Open Groups for Children*

The composition of the play group should be kept intact as much as possible. When indicated, changes should be made during the time of preplacement meetings, or soon after a group has been started. Once transference relationships are developing, removal of a child from a group induces anxiety. Through identification with the "lost" child, others fear that they too can be removed. It is also inadvisable to introduce a new child to an advanced

---

* In group practice an open group is one in which individuals may be added or withdrawn freely. A closed group, on the other hand, maintains its membership intact. Changes made in a closed group's composition are infrequent, and they are dictated by exceptional circumstances.

play group because this can reactivate rivalry and hostility. Further, since the therapeutic experience in the play group is an extended one, a "new" child is, in a sense, psychologically dislocated; he has to work through phases of developmental experience which others have already been through.

Billy, nine years old was aggressive and defiant, both at home and elsewhere. He was very bright but he never worked to his capacity in school. As a matter of fact, he often did no work. He truanted excessively, roaming the streets of the slum neighborhood in which he lived. He violated school rules with impunity. Yet, there was a quality about the child which made most of his behavior appear like a cry for help. In the absence of other resources he was placed in a play group which had been meeting for about two years.

Billy was noisy, aggressive and demanding. He clowned, acted like a "wise guy," spilled food deliberately at refreshment time, and behaved altogether as *might be expected* of such a child when first placed in the permissive setting of a play group. The other boys, however, found him intolerable. They scolded him, and in other ways attempted to limit him. To a certain extent they were successful because, as a group, they had considerable strength. Psychologically, they had a need to deny him the privilege of acting out because they were now making effective, healthy sublimations and Billy, besides annoying them, threatened their more mature level of adjustment. It was not good for Billy to be subjected to rejection by the group.

Billy moved from the neighborhood and this "solved" the problem of grouping. Had he not moved, it would have been necessary to remove him from the play group.

When a therapeutic process requires that a child must have many experiences over a long period of time before ego growth can take place, he cannot benefit when a group denies him this opportunity. *Nor can the group's experience substitute for his.*

GROUP MEETINGS: DURATION, FREQUENCY, TIMING

Group meetings for children who are five to seven years of age should last about one hour. An additional half hour is indicated with older children. In permissive group practices the momentum of interaction between young children is greater than with older children, and the quantum of therapeutic experience in a meeting which lasts one hour is equivalent to that in an older group which meets for a longer period of time.

However, there should be no hard and fast rules determining the length of time a play group meets because special circumstances will, at times, cause the worker to modify it. There are instances when it becomes necessary to terminate a meeting before its scheduled ending. This may happen when the worker decides that acting out behavior is excessive; that intervention by the worker will fail or, has perhaps already failed; that the group is "out of hand" and has become vulnerable. Under such conditions, excessive anxiety may develop or an accident may occur. When a decision to terminate early is made, the worker opens the door and stands there quietly. The children eventually observe this and question it. The worker should then announce quietly, repeating if necessary: *"We'll meet again* at our regular time next week."

This procedure for terminating a play group meeting is an emergency procedure and should be used only to protect a group against itself when its "control system" is inoperative. The children will experience guilt and some rejection but these are minimized by the worker's assurance that the group will continue to meet the following week. It is less damaging to terminate a meeting prematurely than to expose young children to excessive frustration, guilt and anxiety, and possible injury. It also gives the worker an opportunity for reflection about the causes of the extraordinary behavior which necessitated termination of the meeting.

The following situation took place during the twenty-third meeting of a play group composed of six and seven year old boys. It occurred during a phase of group development in which there was considerable acting out behavior.

Burt is a particularly aggressive child:
. . . . They decided to build with blocks. Jack grabbed the truck while Jesus pushed all the blocks to the floor. Burt worked all by himself. After Jack built a structure, he and Jesus decided to "bomb" it. When Jesus picked up a block to throw at the structure, the worker quietly said: "Don't throw blocks." Jack pushed a truck into it instead to knock down the structure. After that he twice demolished the block buildings which Burt had made, after Burt had expressly warned him both times against doing so, adding that he wished to do it himself. Burt became very angry and before the worker could intervene, he picked up a block and threw it towards Jack. Jack ducked, rolled to the floor with much agility. He was not touched. The worker stood at the open door: "Time to go." Jesus said, "We didn't have milk!" Worker remained standing at the door, quietly, waiting for them to leave. Jack and Jesus sat on the supply shelves; Burt began to wash the wall. He then wrote his name on it with chalk. They finally began to leave. On their way out the worker said, "I'll see you next week, at our regular time."

Comment: There are several questionable elements in the worker's management of situations which contributed to the interaction and which eventually made her decide to terminate the meeting. Her injunction to Jesus against throwing a block *at the structure* was premature. This is an acceptable form of aggression. Also, knowing Burt's low frustration tolerance, she should have anticipated the need to intervene, either by becoming more directly involved in the block building with the children, or by initiating another game. However, once the decision to terminate was made, it was effected properly: the children were reassured that they would meet again. Also, the worker did not verbalize the reasons for early termination. She patiently waited out their resistance to leaving.

Group meetings should be held once a week, on the same day. Cancellations of meetings or changes in day or hour should be avoided because they cause disappointment, sometimes anxiety. When a cancellation of a meeting is unavoidable, it is advisable to schedule a substitute meeting on a day *prior to* the regular meeting day. This has much therapeutic impact on the children since it represents for them another demonstration of the worker's concern for their welfare.

The worker had rescheduled the meeting for Tuesday, and had notified the children. Thursday, the regular meeting day, was a holiday. Lily burst into the playroom, followed by the others. She asked, "We gonna come twice?" Worker replied, "No, but I didn't want you to miss a meeting because Thursday is a holiday." For a moment this did not seem to register. Lily repeated the worker's statement, quietly and with a note of wonderment: "She didn't want us to miss it." Then, with more emphasis: "So *that's* why we come today!" The children were pleased.

Comment: Such consideration on the part of the worker is a tangible evidence of love. For Lily, who is more accustomed to rejection in her troubled existence, this behavior on the part of the worker is momentarily incomprehensible. The therapeutic value of such experience should not be underestimated.

Similar reactions are experienced by children to whom the worker mails a personal note after they have been absent from a play group meeting. To children who live under deprived circumstances, such recognition of their personal worth comes with an emotional shock. This is the case in the following episode:

Jack and Pedro came in together. Worker said to Pedro, "We missed you last week." Pedro said, "You did?" Worker: "Yes. How do you feel?" Pedro replied, "I wasn't sick; I didn't have shoes! See, my mother bought me these." The worker asked, "Did you get my letter?" Pedro looked puzzled. "Letter?—No." Then: "You sent *me* a letter? *Just for me?*"

The author has not experimented with play groups which meet with greater frequency, such as twice each week. Theoretically, this might bring about more rapid development of the group but there are possible contra-indications. Children must be able to cope with the separate realities of more authoritative settings (home, community, school) and their antithesis—the permissive play group. If the frequency of meetings is increased, the ability to integrate both experiences might be jeopardized. This would apply, in particular, with young children.

VOLUNTARY ATTENDANCE, RESISTANCE

When starting a group, details are not given to the children about the special nature of a play group or the reasons for selecting them. Troubled children do not relish being "over-told," so to speak, that adults are concerned with them because of personal disabilities. Children, no less than adults, *are aware* of their disabilities, failures, and unhappiness. Further, they are suspicious of the "hand" which is too readily extended and accompanied by excessive verbalization.

The youngest child eventually learns that membership in a play group is the result of a selective process. His willingness to come in the beginning and to continue must be determined by his own motivation, which will be influenced by his reactions to preplacement meetings and the experiences he has with the worker and the children as time passes.

The therapeutic play group parallels other forms of therapy with respect to transient phenomena such as resistance. However, intractable resistance, which is usually expressed through a refusal to attend meetings, is much less frequent a factor in play groups than it is in individual therapy with children. This is so because the therapeutic play group is not concerned with processes such as: uncovering unconscious determinants of behavior, interpretation, and insight formation.* There is no need for the children to verbalize about emotionally charged behavior. As a consequence, the possibility of resistance based on these factors is diminished. Resistance in play group practice does arise when there is *persistent anxiety in the relationship* (transference) with the worker, or, in response to his functional role, particularly his permissiveness.

A child may sometimes manifest anxiety about continuing in a play group, where the real source of anxiety is resistance on the part of a *parent* who is being affected in some way by the changes taking place in the child. In such instances the child's *apparent* resistance is easily dissipated if the parent's resistance can be overcome.

The incidence of intrinsic, unyielding resistance of children has been statistically insignificant in this author's experience during many years of therapeutic play group practice. When it did occur, it was invariably with a child for whom the permissive play group subsequently proved to be contraindicated.

A child who may refuse to continue in a play group because he is being exposed to an excessive amount of abuse or frustration from the other children is not necessarily expressing resistance in the clinical sense of the word. He is merely communicating that something is faulty in the group, in its balance or in the worker's management of his role.

The following case illustrates true clinical resistance:

Steven, eight years old, was referred because he was extremely nervous and timid. His family was beset with problems. The father was unpredictable and aggressive;

* Because the therapeutic effect in the play group depends on a sustained relationship with an idealized, parent substitute, insight in the play group is a derivative based on corrective experience. See p. 96.

he terrorized Steven and his younger siblings. The children often witnessed their father's physical abuse of the mother, who, despite her own fears, once lodged a complaint against her husband with the police.

In the play group, Steven remained isolated from both the children and the worker. He observed everything that went on and continued to be quite tense. He seemed overly sensitive to the acting out of other children, who were testing the limits in this new experience. Steven was worried about what he observed, even though the behavior of other children was never extreme. While he appeared to relax as time passed, he quickly became tense whenever the activity in the group accelerated. He vacillated between attempts to participate with other children and anxious withdrawal. Steven began to verbalize his anxiety by talking to the worker about what the others were doing. His anxiety increased and after several weeks he informed the worker that he no longer wanted to come to the group.

The facts were plain: the permissive group was excessively threatening to him. The worker saw him alone and Steven was reassured that it would be all right for him to stop. Just prior to this, in school, Steven's teacher had begun to notice that he was acting out in class. This change had been a sudden one. In a conference with the mother it was further learned that Steven was becoming increasingly restless.

Analysis: Suppressed aggression in Steven was massive but his defenses were fragile and were becoming less efficient through participation in the permissive play group. The group was contraindicated for this child at this time.

Children eventually become aware of the special nature of a play group but they do not usually see fit to question its meanings in depth. If there is no continuing anxiety in the group experience, children have no need to examine it defensively. The real investment on the part of the children is related to the satisfaction gained in the experience.

There is evidence to show that most children, even the youngest ones, do become aware that the play group has a special purpose, without ever questioning the worker about it.

Awareness of the exceptional nature of a play group and of the worker's essential permissiveness and noninterference is revealed in the following episodes:

From the record of the seventeenth meeting of a play group of boys seven years old:

Gary had been pushing Marty and Grant around. Grant kept asking the worker to intervene; once Marty also complained. The worker chose not to interfere because Gary's behavior was not unusually aggressive or threatening. Gary, of course, observed the worker's failure to interfere. He called Grant a "sissy" and added: "You're on your own here."

An eight year old girl's group:

Lucy took Charlotte's checker as a penalty for "not jumping." Charlotte objected: "I couldn't jump; it would be backwards!" Lucy insisted that she could go backwards. Charlotte: "Only kings can go backwards." Charlotte was obviously right but Lucy insisted on her rule. Linda and Cora overheard the argument and joined in, arguing against Lucy. Lucy was firm: "That's how I play!" Cora turned to the worker for confirmation: "Isn't it true only kings go backwards?" The worker was taking some time to formulate an answer and before she could reply, Louise chimed in: "Mrs. G. doesn't want to say anything!" Worker looked at Louise as she spoke and could not repress laughter because of the impish expression on Louise's face. Louise laughed also.

Another group of eight year old girls—the twenty-eighth meeting:

Ruth started making a pot holder but didn't complete it. She went to the easel, painted a picture and then threw it in the basket. She asked the worker spontaneously, "Why do we come here?" Amy then asked why Judith no longer came to the group. (Judith had moved. Everyone knew that.) The girls looked at the worker for response. It was brief: "So you can enjoy yourself." Justine then said, "Because they say I only play with boys on my block . . . (pause) . . . because there aren't any girls."

Comment: Justine was referred for aggressive behavior. She did play with boys primarily, but for reasons having to do less with her "block" and more with faulty sexual identification. It is interesting that she volunteered this information which was, in a simple way, a close approximation of her basic conflict. No one had ever told Justine that this was why she was placed in a play group.

REMOVING A CHILD FROM A PLAY GROUP

Should it become necessary to remove a child from a play group it arouses anxiety, and the children who remain seek explanations for the change. The worker should give a brief, simple explanation without commenting about negative aspects of behavior which may have prompted the change.

It was decided to remove Paul, six years old, from a play group which had been meeting for six months. He had become very provocative of the others, and aggressive to the point that they could not block him. When it became evident that the worker would have to spend excessive amounts of time with Paul in order to deflect his aggression from the others, or would have to resort to direct limits with him, thus denying her permissive role, a decision was made to remove him from the group.

To effect this, Paul was seen alone by the worker and told that he would now visit the play room by himself. This information did not appear to upset him but he did ask why this was being done. The worker said: "Sometimes I help children by seeing them in groups; sometimes alone. I decided that it would be *better for you* to visit by yourself. You will still play with the same things and you will come once a week, just like in the group." Eventually he was placed in a play group with slightly older boys, who were better able to sustain his aggression.

The children in Paul's original play group asked about him after he had been away for several meetings. The worker gave them essentially the same information she had given Paul. Although some of the boys expressed relief because Paul would not be back, it was also noted that they were reassured in another respect: they were not concerned about the fact that she would continue to see Paul; they seemed to take it for granted.

In the foregoing example, the child who was removed, and the group, were both able to tolerate the change because there was no actual rejection, only a *modification* in pattern of the continuing relationship. Because of the simple but definitive explanation of the reasons for the change and, as a result of the cumulative experiences with the worker, neither Paul nor the group felt sustained anxiety. If *no* provision had been made for helping Paul after removing him from the group, he would have felt rejected, and the members of the group—even those who experienced relief after his removal—*would have* continued to be anxious.

RECORDING

Group meetings should be recorded in detail and, for the sake of objectivity, reports should be written in the third person, using the term "worker" instead of first person pronouns. A verbatim record of all that takes place during a meeting is the goal in recording.

Notes should not be taken during play group meetings; no other persons should be in the room to observe and/or record; devices such as tape recorders should not be used. The therapeutic process demands alert observation, and it is too complex and demanding to permit any reduction of efficiency through the process of notetaking. A worker cannot be accessible to children who may need him, nor responsive to the interaction which takes place if he is preoccupied with writing. Recording should be done after meetings. This may place a premium on memory, but experience has demonstrated that content recall becomes increasingly comprehensive as the worker becomes aware of the significant processes in the play group. Gaps in the record caused by faulty recall are less important than faults in the worker's performance caused by notetaking during play group meetings.

FOOD

Procedures in Serving Food

Refreshments are served at each play group meeting. For this purpose the play room should be equipped with suitable household supplies for use in the preparation and serving of food and for washing dishes.

A round table is preferable for seating the group for refreshments. It should be set attractively, with a clean cover or tablecloth, place mats, napkins, dishes and cutlery. The use of containers, cardboard plates and cardboard cutlery are to be avoided. Such items are impersonal, and they weaken the psychological intent of the process of preparing and serving food. Food is served towards the end of the group meeting in order to convey a sense of termination but this timing may be changed because of unusual circumstances.

It is sufficient to have a dessert type of food and a beverage. Cookies, pretzels, cake, fruits, milk—with or without syrup, juice, and soda are suitable foods. They are varied from time to time. Requests for special foods made by the children should be honored whenever possible. The worker does not distribute the food but serves it in family style so that the children may help themselves. The worker generally pours the beverage but this too may be done by children if they express a desire to do so. When group meetings take place at special times, before Christmas, Easter or vacation, it is a good idea to have a party, with a special treat such as ice cream and an inexpensive gift for each child.

At the first meeting of a play group the children are invited to the table after it has been set, but at subsequent meetings it is not necessary to do this. Children should not be urged to sit, nor to eat, if they do not care to do so. They may come to the table promptly, late, or not at all. They may finish the food they take, sample it, ignore it, and even waste it—all without comment from the worker.

The children's behavior with respect to food and its donor is often meaningfully related to their problems. Since the worker does not distribute the food some children may take more than a fair share, with the result that others either have less or may be completely deprived. At such times the worker does not interfere. Should a child pointedly direct attention to the fact that he has been deprived, the worker replies, "I brought enough for everyone." The meanings are implicit: the worker provided; deprivation is from the group; the worker trusts them to work it out.

The refreshment period is generally the only time during the meeting when a play group assembles as a unit. It is also a time of closest proximity to the worker. In the beginning, the children feel awkward when the worker serves food and sits and eats with them. This awkwardness gives way after a few meetings and, despite the immediate presence of the worker, there is much interaction at the table.

Psychological Factors Related to Food

An extraordinary amount of cathexis becomes attached to food during the early life experience of children as the result of parental errors in the feeding process. The refreshment time in the play group becomes a focal part of the therapeutic process because it is an opportunity for working through problems related to food and to the adult who offers it. The freedom of expression which children develop in response to the permissiveness of the worker becomes evidenced in intensified fashion during refreshments, when the children act out in various ways. Like other forms of acting out behavior in the play group, this also is accepted by the worker without comment.

Some children express hostility toward the worker by not sitting at the table when food is served or by refusing to partake if they do sit; by wasting food deliberately; through other negativistic methods. Eating habits of some children may deteriorate and become infantile. This sometimes exposes them to criticism or ridicule from the group. The worker seldom becomes involved in such situations because group pressure is a potent force. In instances where a child's infantile eating pattern remains static, the worker may have to intervene to foster sublimation. This is the case with very immature children, when they are unresponsive to the group's influence.

The worker's avoidance of control or direction with respect to the distribution of food and how it is used is slowly perceived by the children as implicit trust in their ability to work out their own problems. There are times when special technics become necessary to help a play group through a stage in which the children are experiencing excessive anxiety with respect to food.

Problems relating to food will be resolved if consistent therapeutic procedures are used. The corrective process is relatively slow because of the complex emotional meanings related to food. This is particularly true with emotionally disturbed, young children.

A group's potential for resolving food problems is contingent on its psychological balance and the consistency with which the worker maintains his role as a provider, without being made anxious by the behavior of the children. It is this pattern—repetitive giving of food without *contamination of the process* by the worker through such means as withholding food, punishing for failure to share or for wasting food or refusing to eat, which eventually neutralizes children's anxieties and their distorted ideation about food.

The following samples, extracted from records of different groups, illustrate some of the principles and technics involved in the serving of food in the therapeutic play group:

When food is served for the first time, the children react with mixed feelings. They are pleased but yet awkward about actually eating with the worker. Sometimes there is outright suspicion about the worker's intentions!

This is from the first meeting of a seven and eight year old girls' play group:

The worker began to set the table for snack. The girls whispered to each other, conjecturing about what she was doing. Angela said, "She's going to eat her lunch now." Phyllis said, "No, she must've had her lunch already." The worker volunteered: "I'm fixing a snack for us." She set out five place mats, cups and saucers. "Ooh," said Louise, "five cups." Angela again: "It *must* be her lunch." Patricia was more logical: "It's too many" (cups). Worker again: "It's snack—for us." The girls finally gathered together, stared at the set table, sat down silently, and then began to giggle. The worker sipped milk from her cup. She had poured for all. Angela: "Milk? I have milk!" Louise: "Me too." The worker helped herself to a cookie and each girl followed in turn. "Chocolate cookies," said Angela, "I love 'em!" Later, three cookies remained on the center plate. The girls looked and continued giggling. As the worker arose and was assembling the dishes, Patricia took another cooky and Dora and Louise did likewise. Someone had evidently taken extras because Patricia said, "Mrs. K., there's none for Angela." The worker replied mildly, "I brought enough for everyone." Louise said, I'm taking my decoration (place mat) with me." Angela said, "I'm taking all the others!"

Comment: These children live in an economically deprived neighborhood. They find it difficult to believe that the worker has gone to such lengths to gratify them. The worker eases them into the situation without excessive comment or direction. This is proper technic. Note her response when a child comments that there has been unequal distribution.

The next extract also describes the initial "shock" effect of giving food for the first time; in this instance to a play group of six year old boys:

After setting the table with cloth, napkins, cups and saucers, the worker brought over a pitcher of milk and a plate of sandwiches. She turned to the boys and asked them to sit with her. Jose giggled and hid in the corner. Billy said, "I will if Angel does." They all continued to stare at the food but did not move to the table. The worker sat at the table and again asked them to join her. Instead, Billy joined Jose in building a bridge with blocks. The boys did not speak. Worker sat alone. It was soon time to leave; no food had been eaten by anyone.

The following week, the worker went through essentially the same procedures. The boys were again ill at ease. They simply could not conceive of this phenonenon: an adult setting a table formally, and offering to share food with them! This time the worker was more persuasive: "It's for you. I want you to have it; that's why I put it out." Slowly the children assembled and diffidently they began to eat.

Comment: The worker's offer of food was almost unreal to them. They were quite suspicious because they could not grasp her motivation. When she was more persuasive during the second meeting, they responded. It would have been acceptable to the worker if they decided not to eat even at the second meeting. In that event the correct technic would have been to serve food every week until they realized that it was "for real."

It was not long before this group did much acting out, even at refreshment time. Most of them had been referred because of severe acting out behavior.

It does not take long for the initial reaction to the serving of food to change. Within the space of a few meetings children learn that permissiveness on the part of the worker extends to the refreshment table. Behavior begins to become less inhibited. This is seen in the next extract, taken from the eleventh meeting of a different group of six year old boys:

Stanley sat at the small table, working. Laurence watched him. Mitchell watched worker as she was pouring milk into the cups. Harold yelled excitedly, "You got chocolate syrup. Great!" Laurence: "What kind did you get?" The worker replied, "I bought 'Chico,' the kind you asked for" (at the prior group meeting). Laurence smiled happily. Harold pounced on the plate with the cookies. Again he shouted, "Cherry cookies!" He grabbed *every one of them*. He began to eat them as fast as he could, holding them in both hands. Mitchell watched him but did not drink his milk. He kept calling Harold names: "Pig—selfish." Laurence asked Harold for a cooky but he would not give him any. Mitchell finally snatched one from Harold's hand; Harold jumped up and tried to retrieve it. Mitchell passed it to Jack, then it went to Laurence; from him to Stanley; round and round, with Harold trying to grab it all the time. It became a wild game, with the boys yelling and laughing as they teased Harold. This cooky, and others, were crushed and dropped to the floor as they were passed back and forth.

Laurence took several helpings of syrup. Jack also took an excessive amount. Harold drank some of his milk, then deliberately poured a lot of syrup into his cup and left it without drinking it. Laurence came to the worker and whispered, "Can I leave now?" She nodded. The others left shortly afterward.

Comment: Note the degree of permissiveness on the part of the worker. One child has attempted to take every cooky for himself; food is crumbled; her "gift"—the syrup requested the week before—is deliberately wasted by some of the boys. Still the worker does not interfere. In therapeutic play group practice the process of giving food is symbolically important, but the worker does not distort or exaggerate the value of food itself by withholding it because of misbehavior, nor does she assume responsibility for its equitable distribution. Just as with other problems that arise, she permits the children to work them out.

In the following episode, a play group begins to cope with a similar problem. These boys are all eight years old. Tommy is an aggressive boy who has been able to have his way with the other boys with little opposition. Until now, the twentieth meeting, he has always taken the lion's share of food. The other boys have not attempted to block this, but they have resented Tommy. There have been meetings where Tommy has taken almost all of the food, leaving only the liquid refreshment for the others. The worker, in this meeting, permits the boys to effect their "plan" without interfering— just as he allowed Tommy to snatch food all along.

The worker began to set the table. Morris came over and helped by putting out napkins. Suddenly the worker sensed there was a plot afoot. Tyrone also came near the table and he and Morris warned worker by putting their fingers to their lips, signifying the need for silence. The worker looked at them without changing expression and continued to prepare the refreshments. While this was going on, Tommy had been painting at the easel, oblivious to what the others were doing. Suddenly Morris and Tyrone grabbed all the cookies. Tommy became aware of this when he heard the scuffling; he stood, staring impassively. The two boys laughed for joy at having pulled off this coup. Tommy shrugged and said, "I don't care," and when the group continued to laugh at him he repeated, "I don't care." A moment later though, when Tommy came to the table, he grabbed for Morris' hand which was filled with cookies. In the struggle the cookies were crushed. Morris complained, "I'll tell Mr. G." Tommy abandoned the effort to get the cookies.

In subsequent meetings the boys supported each other against Tommy and a more satisfying distribution of food began to take place. They had defied him and he could not withstand the group's pressure. During this development the worker took no active part.

The Group Worker: Attitudes and Technics

Non-Interfering

During play group meetings the worker remains peripheral to the activities in the group but he is easily accessible to any child who wishes to make contact. The purpose of this is to avoid blocking or unduly influencing the interaction between children. The amount of involvement with the children is determined by them, for the most part, although contact is sometimes made by the worker volitionally in special situations which may require it. Because the worker seldom initiates or directs activities, the behavior of the children is responsive to their own motivation. Further, when the worker is not intrusive, the children are able to observe him from a safe distance. This is especially important with beginning groups, and with withdrawn, insecure children who become immobilized when the adult is too close. The worker's movements about the playroom should be kept to a minimum.*

Inexperienced play group workers are bothered by feelings of "doing nothing;" or, they complain that they do not know "what to do." These are reflections of physical awkwardness in a new role, one which is construed by them initially as being passive and lacking volition. This feeling can be alleviated somewhat by giving the worker a performance "frame of reference." The author generally uses the following: "Everything you do, or *do not do*, has meaning in the therapeutic process. This will be validated as we study the records during supervision. For the present, it might be helpful if you considered yourself a mother (father) at home. Your children (play group) are playing and doing other things. There are chores which you have to do in the home—cleaning, repairing, cooking, serving food. Since you are the "best"

---

* A play group worker who is overly participative is equivalent to a therapist who verbalizes excessively while treating an individual patient, thus interrupting the associative thought processes of the patient.

kind of parent, you trust your children and do not interfere in their activities unless there is real need. This may be determined, in one instance, should one or more of the children become frightened or too frustrated, at which time you should stop whatever it is that you are doing and initiate some action, unobtrusively, to alleviate the situation. Further, any time a child asks for help, drop what you are doing and help him. Then return to your own work. Of course, at all times you must be an unobtrusive observer."

Because the play group process is experiential, non interpretive, the worker's therapeutic role becomes established primarily through his actions. All activities engaged in by the worker during group meetings should be in the service of the therapeutic process. The worker cannot occupy himself with activities unrelated to the group, such as studying records, writing reports, using the telephone. When he is not needed by the children he may repair an item which is broken, hang pictures, make place mats for table settings for refreshments, or become involved in any other activity which is *meaningfully related* to the children, the setting, and the process.

For lack of something to do, one worker decided to embroider a table cloth to occupy herself during the meeting. She sat in a chair at the side of the room for long periods of time. The boys persistently asked her what she was doing and she explained that she was embroidering a table cloth. In a supervision conference it was suggested that she tell them it was for the group. She did so and several times during the next few weeks the cloth was used in its unfinished condition when the table was set. The children were quite impressed with this "gift" made in their interest.

Non-Interference as a Dynamic Factor: Neutral Versus Passive Attitudes

The permissive, noninterfering role of the worker is not a passive one in a therapeutic sense. A truly passive role is one which lacks volition and makes no contribution to dynamic interaction. There are times when a worker becomes more active, because of special situations. Through his action, the therapeutic process is fostered. A truly passive worker *avoids interaction at all times*, usually from a misconception that equates permissiveness with "doing nothing." As a result, a child or group must then cope with extraordinary problem situations without assistance. Inasmuch as situations will arise in every play group which will require action on the part of the worker to maintain the equilibrium of the group, at such times continuing passivity, in the literal sense, can become a destructive element in the group process.

S.R. Slavson has used the term "neutral" in describing the role of the worker in Activity Group Therapy.* He does not use it in the sense that the worker demonstrates fairness in conflict situations between children—which

* Slavson, S. R.: An Introduction to Group Therapy, New York, International Universities Press, 1943.

is also true—but rather, as a quality of being available and meaningful to the children *in terms of each child's unique need*. Each child "makes" of the worker that which he requires. Slavson has made this concept more vivid by comparing the quality of the worker's neutrality to a blackboard, which is neutral in that on its surface the child "writes" his requirements. The need is the child's; the worker is resonant to the need. All group members are accepted equally; no preferential treatment may be given one child over another. Of course, the effect of interaction in a single episode may temporarily make one child feel that others are receiving more attention than he. Conflicts created by excessive demands for attention by individual children are temporized by the group, which defends its own needs. Should the pressure from the group and the worker's attempts to abate excessive attention-seeking both prove unsuccessful, consideration must be given to the adequecy of the group's psychological balance.

Children first discover the permissive quality of the play group through "accidents." This comes about when the children see that the worker does not become irritated by the noise of falling blocks, or by drops of paint on an easel and on the floor, or when a crayon is broken. If two children argue and then push each other in anger, the worker observes but does not interfere. Should a child grab food at refreshment time or even before it is served, the worker permits it. From these and similar incidents, the children develop awareness of the therapeutic adult. Before this perception becomes integrated there is uncertainty and, in some cases, consternation. Some children pointedly focus episodes of acting out for the worker's attention: "Look what he's doing!" or "They're fighting!" or "Don't you see?" The worker responds to such comments or questions only to the extent of indicating that he *is aware* of what is happening. It is not always necessary for him to verbalize in doing this. Looking, when a child is directing attention to something, or a nod, can be sufficient acknowledgement that the worker knows what is going on. Of equal importance is the children's observation that he continues to help even after they have acted out. In these ways the children learn many things: that the responsiveness of the worker is not conditioned by what is good or bad, acceptable or unacceptable behavior; that the worker is consistent in his role; that he is aware of acting out behavior and tolerates it. Permissiveness, continuing acceptance, helpfulness and understanding—these qualities of the worker's role—are the determining forces in the therapeutic process.

Harry asked the worker for the stapler. She gave it to him. Ralph then asked for paper. When he received it he went to the table where Harry was working and took the stapler. Harry yelled, "Hey!" Ralph: "I need it." Harry angrily: "I had it first."

The boys began to wrestle for possession of the stapler. They rolled on the floor, with each alternately getting the upper hand. After a few minutes they arose and Harry took the stapler. Both boys sat at the round table. Ralph stapled something and Harry observed, "That doesn't look like a basket." Ralph replied, "It's not. It's a hat." Then he turned to the worker, who had been observing all that had transpired, and said, "Look at my hat." She did, and smiled at him.

John reached over the easel to help himself to some of George's paint. George said, "Hey, that's mine." John, petulant: "Why can't I use it?" George: "Because I say you can't." Then, George reached over the easel himself and drew a large cross with green paint right across John's picture, spoiling it. John called out to the worker in a whining tone, "Mrs. R." The worker looked up but said nothing.

Comment: The workers avoid becoming involved in both of these incidents. They are inactive but purposefully so. In both situations the elements were such that the children involved were not exposed to unusual degrees of frustration, anxiety, or fear. Therefore, it was correct technic for the workers to permit the interaction without interfering with it. Of course, frustration and anger do occur, as witness the impact on John when George smeared the painting. However, it is not the purpose of psychotherapy to block frustration, or other emotions. Rather, the therapeutic process is more concerned with helping children so that they may safely experience in ways which will improve their abilities to cope more effectively.

The following three episodes also illustrate situations in which the workers chose not to intervene because the experiences were deemed essential to the therapeutic process and were not unduly threatening to children:

. . . Frank, eight years old, took the chalk and started to draw bases on the floor. Jesse became upset and said to the worker, "You're not supposed to write on the floor, are you?" When the worker did not answer, he said to Frank, "You're not supposed to write on the floor!" Frank ignored him.

Comment: Frank knows its "safe" to write on the floor. He had determined the permissiveness of the worker. So has Jesse, for that matter, but he is still blocked in behavior because of an inordinate need to be proper.

. . . Mary, eight years old, took scissors and started to cut the felt. Carla watched her and exclaimed, "Don't do that! Why are you cutting it up?" When Carla yelled out, Leah also observed what Mary was up to. Leah ran to the worker and said, "Mrs. C.—tell her not to!" Then—"Mary, stop! Mrs. C. tell her not to." The worker looked at each girl but made no move. Mary cut a circle out of the felt, brought it to the worker and gave it to her, at the same time smiling shyly. The worker accepted it. Mary returned to the table and resumed cutting the felt.

Comment: Leah and Carla are perturbed by Mary's use of the felt cloth. They are both well behaved children who suppress most of their aggression. Mary, on the other hand, is an angry, argumentative child who has never hesitated to ventilate her aggressions anywhere. That is why she was referred for help. Mary is not afraid of using the felt as she pleases (actually, what she did was innocent enough). Further, Mary does something quite interesting: she gives the piece of felt to the worker. This is almost a conscious demonstration to the other two girls that *they* need not be fearful; that Mary is "sure" of the worker.

. . . William, seven years old, stopped playing the recorder and began to bang the drum. Angie and Gilberto got the telephones and they began to talk to each other in Spanish. Angie picked up a block and threatened William with it because he was making a racket. William stopped beating the drum but he threatened Angie and Gilberto with the sticks. Gilberto giggled, and Angie said, "You wouldn't dare!" Angie then took the drum and he beat it loudly and steadily, for about 15 minutes. Now William was at the paints. He picked up the small wooden railroad cars and began to paint them. Angie, aghast, yelled, "Look, Mr. A., Willy is painting the cars!" The worker did not reply, but he did look as directed. Then Angie went to the easel, took some red paint and began to paint a block. Now it was William's turn: "Mr. A., Look, he's painting the blocks red!" Gilberto chimed in, "He's painting blocks!" All during this activity the worker sat at the table and continued his work. William brought a painted car to show him. Worker looked at it and nodded.

Comment: This is the seventh meeting of the group and the boys are reacting to the worker's tolerance. The children each "announce" the exceptional behavior they observe but they are not really dismayed by it because they then proceed to act in like manner.

Methods of Intervention

When acting out behavior of children becomes excessive, the worker must intervene to restore activity within the group to a tolerable level. The question of intervention by the worker arises whenever it becomes apparent that one or more children cannot cope with frustration or fear, or where there is an imminent possibility of injury to a child. At no time is it advisable for the worker to remain inactive in situations in which there is implicit danger.

Limits which are used appropriately, to preserve the security of children, will be accepted by them and not construed as rejection, or as an essential change in the worker's attitudes. Occasional errors made by the worker may lead to temporary confusion; the children then retest the worker. Unnecessary limits, which originate in errors of technic among other things, are responded to differently, especially when they are used excessively.

Young children are less alert to the possibilities of danger which are inherent in some physical activities because their life experience has been limited, and because they are still much under the protective supervision of adults. This can also be true of older children who have been sheltered and overprotected. The group worker will generally find it necessary to be more concerned with the question of when to use limits with play groups composed of young children.

On the other hand, it has been observed that young children who live in slum neighborhoods—in contrast to children of equivalent ages from middle class areas—are more alert to potential dangers because they are exposed earlier in life to unsupervised experiences in which they must learn to fend for themselves.

Limits Imposed Indirectly

When intervention by the worker is required, it should be managed calmly, without criticism or judgmental overtones.

Indirect limits should be used whenever possible. Untenable situations can often be controlled or converted by the worker's substitution of other, interesting activities. This is a particularly good method because it not only blocks a destructive process but it also provides continuing gratification. Proximity of the worker to conflict situations has a damping effect. Another effective technic which can be used to limit excessive acting out is to alter the "timetable" of the group meeting by serving refreshments earlier.

In the following examples we see how workers intervene to help children:

Dominick, seven years old, was having a lot of trouble with a few of the boys. He managed to provoke them by grasping and retaining toys but he apparently could not sustain himself against the taunting and pushing caused by his own behavior. Dominick wrung his fingers, became red-faced, and finally shrilled at the boys to "stop bothering" him. The worker asked Joseph and Pete, the boys who were teasing Dominick, to help him move the large table. After this was done he became involved with them in a game of pick-up-sticks.

Comment: Retaliation against Dominick is never severe enough to cause actual hurt, but Dominick becomes agitated easily. He really would like to play with other children but he is only beginning to learn how to handle himself in a group. The worker *deflects* aggression by involving himself with the children.

The children were punching the big, inflated figure. It bounced back and forth while they ran around it, striking it from vantage positions. At one point, David grabbed it tightly while the other children continued to punch it. They then tried to pull it away but he clung to it, yelling at them to stop. They yelled louder and were becoming excited. Finally, they began to tease David. He, in turn, became angry, then tearful. The others, unmindful of David's reaction, continued to taunt him. The worker announced that it was time for refreshments and placed the inflated figure in the corner of the room. David went to the table and sat down. The others ran over to join him. While they waited for the worker to serve there was much activity and laughter, in which David did not join.

Comment: David was really becoming too frustrated, and the other children were unmindful of his tears. The worker felt he had had enough teasing. This is a form of intervention by *substitution* of a gratifying activity.

Dennis, 5½ years of age, has been eating his food during refreshment time in an extremely infantile fashion. This has been going on for months. He pours his milk into the saucer, crumbles cookies into it and then leans forward to sip it. In this process the food becomes slopped on the table and on his person. Until now this behavior has not been interfered with. Other children would at times ridicule him but Dennis seemed oblivious of it. A decision was made in a supervision conference to limit this behavior because it interfered with improvement which had become evident in other areas of Dennis' behavior. When Dennis again started to mess with food, the worker quietly poured the contents back into the cup from the saucer and wiped the overflow with a paper towel. Dennis stared at her momentarily; he tried it again. Once more the worker repaired the mess, this time adding quietly: "It's better this way." As time went on, Dennis persisted in acting out but in other ways he continued to test the forebearance of the worker. The worker never intervened when he acted out in less regressive ways.

Comment: Dennis learned that her intervention was not a form of rejection, since she gratified his needs in many other areas. Because the relationship with the worker and acceptance by the other children became meaningful to him, he was able to relinquish much inappropriate behavior. In essence, he eventually surrendered part of his immaturity in exchange for love.

A Failure to Intervene

In the following example, the worker failed to become involved in a situation which required intervention:

This is the first experience in play group practice for the worker. She has met with this group of seven year old boys for about six months. Because she has some anxiety about the boys' acting out behavior, she consciously separates herself from the group's activities to avoid interfering. However, her reactions to the boys' acting out tend to immobilize her, even in instances where she should be more active. This is seen in the following episode:

Arthur is a tense child; at times he becomes visibly agitated. His behavior has been under somewhat rigid control in the play group. It has been observed that he can readily become anxious and he then strains to suppress whatever emotion he may be struggling with. At an earlier conference it was suggested to the worker that she help him whenever his frustration tolerance seemed threatened, or if he was becoming agitated.

. . . Arthur began to paint at the easel. He has done so in the past and seems to enjoy the activity. His output is routine, not creative. Worker noticed this day that Arthur painted outside the margin of the paper, so that part of the easel was spotted. He became more conscious of this and after a moment he ventured to paint spots on other parts of the easel. The other children were engaged in various activities and the group was relatively quiet.

Arthur began to paint the supporting legs of the easel. He did this with increasing energy. He then put a brush mark of paint on the wall next to the easel. This was deliberate. He turned to see the worker and knew she had observed this. The worker did not move from her seat across the room, nor did she modify her expression, which masked any feelings within her.

Arthur became visibly agitated and paint began to drip from his brush as he alternately painted on the easel and the wall. Paint also spattered on his clothes and on the floor, but now Arthur seemed oblivious of this. Several other children now became aware of his activity. First they uttered exclamations of surprise and criticism, but soon they too became "infected" by this regressive activity and within moments they began to paint articles of furniture and other items.

All during this time the worker remained seated, not saying a word. The group observed this and it seemed to provoke greater activity. After a few more minutes, the worker opened the door to the play room and stood near it. The children quickly left the play room. As a matter of fact they seemed eager to do so.

The play room was a multicolored shambles.

Comment: Arthur was permitted to use paint regressively. Psychologically it was indicated that he should feel free to "release" some of his suppressed aggression, but at a time and at a pace which he could tolerate. The worker's error was twofold: she had provided full pint jars of poster color in preparing the room for the meeting. This is not correct; approximately 2-3 ounces of fresh paint in each color is sufficient for one group meeting. Secondly, and more important, she *failed to intervene* at a point where Arthur's behavior indicated the need for it. He became excessively activated, then anxious, finally manic. The worker should have supplemented his controls at the time he painted the easel, and failing that, certainly when he put the first spot on the wall. The technic could have been to spread more newspaper on the floor around the easel, and to offer Arthur a smock. Both methods would have had a compressing effect. Arthur did need to smear but he could not benefit from manic behavior.*

RIVALRY

Psychological "Sibling" Rivalry as a Normal Phenomenon in the Play Group

Rivalry between children is a prominent phenomenon in a play group. It sets in as the worker becomes psychologically meaningful as a libidinal object. It increases in intensity and becomes maximal when transference is firmly established, and it abates much later in the history of the group, as the children mature. Rivalry becomes supplanted eventually by groupism, which is the integrated social manifestation of healthy sublimation.

Rivalry between children in the play group is psychologically equivalent to sibling rivalry which started in the family. In the play group the rivalry problems of some children become temporarily more pronounced in response to transference relationships which simulate those of the primary group. With children in whom rivalry behavior is at first not manifest because it has

* The worker and her supervisor spent several hours scrubbing walls, floor, windows, and equipment. It was salutary activity for both: the worker learned something about frustration tolerance of children and catalytic interaction between group members; the supervisor learned to avoid placing anxious children with inexperienced workers!

been suppressed, it becomes reactivated. Such rivalry does not originate in the play group. It is a renewal of an earlier, unresolved conflict, within the safety of the therapeutic milieu.

In satisfying the needs of all children without showing preference, the worker does not repeat or reinforce the errors made by the real parents, which errors were originally responsible for creating excessive rivalry. The children learn slowly that all are accepted equally in this "family." They will learn to share love when they are no longer anxious about whether they are themselves loved.

The permissive group is an excellent operational "field" in which children may work through feelings of rivalry without anxiety. Because the worker continues to meet needs impartially, *he does not intensify* the existing, affective components of rivalry. Furthermore, if the play group is in good functional balance, formerly blocked feelings of jealousy and anger can be discharged safely.

These boys are 7-8 years old. They have been meeting for almost a year:

. . . Nat said, "I was the first one to see her. I saw her alone!" Grant argued the point, "Oh no! I was the first one. The truant officer took me over to her." Manuel used a different approach; he came directly to the worker and said, "I saw you first, didn't I?" The worker smiled but made no response.

Comment: While the open rivalry to be the preferred child, if not the only child (Nat), is apparent, note that the worker takes no part in the argument. This is so even when the direct question is posed by Manuel. The subject content which acts as the vehicle for rivalry is relatively unimportant. What is important is the fact that the worker's acceptance of the children, and her constantly demonstrated helpfulness, are impartial. Eventually this will surfeit the emotional needs of individuals; then rivalry subsides.

The girls in this play group are nine years old.

Lois and Carol sat at the round table, playing a game. Laura sat alone at the other table while she worked on the horse she was making out of clay. The worker sat near her and Laura often asked advice from her about how she should use the clay. Several times Lois was heard to say, "I wish someone would help me." However, she did not focus her statement directly on the worker. Occasionally the worker moved away from Laura but always, when she would return to her seat, Laura immediately had a question to ask. Finally, Lois said, "Mrs. G. will you help me?" Worker answered, "Yes."

Comment: The worker acknowledged in supervision conference that she has been trying to extend herself toward Laura, who, she feels, needs support. Laura is a sensitive child who lives with foster parents. The worker felt that proximity to Laura would be helpful but not obtrusive. Events proved her wrong—proximity, *if sustained*, will stimulate rivalry.

Children who are Excessively Dependent

When a child cannot forego gratification, and he persistently demands or competes for the worker's attention in the face of group resistance and the unrealistic burden which is placed on the worker, it is questionable whether he can be helped in the play group. With such a child the basic problem is less a question of rivalry with others but more a need to "use" the adult for his exclusive gratification. This need is essentially narcissistic and the child's capacity for frustration is minimal. When such children are continued in play groups, they intensify rivalry behavior extraordinarily. Such children should be seen in individual therapy and if there is reduction in narcissism they may then be placed in groups.

Individual therapy for such children is not sufficient in itself. It is imperative in their treatment that they eventually be worked with in therapy groups, as soon as they develop enough frustration tolerance to make them responsive to the demands of the group.

COMMUNICATION IN THE PLAY GROUP

Verbal and Nonverbal Communication

Communication in the play group takes place on verbal and nonverbal levels, the latter predominating. While there is much verbalization between children and towards the worker, the worker avoids unnecessary speech and should initiate conversation only when situations demand it. If the worker speaks more than is necessary, it has the same effect as if he were physically overinvolved in the play group's activities: it interferes with interaction processes.

The quality of the worker's speech should be median—neither dramatic nor expressionless. This is also true of his facial expressions and movements, since much can be communicated through these pathways. All forms and content of communication from the worker should be determined by therapeutic requirements. Gratuitous remarks contribute little, other than to increase the possibility of functional error. It should be remembered that the therapeutic modality of the play group is experiential. Outcomes will eventually be determined more by "deed" than language.

Factors Which Determine the Amount and Quality of the Worker's Communication

Age of the children. The worker is closer to the interaction in play groups with young children, six to eight years of age, than he is in groups with older children because of differences in their tolerance for permissiveness. The increased proximity of the worker leads to more direct participation with children and inevitably to more speech. However, excessive verbalization is to be avoided, even with the younger groups.

An example of unnecessary communication took place when a worker, in a play group of six year old children, sought to relieve some of the silence during refreshments by asking one of the children about his "new" baby brother. Not only did the child react with suspicion—since the baby represented a threat to him, and he certainly did not appreciate being reminded of it—but the rest of the children at the table began to ventilate in diffuse ways about their own siblings. Since the play group is a psychological parallel of the family, it has its own sibling equivalents through whom the children will, hopefully, develop better relationships with members of their actual families. It is unwise for a worker to introduce content related to the actual family.

Multilingual children. The worker must be conscious of the level of vocabulary he uses with young children, especially with those from multilingual homes. This also applies generally with children from families described as "culturally disadvantaged," where communication is maintained with limited vocabulary. Teachers in kindergarten and lower grade classes, in communities with social and economic deprivation, have learned from direct experience that they must modify their own language content so that it is appropriate to the age and experience of the children. Clinicians and others, when they begin to work with young children or deprived children for the first time, must learn new levels of communication.

A guidance counselor once showed the author a sentence completion series she had developed for use with young children. Her procedure had been to read each question to a child and to record his answer, to insure that he would understand the intent of the question without being hindered by limited reading ability. She was concerned with what appeared to be the bizarre responses given by one child to some of the questions. It became apparent that some of the words used in the queries—which were quite simple and had heretofore proved appropriate for first grade children—were inappropriate for this child. His family was bilingual and further, some of the experiences and meanings involved in the queries were altogether unfamiliar to him. His responses were haphazard, and consequently some seemed bizarre.

Direct intervention through speech. The need for intervention through speech is more common with young children because they are impulsive in their behavior. When the worker intervenes directly in special situations by talking, he should use as few words as are necessary to convey his meaning. An angry six year old boy may lift a block, threatening another child. The worker says quietly: "Don't throw blocks." In one group a young boy climbed on top of a table in his stocking feet and began to slide up and back on the smooth surface. The worker walked to the table and stood there silently. The boy looked down, smiled and said, "Don't worry!" The worker replied, "I'm not worried, I'll be here if you need me." The child continued to slide, gratified by the worker's trust and also his concern for his welfare.

In each of these examples, meanings were conveyed quickly and effectively, with minimal probability of subjective distortion of the worker's intent by the children.

Verbal Acting Out by Children

Acting out behavior has physical and verbal components, both of which are tolerated in the play group. Language content may be angry, defiant, libidinal, and regressive, depending on circumstances. The children may speak of parents, siblings, teachers and others in negative ways in the presence of the worker. When such behavior takes place they will watch the worker for his reactions. The worker permits such ventilation without reacting to it by word or changes in facial expression. He cannot pretend to be unaware of what has been said. This would be avoidance, not permissiveness. The worker's tolerance of verbal acting out does not imply that he sanctions it.

Occasionally the speech of an immature child becomes highly regressive and persistently so, despite criticism from other children. If this pattern is limited to one child, the worker eventually has to intervene. When regressive speech is unremitting, it serves no therapeutic purpose, and the worker should begin to help the child to suppress it. When this is first attempted, the worker may look directly at the child when he uses regressive language. This visual "contact" often can have the same braking effect as physical proximity. If this method is not effective, a more direct limit is used—the worker shakes his head, without comment. Both technics are designed to induce minimal guilt reactions which, in turn, help the process of suppression by the child.

Robert, six years old, has been using much regressive language. Some of the other children scold him but this has little effect on Robert. Until this episode took place, the worker has not limited Robert in any way. However, she decides to do so now because she feels that he has indulged himself sufficiently in this form of infantile behavior and to allow him to continue would have no value. . . . Robert said aloud, "Does anybody want some? This is a frankfurter and pee." He showed the clay which he had been rolling out. Mitch said, with conviction, "You're nasty!" Robert added something else but the worker did not hear it. However she caught his eye and looked at him, without changing her expression. Robert then lowered his voice and whispered. Worker could barely hear the words, "Pee on the floor."

In subsequent meetings the worker used the same technic from time to time and it was sufficient to help Robert control a good deal of his regressive speech. He continued to act out aggressively, but in more appropriate ways.

Communication with Withdrawn Children

Withdrawn children may remove themselves from social contact in the play group for various reasons but, as has been noted, they are sensitive observers of all that takes place. With such children, communication is a one-way process through silent observation.

The amount of communication between a worker and withdrawn children is determined by their tolerance for it. Verbalization is often frightening to them because it is the equivalent of physical contact or aggression, and these are experiences for which they are, as yet, inadequately prepared.

Even when a withdrawn child begins to move from isolation he avoids speech. He may draw the worker's attention to his need for an item by gesture. When this happens the worker should respond to the request without comment and not attempt to elicit conversation. When it becomes evident that a child has moved from self-protecting isolation and is maintaining contact, the worker may then begin to communicate more directly. Such children eventually provide appropriate signals of their tolerance for both verbalization and relationship.

Robert got up from the table where he worked in isolation week after week. He picked up a paint brush, looked about nervously, and then stroked the face of the easel. After a few moments the worker unobtrusively obtained a sheet of paper and moved toward him. She attached the paper to the easel. Robert looked at her shyly as she turned to leave. He smiled self-consciously. No word was spoken.

Carol is nine years old. She is painfully shy and barely speaks to other children. In the play group she usually sits at one of the tables and works quietly and unobtrusively. In this meeting Carol "signals" a readiness for contact and the worker responds to it.

. . . Louise picked up the chain which Carol had finished and said, "Did you make it?" Carol nodded. Louise added, "It's beautiful! Will you show me how when I finish my flower?" Again Carol nodded, still not uttering a word. Carol took some crepe paper and cut some forms. She crumpled them in her hands, arose, walked near the worker on her way to the basket to dispose of the paper. This happened about three times; each time Carol walked close to the worker. The worker looked up whenever Carol passed by and smiled briefly. A little later, Carol approached the worker directly and said timidly, "Can I make that?" pointing to some puppets. The worker said, "Yes," and moved over a bit to make room for her at the table. Carol did not sit down. Instead, she gathered the materials she needed and joined Louise at the other table.

Comment: The worker sensed Carol's readiness because the child had walked close to her, three times. Carol had rarely left her seat during previous meetings. Note, however, that Carol's "experiment" could not tolerate her sitting next to the worker. She became able to make direct contacts more frequently during the next several meetings and she also began to speak freely to both the girls and the worker.

Another type of withdrawal behavior is sometimes observed in children who are suspicious of the worker: they are verbally uncommunicative, but otherwise active. Their attitudes, expressed nonverbally, may be negativistic, hostile, or even challenging. What is involved here is unconscious fear of relationship and, as a result, there is distrust of the permissive worker. The worker must not extend himself toward such children but he should respond to all requests for materials or assistance if they are made, limiting his response to that which has been requested, nothing more. He should avoid initiating conversation.

Children who "defend" themselves against relationship in this hostile manner *need much time* for their defenses to loosen. The play group process is well suited for them because the group acts as an insulator, diluting much of the tension that would otherwise exist if they had no means of maintaining a distance between themselves and the worker.

Mitchell was eight years old. He had been referred because of markedly infantile speech, few contacts with peers, withdrawal behavior, general suspiciousness. In the play group, he avoided the worker completely. He did not speak a word to her for many weeks and when he finally did it was with evident strain on his part. At all times there was something in his manner toward the worker which was unmistakably hostile. At times he would not sit with the group when refreshments were served. When he did join them he often refused the food. The worker "confessed" during a supervision conference, that she was beginning to dislike the boy and that she almost resented his "attitude." It was suggested to her that she continue to avoid all contact with Mitchell unless he came directly to her. Slowly, as Mitchell observed the worker's acceptance of the acting out behavior of the other children, he began to use more direct pathways for expressing his hostile feelings toward her.* Several times he mimicked her voice when she spoke to other children. More frequently he acted out by spoiling materials or deliberately wasting them. Following this he would request replacements or ask for special materials, all of which the worker tried to provide. He began to relax; occasionally he smiled at the worker, and eventually he was able to sustain proximity to her and to converse without strain.

NATURE OF EXPERIENCE: DIRECT AND VICARIOUS

The faults in a child's personality originate, in most cases, from prolonged, mal-experience in parent-child relationships. Unusual or exaggerated fears, anxiety, guilt, general insecurity, and other reactive or symptomatic conditions, are the consequences of repetitive damage to the child during important periods of personality development. These emotional "learnings" have an experiential base; their amelioration is dependent on extended therapeutic reexperience, which attempts to undo, as far as possible, the effects of mal-experience.

* Mitchell's mother was overbearing and rejecting, and the boy's behavior toward the worker was unconsciously a displacement of the anger he felt towards his frustrating mother.

A child's experiences in the play group may be direct, in that he is physically involved in the interaction processes which take place between the components of a group, including the worker. On the other hand, experiences can also be indirect, vicarious. For one reason or another, a child may be unprepared for active participation in the group but he can, and does, observe the interaction which goes on. His perceptions of how others react in the unique setting may modify some of his fears, without producing manifest changes in his behavior for some time. Such vicarious experience is a preparatory phase during which the child becomes sufficiently strengthened to attempt participation in the group's interaction. Vicarious experience of itself, without eventual involvement on more direct levels, has no therapeutic value. If there is to be some remission of the effects of emotional traumatization, catharsis must take place within the framework of transference. Participation in the interaction of the group is a direct form of experience, and such experience is no less necessary in the therapeutic play group than it is in forms of therapy which are concerned with uncovering unconscious material, interpretation, and insight formation.

The Withdrawn Child's Experience Is Initially Vicarious

Withdrawal behavior is ego-defending. In one case it may protect a child from actual or phantasied danger; in another, its purpose may be to spare others from the consequences of anger which has been severely repressed. These are the underlying reasons for social withdrawal of most emotionally disturbed, nonpsychotic children. To a certain extent it probably accounts for the withdrawal of some autistic children.

One thing is certain with respect to the withdrawn child in the play group: whether he remains rooted to one position or isolates himself in a corner of the play room, his sensory apparatus is in maximum use to keep him aware of all immediate stimuli. For this reason, the play room setting should have suitable facilities for isolation, such as a table set in a corner or in an alcove. The withdrawn child tries to keep all persons and activities in front of himself. He literally keeps his "back to the wall" in self protection.

Changes in the behavior of withdrawn children in play groups are rather dramatic, and they evolve in well-defined stages. At first, withdrawal behavior becomes reinforced when the children observe an adult who is so different from those they have known in the past. As a matter of fact, in play groups the first reaction of children of this type is akin to a shock response: they become immobilized. It is unwise for the worker to attempt to alter this situation by approaching such children to put them at ease. Their needs will best be served by maintaining the separation. The perception of the worker as a "safe" person will penetrate slowly as a withdrawn child continues to study him.

Vicarious Experience Yields and Becomes Participatory

Children do not take advantage of the apparently defenseless withdrawn child, who appears to be a prime target for aggression. This is probably due to several factors. The withdrawn child is passive, unobtrusive, noncompetitive and, as a result, he does not stimulate rivalry. Also, other children react with sensitivity to the isolate; they seem to understand his need to be alone. However, when a formerly withdrawn child begins to make contact with others, then, in a sense, he becomes "fair game." His former "immunity" is lessened and he becomes exposed to more aggressive experiences. However, since this change occurs when the child's defensive potential is stronger, he can sustain these new experiences.

As a withdrawn child begins to move from isolation he still requires attenuated experience. Support is often found through relationship with another child.* If he finds continuing satisfaction in interaction then his contacts will extend to other children and eventually to the worker. This movement into the group may take several months and, in instances, even longer. The change in attitude often appears dramatic when contrasted to the original behavior, but it is really only an initial step in the development of transference. It is from this point on that a withdrawn child actually begins therapeutic experience. Until now all prior experience in the play group has been preparatory, supportive, more vicarious than direct, and a prelude to the therapeutic phase.

Don was six years old when he was placed in the play group in which he was to remain for almost four years. When he was referred for help he was extremely withdrawn; he spoke very little at home, never in school. He had no friends and would not participate in organized group activities.

In the play group he remained isolated from everyone; he never spoke but he did observe everything which transpired in the room. He never changed his expression; it was difficult for the worker to guess what Don was thinking or feeling. Interestingly enough, the other children never bothered him.

For the first time, during the twenty-fourth meeting of the group, Don spoke a few quiet words to one child. This occurred shortly before the summer vacation period. When the group resumed its meetings after the summer, Don was just as uncommunicative and withdrawn as he had been at the very first meeting he attended. The worker was quite discouraged. She described him as a "wizened, dried up little man."

The worker began to report some changes after he was in the play group two years. Don began to manifest more expression; his eyes were brighter, and he appeared alert. He remained on the periphery of the group but he now seemed more interested in the aggressive interaction between the boys. He began to speak in response to overtures from others and loudly enough to be heard and understood. Don also began to join in some of the games with the boys.

* Slavson calls this a "supportive ego" relationship.

The worker now took a more active role with Don. She occasionally suggested a simple game, such as ring toss, and Don seemed happy to play with her. Slowly she involved him more and more in activities with the other boys. Eventually Don was able to initiate contact with the worker and the boys.

In the third year it was reported by his teacher that Don was participating in class, where he had never done so before. Improvement was also reported at home. At no time was his behavior aggressive in the usual behavioristic patterns. Don spoke, laughed and joined in games with others, but he remained a marginal participant.

Comment: This is a highly condensed description of the changes in a severely disturbed child, whose self-protecting insulation had the quality of autism. This insulation was eventually breached by the worker, *who had always been under constant surveillance by the child.* Don eventually became assured that she was really permissive, kind and helpful, through observing her behavior with others Only then did he dare to relate to her actively. When he was able to do so and remain "unscathed," then he could attempt other experiences.*

Probing for the Meaning of the Therapeutic Process

The uniqueness of the permissive play group experience initially impels children to test its reality through acting out. Later, they are also prompted to probe for its purposes. They may question the worker directly or rhetorically, viz: "Why do you let him throw clay?"—"They're fighting. Why don't you stop them?"—"Oh, boy! What would happen to him if his mother (father, teacher) saw him!" The worker is attentive to the questions or the observations of the children but avoids discussion. If a child demands acknowledgement, the worker's replies are limited to: "I know" or, "Yes, I see."

The understanding which the children eventually acquire, mainly through nonverbal communication, is that the worker is different from other adults. They learn that the worker's tolerance for acting out behavior is not accidental, but part of his investment in helping them. This unspoken "message" can be detected in their remarks and observations:

Johnny was attending his first meeting with a play group which had already been meeting for several months. He observed the freedom which other members of the group enjoyed and the absence of adult restriction of aggressive behavior. Several times during the meeting Johnny admonished the children because of their quarreling and aggressive play. Finally, in exasperation, Henry told him: "Keep quiet! *He*

---

* Within the author's experience with therapeutic play groups, there has never been an instance wherein children such as this have failed to respond after being maintained in a group for *a sufficient length of time.* The author feels that the therapeutic group has extraordinary potential in the treatment of exceptionally withdrawn children. A critical factor with such children is the psychological balance of the play group: these children must never be subjected excessively to threat, frustration or stimulation.

(worker) doesn't mind." Pedro added: "Yeah, you're new. You don't know it."
(Yet!)

Children rarely pursue a line of questioning which compels the worker to
define in more precise terms the meaning of his role and the purpose of the
specialized group. The reason they avoid doing so—for it is avoidance—is
that they are more interested in the satisfaction *derived from therapeutic
experience* than they are in intellectualization. Young children are pragmatic;
they have little need to fathom the motives of the worker or the implications
of therapeutic group practices. Whatever uncertainty they may have had,
when first exposed to the permissive experience, is dissipated by their direct
tests of the worker during early group meetings.

Occasionally there are children who insist on more detailed information
from the worker. In such cases it is usually because they find the therapeutic
experience momentarily anxiety provoking. Those who have need to inquire
in depth are generally children who are developing neurotic or character-
type personality disorders. The psychological impact of the group, particularly the developing transference relationship with the worker, makes them
feel uneasy. This uneasiness is probably the result of alterations taking place
in their ego-defenses. The worker should respond to questions from such
children with answers which are specific but uncomplicated.

Marshall, seven years old, asked the worker, "Why do we (really 'I') come
here?" The worker replied, "To play." Marshall was not satisfied: "Do I have to
come if I don't want to?" Worker: "No, but I like you to come." Again Marshall
inquired, "But why did I start to come?" The worker paused a moment to reflect and
then said, "I wanted to *help* you have friends and be happy." Marshall pondered,
then said, "Oh." The questioning ended.

Comment: Actually, all of Marshall's questions have one element: "What
is the meaning of this special experience and why am I part of it?" When
the worker realized the child's need for information she provided it. Her
answer was simple, yet quite accurate. It was also sufficient; Marshall knows
he was unhappy and had no friends. It would have been pointless for the
worker to explain that the play group might also help him work out some of
his jealousy of his younger sibling and his feelings of rejection by his mother.

When a worker fails to respond to the persistent questioning he engenders
even more anxiety. This is illustrated in the following extract:

Carl, eight years old, is very bright, gentle, and manifestly effeminate in speech
and carriage. He has been a member of a play group for many months. This group
was conducted in a school. In this meeting, the thirty-second, he persistently
questions the worker about the meaning of the play group. Carl is probing from
anxiety, which has recently become heightened as his behavior in the play group
began to fluctuate between passivity and aggression. For Carl, aggressive acting

out has been a newly discovered experience, and one not without elements of anxiety. His uneasiness about this makes him think more about the phenomena in the play group.

The worker attempts to skirt the situation but only gives added impetus to Carl's search for answers. Further, Carl's frustration, and the worker's continuing evasiveness, infect the other boys. They also become involved in questioning her, even though they do not share Carl's motivation.

. . . Victor and Robert went to the bench and began to work on their wood projects. Carl stood by, watching them. He looked toward the worker, walked to the table near where she sat and said, "My mother wants to know why I have to come here" (The fact is that his mother was eager to have him a member of the play group). The worker replied, "No one has to come here." This exchange was overheard by the other boys. Carl was evidently not satisfied; he had a strained expression on his face. Again he asked, "Why do we have to come here?" The worker hesitated. Now Robert, Victor, and Mitchell became interested in the conversation. Victor asked, "Why do we come here?" The worker began to explain further, telling them that she sometimes saw children individually and sometimes in groups (evasive). Carl continued: "I'm the only one who comes from my class. Why am I the only one?" Mitchell: "Why am I the only one from my class?" The worker answered "Other children come from your class." (This is still evasive; not responsive to the intent of the children's questions. The worker does not know how much to tell the children, and she is altogether "hung up!") The children now continue to probe, because her evasion has made them either curious or anxious. Robert called out: "Yeah, I know. You're the guidance counselor. We come to get better in school. Is that the reason?" (He could not have been more perceptive—and helpful to the now perturbed counselor!) She replied, "Some children come here for that reason and other children for other reasons. Some come so they will feel happier; some to learn how to do better work." (The worker is obviously fearful that the children cannot tolerate information to the effect that she wishes to help them because they need it.) Carl persists, despite the discomfiture of the worker: "But I *am* happy, and I *do* good work!" Mitchell added, "Yeah, I'm happy too! I used to come here alone when I was in the second grade because I used to jump around in class." At this point the boys were moving about actively, but close to the worker (agitation). Carl again: "Is this a special kind of speech group?" (He knows it is not. However, children do go from class to special groups, such as for speech correction. Carl is trying to get the worker to say it is "special" in the play group, by borrowing from any experience he knows). Mitchell: "I used to go to speech because I have trouble with my 'l's.'" Then Carl asked, "Why do children go to reading?" (Another "special" group experience). Worker: "Some children need help to read better."

The conversation terminated. The children were restless. There was considerable activity on their part during the remainder of the meeting. There was much smearing of paints and banging of wood at the workbench.

GROUP AUTONOMY IN PROBLEM SOLVING

Improvement in behavior is reflected in increased cooperation between children and more communication with the worker, whose role in the group slowly becomes modified. When this developmental point is reached, the children's capacities for efficient sublimation have increased and they are better equipped to resolve intra-group dissension through discussion instead

of through acting out, as in the past. This is seen most pointedly at the refreshment table, where discussion of many topics takes place. The worker
may participate in discussions but he should still avoid over-verbalization,
particularly when questions involving group decisions arise.

Following is an extract from the seventy-eighth meeting of a boy's play group.
The boys are nine to ten years old. They have already had several meetings outside
the play room. In this meeting the question arises as to whether the group should
go outside. Two of the boys, Mike and Pete, resist the idea of leaving the play room
at first. The worker avoids interfering in the argument.

The boys in this play group have matured considerably. Originally it was an
activated play group, with much dissension, rivalry, and fighting.

Felix who was bouncing a ball, said, "Hey, could we go to the 10th Street playground?" Worker said, "It's up to you boys." Moe said, "Let's go!" Jorge, who was
drilling some holes in wood said, "Yeah, let's." Pete, however, said, "I'm staying
here!" Mike added, "I don't want to go." The boys argued back and forth. Pete
finally capitulated: "All right! If you all go, I'll go." Felix then appealed to Mike,
who still objected to leaving the play room. Moe said," I'm hot." Mike responded,
"You know why you're so hot? You play too much!" (Note: Mike's resistance to
the idea of going to the playground was probably due to the disappointment he
experienced on another occasion, when he did poorly in a competitive game. He is
not as skilled as the other boys in ball games.) Moe turned to the worker: "You ask
him. Maybe he'll do it for you. He won't for us." Felix finally said, "O.K. You can
stay here—I'm going. Come on Moe." Both boys walked toward the door. The
worker said, "I can't go with only part of the group." The argument between the
boys continued. Moe teased Mike, "You want to stay here with girl's work—
painting!" (Moe senses the basis for Mike's resistance.) Mike mimicked Moe, in
turn. Now Peter said in anger, "You keep talking and then it'll be time for our
snack and then we'll all have to go and I'll punch you in the mouth!" He walked
toward Mike in a threatening, crouched over manner, then smiled and went back to
his seat. Mike said finally, "All right—as soon as I finish cleaning up." Jorge said,
"I'll help you." Mike was using delaying tactics: "I've got to get my coat." Moe
said, "What for? It's hot!" Finally the group left. At the door Jorge asked for the
key and he locked up.

. . . Later, the boys returned to the play room and immediately began to set the
table. Jorge pulled the table to the center saying, "Good old snack! Good old little
snack!" Moe got the pitcher, worker the cups, Pete the plates. Felix sat and said,
"I'm thirsty." Worker poured. Pete said, "Do we have cookies?" Worker said,
"No, today I brought a cake." Mike added, "Thank God. You know what happens
when we have cookies!" Worker cut and served the cake. Felix volunteered: "Gee,
I'm hot. I could go swimming." Jorge said, "I went swimming on Sunday." The
boys' conversation turned to swimming in the East River.

Comment: The group has the capacity for resolving problems and conflict
situations.

During the long phase of therapeutic experience in the play group, the
worker studiously avoids unnecessary involvement or conversation with the
children, does not interfere in the interaction between them, nor direct them

in their work or play. Later, when the children have begun to demonstrate their maturation on individual and group (social) levels, it is even more important that the worker continue to avoid over-participation, verbally or otherwise. It would be illogical for the worker to assume a leadership role at a time when the group has become more autonomous and self-regulating and has evolved its own leadership potential.

MATURATION AND TRANSITION

For an extended period of time, the length of which is dependent on the nature of the original child problems and other factors, the children seek gratification primarily from the worker. This is a period of nurturance, a regressed phase. As the children are strengthened in the therapeutic process they become able to subordinate individual needs in exchange for other important gains.

The children find gratification on higher levels: through recognition from other children and from status in the group. In order to maintain these important outcomes they must become more responsive to group decisions. As this maturational process evolves, a group is seen as a dynamic gestalt, perhaps for the first time. This change is subtle and deceptive, and workers sometimes begin to describe behavior as if the group were a unitary object with its own unique motivation and volition, independent of subforces. This is not so. The improved performance of the dynamic group is not a group phenomenon. It is a composite outcome derived from improved interaction between individuals. It is based on the maturation of individuals and their separate but interacting capacities for goal determination and self-regulation.

Constructive processes replace destructive ones. A reduction in the incidence and intensity of rivalry and a corresponding increase in cooperation may be seen, in games, sharing of materials, and decisions worked out by the group. At refreshment time, competition for food, wastefulness, and other negative forms of behavior yield to more acceptable patterns. Conversation at the table is more fluid, less argumentative. Many of the chores related to preparation, serving and cleaning, which the worker has been doing from the beginning, are taken over by members of the group.

The children's interests and skills expand, and materials are used more purposively. Some of the aggression which was formerly exhibited in hostile interaction is converted to creative output. At this time the worker must supplement the supply shelves with new materials to satisfy developing interests.

MODIFICATIONS OF THE WORKER'S PERMISSIVENESS

The worker's role changes perceptibly; it keeps "in step" with the growth of the children. Where the worker was, heretofore, a source of almost unlimited gratification, he can no longer be so. In the evolving group, there must be a change in the children's ideation about the therapeutic worker, who has been unique in their life experience.

Transference passes through stages of varying intensity during the life of the therapeutic play group. It becomes more dilute as the identification of the worker moves closer to a reality context, and as the play group loses its exceptional nature and begins to assume qualities of "normal" groups. In this process of change the worker becomes less permissive, to help the group make the transition to other levels of interaction.

The children accept the changes in the worker because of the extensive gratification they have experienced in their past relationships with him and because their *present* need is to adapt their ego gains to levels of higher social functioning. Frustration tolerance and sublimation become used in the service of maturation—planfully by the worker, less consciously by the children. The children are less dependent and are now responsive to re-educational forces, *some* of which are mobilized by the worker in the interests of the children.

It would be altogether incorrect to visualize the workers' role as one which is permissive to start with, and later, prohibiting and directing.

The worker begins to use innovations to provide a *modus operandi* for reality testing, but he does not direct behavior. He is still permissive, but the quality is different. In the beginning, permissiveness was used by him in a generalized manner, to help children relax and to induce free expression of blocked emotions. Now, a more discriminating use of permissiveness permits the group to function autonomously in the management of its problems by capitalizing on the acquired strengths of its members.

A quality of group allegiance sets in as the children share the "profits" of social maturation. The play group has come to have special meaning because it was the vehicle in which growth took place. The group becomes a social structure in which democratic processes are meaningful because they have *evolved* from dynamic interaction. They have not been superimposed by adult authority.

In the advanced play group, the interaction between group members is cooperative, mutually supportive, and often characterized by a spirit of camaraderie. These qualities are illustrated in the following extract, taken from the fifty-fourth meeting of a boys' play group. These boys are nine to ten years old.

Orne: referred as a moody, suspicious boy, who resisted relationships with anyone—child or adult.

Nickie: originally a hostile, provocative boy, always involved in fights with other children.

Sam: bright, sensitive, and creative, but unhappy and underachieving.

Ramon: a passive, lonely boy.

... Worker joined Nickie at the table and helped him with his project. Orne meanwhile joined the other boys who were playing ball. Sam called to Nickie: "Want to play?" He replied, "As soon as I finish this." Sam walked over and voluntarily helped him. Then he said, "Let's play baseball. Where's a pencil?" Nickie offered his. Sam: "Now we need paper and we're ready." Worker got some paper and gave it to Sam. He ruled it off, gave the pencil to the worker and said, "You sit here and write what we tell you." All the boys began to play a modified game of punch ball, making up rules as they progressed. They occasionally made announcements: "From now on if the ball goes here it's out,"—and—"Forty points wins." The boys continued the game, occasionally haggling over "outs," or teasing each other about who was going to win. At a natural break between innings, the worker announced, "Time to eat." Sam said, "Can we stay and play late?" The worker replied, "I can't today, but you can continue next week."

At the table they talked about the game, their respective abilities, how much fun they would have when the snow cleared and they could go out to the playground. When they finished eating, Sam again asked, "Is there time to play some more?" The worker said, "For a few minutes." Orne yelled, "Oh boy, let's play!" Sam scooped up the cups and brought them to the sink. Ramon was still dunking cookies into his milk. "Come on boy, drink up?" Sam said, reaching for his cup. Ramon gulped the rest, Sam grabbed his cup and added it to the others. As he did so he said to the worker, "It was good—that chocolate milk." The other boys moved the table and chairs back and the game was resumed. There was a lot of good natured yelling over foul balls, scoring, etc.

In the beginning, the unique elements of a play group distinguished it markedly from normal groups. It was a specialized experience and its phenomena were atypical as compared to all other groups. Later, the exceptional quality diminishes. When the play group, as a gestalt, finally demonstrates real maturation in social behavior, it is valid to assume that the members of the group have been modified through the therapeutic process. Such growth can be detected even though there may be variances in the degree of improvement of different children.

PROCEDURES FOR TERMINATION

The decision to terminate a play group should be implemented at a time of the year which children normally associate with ideas of change: the end of the calendar year, or in June, just prior to the termination of school for the summer vacation.

An announcement of impending termination should be stated simply, when the group is assembled for refreshments. It is sufficient to say: "We have been meeting for a long time. We have had a good time and I was very happy to be with you. However, it will soon end and we shall no longer meet here. We shall have our last meeting just before vacation."

The children will elicit other information from the general discussion which will be prompted by the worker's remarks. The worker's announcement usually has immediate impact but the knowledge of termination is not altogether unheralded. In all play groups, questions of eventual termination are raised and discussed by the children from time to time. Despite this, however, the reality of termination does create moderate anxiety which, in turn, leads to mild acting out. It is as if the children are demonstrating that they are not yet ready for the separation. Such behavior is transitory.

It would be surprising if the knowledge of termination did not stimulate feelings of separation and loss. The therapeutic experience has been sustaining in its effects. Of course, the manner in which the children adjust to this last and most frustrating experience of all becomes another measure of their real growth.

The following record describes the effects of a worker's announcement of termination. It takes place during the seventieth meeting of the group. The reactions of the boys are interesting. One of them disavows the worker's explanation that they are ready for termination. Another child unconsciously depicts his anxiety about the coming separation by talking of injuries, e.g., loss of tooth and hospitalization. A third child verbalizes about his behavior at the time he started to attend the group. And again, a boy recalls his first visit. All of these reactions to the termination are moderate manifestations of anxiety. In this case they were transient and when the group was finally terminated the boys made adequate adjustments.

. . . Fred entered. He went to the work bench, picked up some wood and said, "These are mine." When Max came in Fred gave him a piece of wood. Max asked him for the hammer "for a minute" and began to use it. Morris and Fred now worked together on their pigeon coop. Ted and George played ball but then they pulled out the swivel chair and they took turns spinning each other around. Max joined them. . . . Worker began to set the table. He waited until Ted returned from the bathroom before serving the ice cream and soda. Fred spotted it and yelled, "Oh boy, soda!" When they were seated, the worker began to speak, pouring soda as he did so: "You know, summer will soon be here and school will be over. You have been coming here for a long time. You are all so big now, and you will not need the group anymore; so we won't be meeting after the vacation."

George was the first to react: "Oh—no more?" Then Ted: "*I* still need it!" Santo said, "Suppose I get left back in school—can I still come?" The worker smiled at this and Santo himself laughed, aware of the almost contrived meaning. Ted commented, "I remember the first time I came." Somehow Fred turned the conversation to polio and sickness. "I don't like 'shots.' I don't like my teeth pulled neither. Once I had teeth pulled; they gave me gas. You can die from gas." George said, "Oh no, silly. If you go to a hospital they don't give you poison gas."

Santo asked, "What will you do with the toys and the tools?" The worker replied, "Well, you know you came here because I wanted to help you. There will be other children who will need help and I will use these for them." George asked, "No more? We won't come here no more?" The worker replied, "Yes, you will come until the end of June."

The boys left the table and returned to various activities. Max, at the easel, said, "I used to splash paint on the paper like this," and demonstrated it. He began to hoot aloud, until several of the boys told him, "Shut up." (It is interesting that Max chose to demonstrate several things he used to do during a highly regressive period of earlier behavior.) When it was time to leave Fred took his woodwork and said, "I'll see you next week." The others followed.

3 The Play Room—Furnishings and Equipment

REQUIREMENTS OF AREA AND DESIGN

In activity type, noninterpretive group therapy practices with children, the setting is no less subject to the requirements of specialization than are the technics of the practitioner. The setting is an integral part of the clinical process; the size and shape of a play room, the furniture, equipment, and the play materials, are desiderata which have meaningful relationship to the interaction in the group. In the absence of optimal physical conditions for therapeutic group practice, it may be possible to make some concessions, but if any unusual circumstances in the physical setting block the worker's ability to maintain the permissive role which is essential, then the setting is inappropriate.*

An optimal floor area of a play room for five or six children would be approximately 300 square feet. An efficient unit of measurement in planning is 50 square feet per person, the worker included.

An irregularly shaped floor area is better than one which is geometrically uniform, such as a square or rectangle. A small entrance foyer, an alcove, or an empty closet (without a lock) are features which lend themselves to special kinds of play and other activities.

To accommodate shy children, who need the protection of partial isolation, at least one part of the room should be apart from the open floor area. On the other hand, the larger floor area should be unencumbered so as to permit free movement for active games and to meet the special needs of hyperactive children. Confinement for them would be oppressive. A room which is too large reduces the opportunities for interaction between children.

Physical conditions which are potentially hazardous to children must be eliminated, or, if this is not feasible, treated in such a way as to reduce the possibility of accidents. Glass in doors or partitions can be removed and replaced with wood. Exposed pipes which extend into the room, swinging doors, and low window-sills are examples of other structural conditions

---

* This was the case in a clinic which attempted to use one large room for several purposes. During most of the week, four social workers used it as a common office. At other times it was used for activity type therapy groups. At such times, the desks, cabinets, and other items used by the social workers were pushed against one wall. Ostensibly they were to be inviolate. The group therapist became involved repetitively in protecting the setting.

which should be remedied. A nail driven into a window frame will prevent the opening of a lower window; a swinging door can be made safe by changing hinges or adding door checks; exposed pipes can be enclosed or covered with padded materials.

Figure 2 shows simplified floor designs of regular and irregular play room areas. The shaded parts represent structural features which are not within the play room:

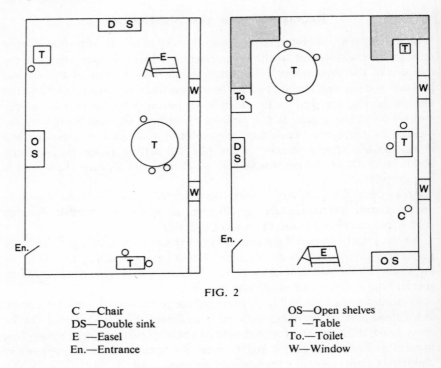

FIG. 2

C —Chair   OS—Open shelves
DS—Double sink   T —Table
E —Easel   To.—Toilet
En.—Entrance   W—Window

FURNISHINGS

The need to match furniture to the children who use it cannot be overstated. The requirements for tables and chairs are that they be of proper size and sturdy. For the purposes of therapeutic group practice, used furniture is better than new.

Three tables are sufficient for a group of five or six children. One should be round and large enough to accommodate all the children and the worker at one time. Two smaller tables are necessary; one to accommodate two children, and the other of the same size and placed in a corner of the play room for a child who needs to withdraw.

Supplies, games, and other materials are exposed in an open cabinet or on bookshelves, and easily accessible to the children. Blocks may be kept in sturdy cartons. A double easel is best located in a well lighted corner of the room. Where floor space is limited, a double easel can easily be separated into two single units, which can be set side by side and attached to a wall. The wall adjoining the easel should be covered with oilcloth, and the floor beneath with newspaper. Oilcloth should never be used on floors since it becomes slippery when wet.

A play room should be well-illuminated and adequately ventilated. Preferred wall colors are pastel shades, such as green, yellow, blue, or pink; gray or brown may be more utilitarian, but they are depressing colors. If decorative pictures are used, framed or otherwise, they should be neutral in content.* Much of the wall space in a play room is eventually used to display the finished art work of the members of a play group.

A double sink with one, large, deep-well section is important for several purposes: washing, water play, particularly for young children. Where no sink is available, large containers of water may be used, several for washing hands and some for cleaning brushes and other items. Housekeeping implements are always necessary in a play room: broom, dust pan, mop, pail, dust rags, wastebaskets, old newspapers, etc.

Children are imaginative architects; in the permissive play group their play needs prompt them to make spontaneous alterations of the setting to fit immediate plans. Thus, tables and chairs are often readily moved about to make forts, ships, and barricades. Even fixed furniture becomes incorporated in play. One group, for a period of time, would clear out the bottom shelf of a large, metal cabinet, and this then became a "hide out." A swivel chair was used by another group as a wonderful merry-go-round. More aggressive games—"cops and robbers," "cowboys and Indians"—convert toilets, closets, and chairs into "hide-outs," houses, or automobiles.

This ready manipulation of the environment is one fascinating expression of children's imagination, and it depicts their capacities to change the setting so that it can be used to complement play activities or as a vehicle for expressing aggression and other feelings.

As noted earlier, some modifications can be made in the basic setting and furnishings of a play room. Imagination and good therapeutic practice can transcend the limitations of some settings; poor practice cannot succeed in optimal physical surroundings.

---

* One play room visited by the author had a series of highly stimulating posters on a wall, one depicting an angry father chastising his son. It is conceivable that such content could be used profitably in some clinical settings, but it was entirely unsuitable for a play room. The author feels that a play room, initially, should be devoid of pictures or posters. The eventual use made of the wall areas will be determined by the needs of the children.

PLAY MATERIALS, GAMES, CRAFTS

Criteria for Selecting Play and Other Items

Play, game, and craft items which are used in therapeutic groups are selected purposefully; they are not simply an aggregate of "things" which children like. While it is important that all items have intrinsic interest for children, they must also be of a nature to contribute to the therapeutic program. Complicated toys and games, which tend to capture attention but which are not expressive media, are self-defeating.

Items have therapeutic value if they serve one or more of the following purposes: to facilitate communication; promote interaction; satisfy creative needs; develop manipulative skills; provide relaxation.

Valence: A Measure of Therapeutic Value

The term "valence"* may be used to measure the potential an item possesses for inducing communication, which is of fundamental importance in experiential, activity-type therapeutic processes. High valence play objects can be toy representations of persons who are significant in the lives of children. In contrast, low valence items are not identifiable with significant persons or experiences but are used by children for creative output and in developing new skills. Thus, father, mother, brother, sister, and infant dolls and hand puppets are high in valence; while a loom used for weaving and a paint brush have low valence. A low valence item may have higher value momentarily if it is used in ways other than its intended purpose, usually in the expression of impulsive feelings. A child who uses a loom or a wet paint brush to threaten another child invests these objects with other meanings.

The valence of materials is also influenced by the quantity which is made available to the children. If too many dolls or puppets are used, the motivational strength of the media becomes diluted. Thus, if there are multiple sets of dolls and puppets—depicting family members, doctors, policemen, nurses, truck drivers, "walking-talking-wetting dolls,"— their communicative value, even as high valence items, is lessened. Further, interaction between children becomes impeded or unproductive whenever a play group is over-supplied with materials.†

---

* In chemistry, valence is a measure of the combining powers of elements.

† Uncritical and exorbitant use of materials in play group practice may be due to inexperience but it is sometimes an unconscious expression of insecurity on the part of the practitioner. In the latter instance, the practitioner unconsciously "hides behind" the equipment. This also applies in the practice of play therapy with individual children.

Categories of Items Used in Play Groups

The objects used in play groups may be grouped into the following categories:

Objects representing significant persons and animals: dolls, puppets, a large, inflatable plastic figure, face masks.

Objects which are identified with significant persons and their activities: adult "dress-up" clothing, crib, carriage, refrigerator, sink, toy size house furniture.

Plastic, multifunctional media: poster paints, finger paints, plasticene clay, self-hardening clay, blocks, water.

Manipulative skill and craft materials: lumber and basic wood working tools, looms for weaving, leather craft, materials for sewing, knitting, crocheting.

Recreational supplies, toys and games: ring toss, a soft rubber ball, a simple boxed game which two or more children can play at one time, dominoes, checkers, pick-up-sticks, Nok Hockey, truck, auto, airplane.

Not all of these items are used at the same time in all play groups. Differences in age and sex, plus other special determinants, are the controlling factors, and these will vary from one group to another. Finger paints, for instance, can be highly regressive media for some children and sublimating for others. Therefore they should be used only after consideration has been given to the potential effects on all the members of a play group. "Dress-up" clothing must be appropriate to the sex of the group. It would certainly be a serious error to make female clothing available to a boy who has problems in sexual identification. Nor is it wise to have knitting and crocheting materials in boys' groups, or woodwork in girls' groups.

OBJECTS REPRESENTING SIGNIFICANT PERSONS AND ANIMALS

Such objects are high in psychological valence because they induce individual and group play in which children reveal their feelings and attitudes about parents, siblings, and other persons. Reactions to authority, hostility, fears, and wishes become more easily expressed through the use of psychologically significant play objects. Puppets which are representative of a family, nurse, doctor, policeman, alligator, and tiger, are used in play in the identities which they manifestly depict, and sometimes in symbolic ways. Thus, the alligator or tiger may be used aggressively by a child in acting out his own hostile impulses, or, they may represent, in less conscious fashion, the imagery of a parent as a threatening object.

Hand puppets of molded rubber are more effective in expressing emotionally charged feelings than are dolls. Placement of the hand within a puppet, in order to manipulate it, promotes identification with the puppet and facilitates communication. Multiple roles can be enacted by one child through the use of two or more puppets. The persistent use of a particular puppet or doll, over an extended period of time, may be a clue to significant areas of conflict in a child's life.

Doll figures are frequently used in combination with other play items, such as blocks and house furniture, in playing out more complex situations. For this purpose, simple one piece dolls of molded rubber or plastic (with painted clothing) are better than complicated ones which can walk, talk, cry, blink, and wet in confusing, unbiologic ways. String puppets should be avoided entirely because they require advanced skills and are frustrating to young children. Also to be avoided are amputee-type dolls, which permit arms, legs, and heads to be torn off and replaced. Such dolls can create great anxiety in some children when their hostility expressed in play terminates in actual dismemberment. Symbolically this could be equivalent to castration or death.

In girls' play groups, several larger dolls with real clothing are suitable. A carriage, crib, and other furniture items for house play with these dolls should be available.

George and His Frog!

George was seven years old when he was placed in a play group. He had a fraternal twin who seemed to be making a better overall adjustment. George was very immature and dependent on his mother, to whom he clung. He had no friends; he seemed to be satisfied with isolative play; he was preoccupied with his own thoughts. When he entered kindergarten, he separated from his mother with much difficulty. In the first grade, his teacher described him as overly dependent on her and completely disinterested in learning.

Surprisingly enough, George did not appear frightened when he came to his play group for the first time. He was intrigued by the play materials, in particular with a rubber hand puppet, shaped like a frog. This became his *alter ego;* for the next four months this frog puppet was used by no other child in the play group. The moment George entered the play room, he would run to the shelves and grab the frog. He seemed oblivious of the other children and the worker as he enacted various phantasies. George was far from lethargic under the magic influence of the frog. He moved about the play room rapidly, making different sounds to accentuate the particular roles that the frog (George) assumed. Once, with a small, cloth cape which he made and attached to the frog, George became Super Frog, zooming through the air from one end of the room to the other, occasionally taking off into flight from the top shelf of the supply cabinet. Other times the frog became aquatic, as George played with water in the deep well of the sink. George even ate refreshments by having the frog hold the cookies, cake, or fruit which were served by the worker.

The other children accepted George with amused tolerance. A few times when he was threatened, one of the more aggressive boys in the group came to his defense. From that point on George was no longer provoked by others.

One meeting George and his frog were very busy at the window. It was only when he left that the worker could determine what he had done: George (frog) had hung a rubber figure by the neck with the cord of the window shade. It was the father figure. (In reality, George's father showed open preference for his twin brother, who was more active and aggressive.) The frog (George!) for many meetings thereafter, visited different forms of mayhem on various and sundry puppets, dolls, and finally, objects indiscriminate. George never missed a group meeting.

By the end of the first year, the worker reported that George was much more involved with the other children. He seldom used the frog, or any other puppet, in his play activities. He provoked other children through mild teasing, followed by running away. The boys still tolerated him, as one might react to a mild irritant. More and more he began to join them in games and block construction. George's mother reported marked changes in his attitudes and behavior at home; his teacher confirmed this observation.

Comment: George was a child who had suppressed aggression. Internalization led to tremendous ruminative phantasy. This was manifest in his facial expression; he always appeared "removed" from peripheral stimuli. His eyes were often blank, even when someone spoke to him. In the permissive group he slowly converted aggression which had been limited to autistic phantasy into action—through the frog. Through identification and magic—the latter being the process which makes the unknown, or the feared consequence tolerable for young children—the *enactment* of aggression became safe. It then became only a matter of time before this puerile aggression became stronger and more direct in its manifestations.

Face masks are interesting and productive play items. Two are sufficient; one to represent a "bad" symbol—witch, devil; the other a "good" symbol—policeman. When masks are used, children will invariably play in pairs, and the process of role selection and the subsequent verbal content can be informative.

The meanings which are conveyed through play with dolls, puppets, and other high valence play items are often symbolic, and the children are essentially unaware of the unconscious origins of the emotions which accompany their play. However, children can also be quite direct in play and conscious of its reality basis and their feelings. At such times, because children are well aware of the identities of the play objects and the roles and feelings which they attribute to them or enact upon them, play becomes an important pathway for the discharge of strong feelings. There is therapeutic value in the ventilation of affect through play, *even in its symbolic, unconscious form,* particularly for children who have previously had inadequate or inappropriate outlets for suppressed emotions.

The following examples, extracted from records of different play groups, illustrate how high valence items become used in meaningful play:

Eli is eight years old. In the play group he has been playing with dolls and puppets constantly, ignoring the games, construction materials and painting. During this particular meeting he picked up the small, rubber, family dolls and played with them on the floor. While he played he gave a running commentary in a squeaking voice. At one point the worker overheard: "He's my husband!" Then, in a falsetto voice, obviously mimicking another person, "No. He's my husband!" Finally: "Let's share him!"

Comment: Eli's parents were having marital difficulties, and the child was obviously distressed by the bickering he observed. In his doll play it may be that Eli was unconsciously expressing preference for his father in this conflict situation. His "solution" of the problem was simple and childishly pragmatic. There is a further possibility that Eli's "solution" may indicate a deeper problem, one having to do with his own sexual identification.

Roger is ten years old. He has experienced extreme rejection—first from a father who deserted; then from his mother, who has little interest in either Roger or his siblings.

During this group meeting Roger sat at the supply closet and played for awhile in isolation. At times he appeared to be oblivious of his surroundings. He picked up the toy telephone, dialed, and whispered: "Hello, hello, calling all cars! Hit and run driver . . . corner 93rd Street. Go to the accident! Hello, hello." Then, more reflectively, Roger whispered: "Hit and run, *mother*." A moment later he picked up a mother goat and a baby goat. These were small, molded, rubber figures. Roger had the baby goat nuzzle the teat of the mother. Then, impulsively, and for a brief moment, he put his own mouth to the teat of the goat. Suddenly he seemed to become aware of what he was doing. With a self-conscious laugh he threw the goats to the floor, shrugging his shoulders as he did so. He ran to the worker, took her arm and engaged her in conversation.

Comment: The content speaks for itself. Roger's contact with the worker immediately after the dramatic—and tragic—play, is an obvious act of drawing emotional sustenance from the relationship.

Sam has attended 47 meetings; he is nine years old. When referred, he was fearful and passive. Recently he has been able to act aggressively in the play group. In a puppet show during the forty-seventh meeting, Sam, for the first time, enacts his hostility towards his sister:

. . . Suddenly Sam said: "I'm going to do a puppet show." He asked the others to join him but they refused. He said he would do it by himself. He took puppets and sat on the floor near the worker, who watched. He named the play: "Ledge of Danger," and said it was about a boy and a girl who went mountain climbing. They climbed very high so "if they fall it would be about 5,000 feet up." Frank laughed at this and said to him, "5,000 feet down, you dope!" Sam giggled and corrected himself. Meanwhile, in the enactment with the puppets, the parents worry and the father climbs after the children. Suddenly the boy trips and holds onto the edge by his hands. His sister tries to help him but she falls down the mountain and is killed. Finally father arrives and rescues his son. The ambulance comes and takes the girl, but she is dead. Sam took the xylophone and played a funeral march.

Comment: Heretofore Sam has had need to suppress hostility and anger. As a consequence, he withdrew from others to fortify his defenses. He is learning through this puppet play, and through other experiences and observations he makes in the play group, that aggression can be expressed safely, without danger to himself or others.

From another record:

Carl is in the first grade. About two months ago his mother lost a child at birth. Shortly thereafter his father died suddenly of a stroke. Prior to this extract—from the twentieth meeting of the play group—Carl had never demonstrated an interest in puppets. There were a few times in the past when he pushed them off the shelf aggressively, but then he moved on to other activities.

. . . Carl brushed the puppets off the shelf brusquely, then picked them up, punched and squeezed them. He took the baby puppet, folded it roughly and said: "I'll make a house that'll satisfy him." He placed the puppet on the floor, built a structure with blocks around it and then covered the top, completely enclosing the baby. The other puppets lay on the floor nearby. He picked up the father and placed other puppets around his block building (grave)—persistently handling them in an aggressive way. At one point he placed the mother puppet face to face with the father and said: "She's making him have a stroke." He then separated the mother and father, as in a prize fight ring, placed the boy and girl puppets in the middle, and mumbled something to the effect that they were fighting.

Comment: Carl enacts the deaths of the infant lost in childbirth and also his father's, at the same time manifesting anxiety and confusion about the tragic events which actually took place. Further, he demonstrates hostility toward his mother, whom he holds accountable for his father's stroke. He reveals his unhappiness about earlier parental bickering by placing the boy puppet (himself) between the parents. It is also possible that there is an element of projection of his own guilt feelings upon the mother.

During this revealing puppet play Carl sometimes watched the worker to observe her reaction. She made no comment at any point. Carl seemed more relaxed when he discarded the puppets to join David in another activity.

From the records of another group:

Danny entered the play room and immediately picked up the puppets. He spoke aloud as he played with them. When Peter arrived, he joined Danny. At first the boys made the crocodile and the bird puppets fight with each other. Danny then picked up the family puppets and said: "The mountain was high and the mother

died." He threw her on the floor. The father puppet came to take her away but the
bird devoured them. Danny said: "Only the bones are left!" Among other disasters
he visited on them were: "Everyone was burned up" "Later they all froze to death."
Peter, meanwhile, attempted to "rescue" the persons who were being "killed" by
Danny by having his bird puppet pick them up. Danny ignored this and continued
his hostile play. It was quite evident that Peter was being made anxious and was
trying to block Danny's open hostility.

Quite similar to this was the interaction between two other young children
in another play group:

Lately Kevin has been playing with the small doll figures. Under the easel there is
a pail, partially filled with water which is used for cleaning brushes. Kevin painted
some of the family figures and then announced rhetorically that he was "cleaning 'em
up." To do this he plunged the small dolls deep into the water in an aggressive
manner. Soon the pattern of painting and cleaning became modified and Kevin was
very obviously drowning the father, mother, and children by having them fall or
dive from great heights into the water. Karl was alarmed by this play of Kevin's. He
had been studying it while squatting next to Kevin. Suddenly Karl began to retrieve
each figure from the water as Kevin was preparing different ones for immersion.
Using the cloth smock, Karl carefully dried (saved!) each doll.
This play persisted in almost identical form for some part of several play group
meetings which followed.

Comment: The meanings in both of the preceding examples are almost
exact. Kevin and Danny are able to ventilate their hostilities openly and
vigorously. On the other hand, Karl and Peter, dismayed by the intensity of
this destructive acting out, are mobilized into actions which attempt to
block it. Such play induces anxiety which is intolerable to Karl and Peter,
and they must *deny* their own suppressed aggression by "saving" the figures.
Eventually they will be able to act out some of their severely blocked feelings,
as they develop assurance (consciously) that the act—in play—is not equivalent to the wish. Later in the therapeutic process their aggression will find
even more direct focus against the worker, in the transference relationship.

In play situations, emotionally disturbed young children actually alleviate
feelings of anxiety, fear, and confusion, all of which are associated with
traumatic life experiences. This becomes possible through play because
diffuse and disabling emotions are given form and substance by being concretized through enactment with material substances, e.g., dolls, puppets,
blocks, etc.

In essence, through such play, a child unconsciously extends affect-laden
experience beyond himself, thus becoming able to see it and also to manipulate it. Having made it more tangible, he then acquires at least partial control
over the overwhelming emotions attached to traumatic experience. This is a
"natural" pathway of expression for troubled children; they are unable to

cope with extraordinary stress situations through intellectualization, as do adults.*

The enactment of a "charged" experience through play, *in the presence of the accepting group worker*, has an additional therapeutic advantage of reducing the guilt which a child feels as he converts hostile phantasies into activities. The permissive worker relaxes the over-strict superego, freeing the child so that he can express his emotions.

The relief which is experienced by children through play may be of itself a sufficient discharge of emotional stress. This is so if the personality has not been severely distorted in structure and function by disturbing experiences. When traumatization has been such as to effect persistent disturbance in ego functioning, play is not sufficient; it becomes necessary for the therapist to help children explore and verbalize about the manifest and latent meanings of their dramatic play.

OBJECTS WHICH ARE IDENTIFIABLE WITH SIGNIFICANT PERSONS

Adult "dress-up" types of clothing are excellent expressive media. They have the quality of hand puppets in that they facilitate the process of identification. It is important that "dress-up" clothing be appropriate to the sex of the children in a play group.†

In play group practice the following items of "dress-up" clothing are sufficient: for boys' groups—a man's felt hat, jacket and shoes; for girls' groups—a lady's hat, short coat, purse, and high heels. Long dresses should be shortened so that children will not trip.

The foregoing items have a pronounced influence on the content of children's play. Children invariably depict parent behavior as it exists in reality or, they express in phantasy their wishes for change in parent attitudes. In such play children are drawn together and a shifting of roles is a prominent feature of their play. As children play together, they will often criticize each other and give explicit judgements as to the correctness or inappropriateness of "parent" behavior.

Spontaneous role enactment by children has several values in the play group process. The worker is able to learn more about interaction in the children's families and about children's attitudes, expectations, and wishes

---

* Even with adults, cognitive processes offer insufficient relief from the extraordinary emotional impacts of experiences such as death, or other traumatic forms of separation from persons in close relationship to them. Children fill emotional vacuums with phantasy and play; adults are dependent on more complicated, ritualistic procedures.

† Many children—disturbed ones in particular—have enough difficulty in psychosexual development without having it made more confusing through the use of inappropriate symbols of sex identification. Both male and female "dress-up" clothing should be available in heterogeneous play groups of boys and girls, where a worker team is present.

with respect to parents and siblings. Also, through sublimated pathways, the children have an opportunity to express love, anger, rivalry, dependence, independence, and other personal needs. Such play also helps in solidifying sexual identification. It is also conceivable that young children may acquire a degree of empathic understanding of their parents through role play.

INFLATABLE PLASTIC FIGURE—AN INVALUABLE PLAY ITEM

These may be obtained in different sizes. For play groups it is best to use the largest, which is about four and a half feet in height, with a sand weighted bottom to hold it erect. It is made of heavy-gauge plastic and is painted to represent various characters, such as a prize-fighter or a clown.

Experience with the large, inflated figure in play groups has shown that it has high valence as a therapeutic tool. As children use the figure, and in their associated verbalizations, they consistently demonstrate that the figure is conceptualized by them as a representative of living persons. The manner in which different children "play" with the figure can be an index of their potential for aggression and further, of consequent guilt or anxiety. Workers observe massive bursts of aggression by some children against the figure, accompanied or followed by revealing somatic signs, such as flushing, lip biting, perspiration, and panting. After impulsive assaults on the figure, children may display compensatory guilt reactions. This can be seen most dramatically with children who are grossly immobilized when first referred for help and who cannot use even an inanimate plastic figure as an outlet for aggressions. When such children eventually become capable of expressing anger, the compensatory behavior which follows is quite overt. This need to compensate diminishes with time.

Children would probably be more constrained in using plastic figures as outlets for aggression if they were too easily invested with the identities of persons who are significant in the children's lives.*

The plastic figure is invaluable in the therapeutic process because it permits activated aggression without fear of retaliation. Children benefit from the release of aggression against the *symbolic* representation of the parent, sibling, teacher, and group worker.

Peter, eight years old, was intrigued with the figure when the worker first added it to the equipment of the play group. After several exploratory pushes, he moved back in a boxer's stance and proceeded to jab and punch the figure vigorously. At one point Peter paused, looked pointedly at the worker and said, "He's big, just like you!"

* It is probably not altogether fortuitous that manufacturers of such plastic figures avoid making them as replicas of real persons—male or female. The designs are undoubtedly influenced by unconscious forces. Another example of this influence is the multitude of dolls of all sizes and types—but all without genitals!

Assault on the person of the worker rarely occurs. It may take place with very young children, or with older ones who are psychopaths or schizophrenic. They should not be in play groups.

There are times when hostility directed against the plastic figure becomes so massive that a child may be unable to control his impulsive anger. He may try to strike the figure with a block or a hammer, or attempt to stab it with a pencil or another pointed implement. The worker must limit such violent attacks because they are symbolic forms of homicide. If permitted free expression, such behavior engenders massive guilt and anxiety and sometimes brings about panic reactions in children.

Carlo, seven years old, was punching the large plastic figure (prize-fighter) vigorously. His attack upon it became more violent; he began to kick it and he, even picked it off the floor and threw it about several times. He was red-faced, perspiring, and seemingly oblivious of what the other children were doing. After one particularly heavy assault, during which he kicked the figure viciously near its base, it suddenly deflated and collapsed. Carlo stepped back in utter dismay, fear imprinted on his face. The worker walked over, picked up the figure and placed it in the corner. She said: "*It's only a toy*. They often break like this. I'll fix it or get another."

Comment: Carlo was terrified because he had "destroyed" the puppet. Perhaps his anger had an accompanying phantasy in which the puppet was identified with someone he knew. The worker's remarks reduced Carlo's anxiety and guilt.

Kyle, age seven, was referred because he was hyperactive, aggressive, and highly provocative. In the play group he was infantile, impulsive, and he demanded much of the worker's attention. His interest span was minimal; he flitted about the room from one thing to another. He abused the plastic figure constantly, often prohibiting others from using it. One day he punched it with great intensity, then reached down and yanked at the valve. It tore out and the figure immediately deflated. Kyle was shocked and seemed ready to panic. The worker picked it up, put it in the storage closet and said, "I'll fix it; *It's a toy*." In this instance the worker again reduces anxiety by restoring the reality identity of the toy—thus denying the consequences of aggressive phantasy against the symbolic adult.

Other emotions are communicated through the large figure. There are times when it is hugged, kissed, and handled affectionately. Some children caress it while sucking their own fingers, like infants. Others may straddle the figure, lie on it, or place it over themselves on the floor. Whenever the figure is used in acting out to an extraordinary degree—whether the acting out be hostile, immature or libidinal—the worker should limit it, or convert the activity to levels which are therapeutically purposeful.

Charles, seven years old, often attacked the plastic figure, which was at least a foot taller than he was. One day, while punching and mauling it vigorously, he exclaimed aloud about what he was doing to "baby!" Several times he tried to strike the figure on the head with a block. The worker limited this.

Nancy is seven. She is preoccupied to an unusual extent with libidinal stories and phantasies. In playing with the other children she often speaks of "getting married," and "boy friends." Her behavior with boys is exaggeratedly feminine and seductive. In the play group her behavior is of a social contact type, with much verbalization. During one meeting she began to manipulate the plastic figure. After rocking it back and forth she pushed it prone, holding it so that it could not come upright. Then she sat on it, straddling it with her legs. For a short time she bounced up and down, then lay on it with her legs still astride it. Slowly, in rhythmic manner she began to rub her body against the figure. The worker walked over and invited Nancy to play a game with her.

Comment: It was necessary to interrupt Nancy's erotic, masturbatory activity. It could also have over-stimulated the other children.

There is an anxiety reaction which is commonly observed with children who are initially very passive. When they become able to act out aggressively, they do compensatory "penance" for their guilt by forcing the figure to punish them.

Yvonne, seven years old, was referred as a timid, frightened child. She was uncommunicative and for a long time, occupied herself in isolated play in the group. As she became more secure she also became mildly aggressive. In this meeting she began to push the plastic figure to and fro in a rocking motion. Finally she gathered enough courage to strike it. After a few minutes of this mildly aggressive play, she grabbed the figure, pulled it sharply toward herself, making it "hit" her in retaliation. Then she herself deliberately fell to the floor, as if she had been beaten. She smiled as she did this.

One group of children had subjected the figure to such abuse that it leaked and collapsed. Lily seemed to be particularly upset, perhaps because she had been most active in assaulting it. The worker was unable to repair the figure for several weeks. Every week Lily inquired about it. She even wondered if it was "in the hospital!" There was manifest relief when the figure was replaced.

Max is nine years old and has been in a play group for two and one half years. He was overprotected by a demanding, overwhelming, driving mother. When referred, Max was constantly teased by children who called him "sissy," among other things. He had no friends. During the time he has been in the play group he has become less fearful and dependent, and he has made friends in the neighborhood. In the play group itself he is more aggressive. When the plastic figure was introduced, Max was intrigued but he could only touch it in a diffident manner, retreating when it rolled back toward him. With each succeeding meeting he became braver; finally he struck it with violence. This blow unleashed hostility which had slowly been coming close to the surface. He became flushed and excited as he started to belabor the figure.

It is interesting to note that in a following meeting, when the worker inquired about bruise marks on his face, Max told her *pridefully* that he had been in a fight on the street.

An extract from another meeting of this same play group reveals Max's aggression, some indication of his anxiety after acting aggressively and awareness on the part of other group members of Max's growing strength.

Max said to the worker: "What do you think . . . pretty good, eh?" He showed the worker an airplane he had made from wood. Holding the airplane (masculine achievement) under his arm, he approached the plastic figure saying, "Now it's *my* turn." He socked it once and said, "Pretty good." He walloped it again and again. George looked and said, "Hey, you *can* hit it!" Max giggled; he continued to punch it. John, who was seated, watched Max hit it so hard that the figure actually bounced off the floor. He and George exclaimed spontaneously: "Wow!" Max put his hand to his mouth in utter surprise, then laughed. George said, "You're strong, Max." Max replied politely, "Thank you." He continued punching, then walked away from it and said, "I wouldn't hurt it *if it was a real person.*"

PLASTIC MEDIA—MULTIFUNCTIONAL, VARIABLE VALENCE

In this category are poster and finger paints, plasticene clay, self-hardening clay, construction blocks of different sizes and shapes, sand, and water. As determined by the varying needs of children, such materials will be used aggressively, regressively, or creatively. Psychologically they have great latitude as expressive media. In contrast, a toy plane would have more restricted functional use and meaning.

Liquid and semiliquid materials have additional values for young children. They are at an age when experimentation with color, form, and consistency is helpful, not only in the process of learning but also in the sublimation of infantile behavior. In play groups it has been noted that immature children are particularly interested in working with liquid media.

In permissive group practices the question of intervention arises because liquid materials lend themselves too readily to aggressive and regressive acting out. Some limits can be "built in" by the worker through judicious control of the quantities and types of materials provided, and through protective (limiting) paraphernalia, e.g., smocks, newspapers under an easel, rags for cleaning, clay board.*

Poster color paints should be provided in reasonable quantities; small, plastic cups, each containing about one inch of paint, will be sufficient for one group meeting. It would be reckless to provide full pint or quart jars of paint. Fresh paints should be available at the start of each group meeting and mixed colors discarded. Five different colors are sufficient in poster paints, and finger paints if they are used: black, white, red, yellow, and blue. Paint brushes about one inch in width, with short bristles, and large sheets of

* There are times when the worker may have to use more direct intervention, especially when young children use paints, water, sand, and clay when they act out.

paper are necessary. Young children draw and paint using large muscle movements; they have not developed sufficiently to do small line, detailed work. A roll paper dispenser with a heavy grade of newsprint is invaluable for art work.

FINGER PAINTS USED WITH DISCRIMINATION

There is no question as to the value of finger paints as an exploratory and creative medium for normal young children. They are able to use this form of art expression successfully, even before they have developed sufficient muscular dexterity to manipulate the tools necessary for more advanced forms of art work. For children finger paints have a sublimating value also in that, through their use, smearing and messing become channeled into more acceptable social expressions.

Whether to use finger paints with emotionally disturbed children in therapeutic practices, particularly in the play group, should be determined only after consideration of several variables. These are: the nature of the child problems in the group; how the children affect each other in the interaction. To particularize: one child in a play group might benefit from the use of finger paints; in the same group, however, finger paints may be contraindicated for another child, or because of the interaction which is currently taking place.

The worker should know which children have need for materials with high, regressive potential which are necessary to resolve elements of their problems. At the same time, in his assessment of all the children in the play group, he must also know the children who have made effective sublimations and who might become uncomfortable if they observe others smearing with finger paints. Further, he must decide the extent to which the need to handle liquid and semiliquid materials is already being satisfied through the existing play materials in the group, e.g., clay, water, sand, poster colors, paste.

Finger paints should be used on an empirical basis; they should not be considered a standard item of supply for all play groups.

Maria was six years old. She was blocked in all levels of communication—mannerisms, facial expression, and speech. She was not mute; she spoke to her parents and siblings, although she was constricted even at home. In school she never spoke, even after a whole year in kindergarten. Maria was a pretty child, and she was always dressed like she was ready for a birthday party. She was never relaxed; her movements were slow and ungraceful.

Maria was placed in a play group made up of three boys and three girls, with a worker team of a man and a woman. For many months Maria behaved as anticipated: she never spoke; her expression was neutral, never revealing thought or emotion. She observed all that transpired between children and the workers, but she herself never ventured into contact with anyone. She permitted children to make contact with her but she did not talk to them. Maria could work side by side with another child who chose to sit next to her. Maria fingered many of the play objects but she always avoided paints, paste, and any other liquid or semiliquid material. Maria was always conscious of the need to be orderly and clean. The other children did not bother her; they sensed her need for isolation.

The workers introduced finger paints: some of the children were fascinated, they had never seen such paints before. Several of them worked intently with the finger paints, week after week. The female worker would always help them set up; she put smocks on them; opened up the jars when necessary; wet the special paper used for finger paints; supplied them with plenty of paper towels for cleaning. Maria watched in fascination—but she *would not sit* at the table where other children were using the paint. It became apparent, as weeks passed that Maria was in a quiet struggle with ambivalent feelings about the finger painting. She observed a few episodes of acting out with the finger paints by some of the others, but this did not represent a problem requiring direct intervention by the workers.

One meeting Maria sat next to another girl who was using the finger paint. She watched. The other child silently offered to let Maria participate; she did not respond. Even more weeks passed before Maria gave the slightest "signal" that she was ready for the experience. (The worker's technic, at such time, had already been discussed in supervision conference—as had the original question of introducing the finger paints.) When the worker discerned a slight movement by Maria to touch a piece of paper on the table, she approached her and, without a word, helped Maria into a smock, then spread a piece of paper before her with opened jars of finger paint. Maria glanced up and saw only the back of the female worker, who was already moving on to something else. Maria then stared at the child next to her, who was blissfully engaged in smearing away with hands colored to the wrists with bright paints. Her eyes then wandered to the paper before her, the paints, then her own hands. She stood up, went to the easel, appropriated several paint brushes, sat down and began to paint straight lines with the brushes dipped into finger paints! When she finished, she replaced the brushes in the cleaning can. Later, the worker hung Maria's paper on the wall, as was the practice with the art work done by all the children. In a few more weeks Maria became able to touch the finger paint with her fingers, first one at a time—experimentally, then with the palms of one hand, and finally with both hands together. The workers began to detect noticeable changes in Maria's body movements; she became more fluid, relaxed.

For Maria, the use of finger paints became the first important "breakthrough" in an already, highly organized, compulsive pattern of order, neatness, and cleanliness.

Another play group of six-seven year old children had reached a point in group development where much interaction was taking place. The meetings were characterized by much excitement, with games involving chases around the room, pushing chairs, yelling and other energetic forms of activity. The worker had correctly interpreted this activity as a phase of testing and exhilaration on the part of the children because of the "discovery" of the permissive adult. However, she felt that it would be wise to impede the momentum of this behavior because it was beginning to have a manic quality. She thought that the introduction of new play materials would act as a method of capturing attention and diverting some energy into less manic behavior. She was correct: her only error was to include finger paints as one of the new items. Within five minutes, despite her best attempts to retrieve the situation, every child in the group was a hand painted "Indian" on the war path, looking to paint up another "Indian." Of course it became difficult for the worker to get more finger paint for the next meeting!

Large crayons and tempera chalk are good media for children to experiment with in attempting more detailed drawing.

Sculptor's self-hardening clay can be kept indefinitely in a covered metal can or crock if it is moistened from time to time. Plasticene, an oil clay, will remain pliable if stored in a metal box in sunlight on a window sill or on a radiator. Both types of clay are excellent creative media and they can also be used safely in aggressive play.

Sand and water should be available for children five to six years of age. A divided sand box, with one compartment suitable for holding a few inches of water, is ideal. Several shovels, pails, and some small, floating toys may be kept in the sand box. The water-sand box is best located in a corner of the play room so that three of its sides are accessible. Besides satisfying important experiential and sublimative needs, the interaction which takes place at the sand box between children helps them develop a capacity for shared play.

BLOCKS—VALUABLE AS EXPRESSIVE, CREATIVE, SUBLIMATIVE MEDIUM

Construction blocks are resistive media but they are functionally very flexible. They are included in the category of plastic materials because the uses to which they are put are almost without limit. They also stimulate interaction and communication between the children.

While blocks are high valence play items, they are more sublimating than other plastic media such as paint, water, sand, and clay. Aggression released through block play is less regressive than that which is set in motion through liquid or semiliquid media. It is the fixed forms of blocks which lead to more integrated, functional output.

Children are intrigued with blocks because they can be used to duplicate elements of their expanding world: buildings, ships, trains, airplanes, and other, more complicated structures. There is much satisfaction in block play, and children develop feelings of power through block construction because the things they create are tangible equivalents of the "grown-up" world.

Blocks can also become part of more symbolic play with the addition of dolls and puppets. As with the sand-water box, blocks draw children together, and the ensuing problems and clashes, successes or failures, become opportunities for important learning experiences.

More than other materials in the play room, blocks are invaluable in testing the permissiveness of the worker. A tall building which falls because of faults in construction, or because it is "accidentally" pushed, makes a devastating racket. Since there is no danger, the worker does not impose limits, and the children experience a dramatic example of tolerance.

In a play group which had been meeting for about one month, several boys were playing with blocks. These boys, eight years of age, were busily occupied in constructing various buildings on the floor. One of them decided to transfer his work to one of the tables, which was about two and a half feet high. He was joined by another child. They began to make a tall, tower-like structure. The four other boys who were present became aware of this structure, which had assumed dramatic proportion; it was now taller than any one child. They all assembled; excitement rose. In order to increase the height of the building, which was being described variously as the "Empire State" building and a "mountain," the boys stood on chairs, and even on the table itself, as they added blocks to the structure. Occasionally there were shouted warnings from one to the other as the project swayed perilously. Many times the boys stole glances at the worker who was busy in another part of the room. The worker knew what was going on; the boys became aware that the worker was not going to interfere in their "experiment!"

The inevitable took place: the thunder of crashing blocks reverberated through the room; the floor seemed to shudder under the impact. Even the boys covered their ears to mute the ear-shattering noise. The boys studied the worker, who had looked up when the crash took place. The worker returned to cleaning the shelf. The boys, on the other hand, returned to rebuilding the tall edifice of blocks and then proceeded to "dynamite" it by throwing blocks at its base.

For several weeks thereafter this type of activity continued, with several or all of the boys participating at different times. The worker "survived" this period of acting out, at the cost of several corking headaches and a number of aspirins!

MANIPULATIVE SKILL MATERIALS—CRAFTS

Children need outlets for creative expression through manipulative skills which enable them to fabricate tangible objects. Achievement through crafts work is edifying and ego strengthening. Because such activity is interest binding, it also provides an opportunity to relax from tension and emotionally charged experience. Where high valence materials tend to stimulate emotional responses and interaction, crafts materials, because of their more neutral quality, become invaluable as diversions. Children need to escape from stress no less than do adults, perhaps more so.

Interest in craft work grows and is maintained on a productive level when a play group is advanced in its development; when the interaction between the children becomes more constructive in its effects. This comes about after there has been an amelioration of the problems which brought about the need for a therapeutic program. As relaxation supplants emotional turmoil, more energy becomes available to the ego for creative pursuits.

The types of craft materials which are suitable for play groups are governed by interest, age, and sex of the children. Weaving, sewing, knitting, leather work, plastics, woodwork, metal embossing, and wood burning are typical craft activities used in play groups.

It is necessary to replenish and supplement the crafts materials in a group as the children apply themselves. This replenishment is no longer a process of psychological "feeding," such as takes place earlier in a group's evolvement, when the children had need for gratification through receiving tangible evidences of "love." Instead, it is a realistically determined question of renewing supplies and materials as they are consumed and adding new craft media to accommodate expanding interests.

WOODWORK—PARTICULARLY VALUABLE FOR OLDER BOYS

Of all the materials used in boys' play groups, lumber is the most resistive, and it is also the most challenging craft experience. The development of skills in woodwork and the exciting end products have formidable influence in fostering masculine identification. Activities like hammering, sawing, and drilling are, in addition, good outlets for aggressive energies.

A woodwork bench of suitable size, with two fixed vises, is a basic item. The bench should be screwed to the floor to prevent it from moving; children cannot be expected to saw wood with a work table that is unstable.

The woodwork tools supplied should be appropriate in size and weight; full size hammers and saws are unwieldy. The following tools would meet most needs:

> two claw hammers; 8 ounce weight
> two saws; about 18 inches
> one keyhole saw; not too narrow; heavy duty type
> one small finishing plane
> one brace; with an assortment of wood bits
> nails and brads of various sizes

Wood which is supplied for use should be cut in advance into short pieces, six to twelve inches long. Soft pine is necessary for children; other woods are too resistive. Pieces of thin plywood and dowels are also helpful.

Woodwork can be introduced into a play group when boys have reached a level in physical growth which permits mastery of the tools which are made available. Children who are seven and eight years old can acquire sufficient skill with basic woodwork tools to fabricate simple but satisfying projects in the forms of games and toys.

In the beginning, children will be dependent on the worker in learning how some tools are used, and all requests for assistance should be met. Even when they begin to work more independently, it would be wise for the worker to anticipate frustration and to offer help to children, to forestall or overcome difficult steps in their woodwork projects.

If woodwork is used in play groups with emotionally disturbed children, regardless of their ages, adequate consideration must be given to all factors involved in safety, including the impulsivity of some children.

With young children, in particular, the worker should be mindful of the fact that, in most instances, they may be using tools for the first time. It is advisable for the worker to give simple instructions in the proper manipulation of the tools and to point out the potential hazards. Because of limited experience, young children are less aware of the possible consequences of their mishandling of tools upon themselves or others.

For example, in sawing wood which is clamped in a vise, a child has to learn not to hold his hand close to the saw's cutting action; and not to place arm or hand in front of a saw. On the other hand, two young children who may be tugging at a saw from either end in struggling for its possession, are momentarily unaware that the teeth can cut.

The worker needs to be alert but not anxious; adult anxiety is pervasive and affects children. They sense ambivalence in adults who are excessively cautious; children "read" this as distrust. Children will generally accept reasonable suggestions and limitations, if they are realistically determined.

Woodwork has such unusual motivating value that it catalyzes latent strengths in individuals and accelerates interaction in the play groups. As a result, there will be episodes of intensification of interaction. Arguments over possession of lumber and tools are common; rivalry is stimulated. On the other hand, the demands of some woodwork procedures bring about constructive effects; children often solicit help from each other or cooperate in common projects. In the presence of the worker's consistent tolerance and helpfulness, conflict situations which may have been intensified after the introduction of a stimulating craft medium are worked out.

The following episode illustrates how woodwork influences interaction:

Gary is the most aggressive boy in a play group of eight year olds. After 18 group meetings the children have begun to resist his demands and react to his aggression. The worker recently introduced woodwork and the boys all become exceedingly interested in it. Gary consistently monopolized the tools, often retaining some when he had no immediate use for them. During the twenty-first meeting, George told the worker several times that Gary would not give him the hammer. Gary kept the hammer under his foot while he sawed. The worker listened to George's complaining but did not become involved. George finally approached Gary, bent over quickly and snatched the hammer away. Gary stopped sawing wood momentarily but he let George take it.

The next extract describes how success with woodwork can enhance and solidify the gains made in sexual identification:

Max, nine years old, has been in a play group about two years. When referred he was described as "effeminate," a "mama's boy." He had no friends; children disliked him. He was seldom permitted to play in the street so he joined his younger sister and her friends when they played at home. During the two years he has been in the play group he has shown much growth. This did not come about without pain and stress. Max had to undergo multiple trials in his relationship with the group members. He was immediately fascinated by the woodwork when it was introduced and he has been working at it assiduously, at times competing aggressively with others for possession of tools. The material which follows is taken from the record of the seventy-fourth group meeting:

Max came in saying, "Hi, Mrs. T. How are you?" The worker smiled, said, "Hi," Max ran to the bench saying. "So much wood! Lots and lots of wood!" John walked in next and Max said, "Hey, look at all the wood, Johnny! Don't take this piece; I need it. I'm going to make an airplane. Last week it was just a cross piece but this time it *will* be an airplane." He asked the worker to help him hammer a nail because it was short. "Don't you have any other nails besides these shrimpy ones?" he asked. *The worker helped him partially*, and then said, "You can finish it." He repeated: "I can finish it?"—then hammered away. Another boy was waiting for the hammer and Max kept saying, "No, you can't have it yet. You'll just have to wait."

. . . Later Max said, "If I don't hammer this nail in I'll get mad—fighting mad!" When he finally finished, John said, "Say—that's good, Max!" He replied, "Yeah, it *is* pretty good. How about that—Mrs. T.? I know I'm going to be a carpenter when I grow up." . . . Later, when the group was having refreshments, one of the boys asked, "Max, what will you be *when you become a man?*" Max answered, "Well, I'm pretty good with wood and tools, so I'll be a carpenter."

Comment: Note that the worker helped Max to a limited extent and then turned the work back to him. This was correct technic. She helped him over a point of frustration, without depriving him of the opportunity for fulfillment.

Of some interest is the awareness on the part of other children of the growth which has taken place in Max. This acknowledgement from the group members, who had for a long time challenged, teased, and abused him, was immensely fortifying to the boy.

The following incident illustrates the importance of using suitable materials:

The worker in a group of eight year old boys considered herself quite fortunate when she obtained, without cost, a large quantity of wood from a nearby manufacturer of furniture. These were irregularly shaped, scrap pieces of hardwood, ¾ inch in thickness. The boys were quite excited when they saw the interesting shapes of wood, and they spoke in eager anticipation of the different objects they would make. Their pleasure was short lived and their frustration was matched only by the worker's when the wood proved to be completely unworkable. It was so hard that a nail could not be driven into it; saws could barely cut it; planing it was hopeless. The worker disposed of the wood and purchased pieces of soft pine for the next meeting of the group.

RECREATIONAL SUPPLIES—TOYS AND GAMES

These items serve a variety of purposes, one of the more important ones being to promote contacts between children. Therefore, games and toys should be types which draw children together. Two or three games are sufficient for a play group; providing in excess of this amount has the effect of diluting the outcomes which are sought. Games with complicated rules systems are also not suitable because they tend to be unwieldy. They promote dissension between children and involve the worker excessively in the role of an arbiter. Depending on the ages of the children, such games as dominoes, checkers, picture lotto, ring toss, pin ball, "Chick-in-the-Coop," "Candyland," and others, are suitable.

There are games which are particularly valuable in helping children sublimate aggression through physical activity. One such is Nok Hockey, a competitive game which two children may play and which requires each to score goals by hitting a wooden puck with a small paddle. It is wise to place the wooden board—which is the field of play—on the floor, so that the puck is close to the ground should it fly off the board when hit too vigorously.

Toys such as trucks, cranes, bull-dozers, airplanes, boats—all preferably with working parts—are ideal for supplementing the children's play with blocks. These toys should be made of hard wood, not sheet metal or thin plastic, which break easily, leaving sharp edges. Some of these toys are made large enough for children to sit on.

Most children find jigsaw puzzles interesting. Puzzles also have a special purpose in the group. They help a withdrawn child who may need a passive activity to sustain himself and to insulate himself from the group. Such children need something to do, even in their self-imposed isolation, and jigsaw puzzles occupy them while at the same time they are free to observe the group. Puzzles should be made of wood; they should be challenging but uncomplicated. Six are sufficient, with occasional substitutions of new ones. When pieces are lost, puzzles should be discarded. A "catch-all" kind of box, in which pieces of many puzzles are mixed together would be frustrating to an adult, certainly more so to a child.

In girls' play groups, it is important to have dolls and other items such as dresses, a carriage, and a crib. A toy house, with furniture and appliances, should also be available.

CRAFT MATERIALS FOR GIRLS

Special craft activities which can be used successfully in play groups for girls are sewing, knitting, crocheting, and weaving. Materials such as felt, cotton cloth, denim, and crepe paper are excellent in that they serve a variety of purposes from making doll clothing to decorations. Some craft materials which are used in boys' groups are also suitable for girls, e.g., embossing, leather, plastic, and reedwork.

For the transitional group which is moving towards termination, it is important for the worker to introduce sports activities within the play room and also in a park or playground. Such activities lead to performance skills which are important to all children in the more highly competitive groups in which they participate, in school and elsewhere. Basketball, punchball, baseball (softball), rope-skipping and similar activities, should be used with advanced play groups.*

The importance of the proper therapeutic setting, furniture, equipment, and supplies in play group practice cannot be overstated. Much of the interaction which takes place in the dynamic group is influenced by the setting and equipment. The efficiency of therapeutic practices with children in general is markedly influenced by the functional "tools."†

* At this stage it is good practice for the worker to participate more with the group, even to the extent of teaching advanced skills.

† Ginott, Haim: A rationale for selecting toys in play therapy. J. of Consult. Psychol. Vol. 24, No. 3, 1960.

4 Elements of Individual and Group Psychotherapy of Children in Early Latency

PROBLEMS IN DIAGNOSIS OF YOUNG CHILDREN

An optimal program of psychotherapy for any individual is dependent on information obtainable from various sources which can be utilized in establishing a diagnosis and in determining a plan of treatment. The following procedures are basic in clinical practice: elucidation of the significant elements of a presenting problem; a hypothetical construct which points up the relatedness of the problem to etiology; a clinical diagnosis or, in the absence of a definitive diagnosis, an assessment of diagnostic factors; and finally, based on an evaluation of the foregoing, the selection of the indicated treatment process.

From a nosological frame of reference some emotional disorders present few variables to complicate the processes of diagnosis and treatment planning. This is particularly so with respect to the psychoses, which can be more readily diagnosed because of the obvious pathology, which differs so markedly from normality. It is another matter with nonpsychotic disorders, because the qualities which distinguish them from normality are not as sharply delineated.

Problems of diagnosis and treatment planning are even further complicated with emotionally disturbed children who are approximately five to eight years of age, in the early period of latency. Diagnosis, in particular, is made difficult because of the relative absence of discrete symptomology, and because behavioral patterns have not been fully crystallized in young children. Their emotional responses are fluid; they are markedly labile. Their ego defense mechanisms are tangible, but they have not been fully determined, neither in type nor degree. A young child's personality—be it deviant or normal—has not been reinforced through elaboration and habituation. It is this factor, more than any other, which makes comprehensive and definitive diagnoses of young children difficult.*

* Exceptions to this are young children with acute symptoms and gross pathology, e.g. anxiety states, phobias, psychoses. In such cases, diagnoses can be made with critical degrees of accuracy. Fortunately, such pathological disorders during childhood are limited in frequency as compared to other, less severe emotional disturbances.

Symptomatic Behavior of Children May be Deceptive

Hyperactivity and Hypermotility

The delineation of atypical aspects of development in children is not made any easier by virtue of the fact that behavior which is indicative of emotional disturbance is not uncommonly camouflaged by qualities which do not appear exceptional. For example, most young children are physically active and capable of expending large amounts of energy over short periods of time. On the basis of this factor alone, it becomes difficult to differentiate between children who are normally quite active and others in whom physical over-activity may be an indication of deviant behavior.

The term "hyperactivity" is used, often too loosely, to describe the physical behavior of children. Hyperactivity is a form of agitation—a consequence of tension created by anxiety. It is one outlet through which the ego frees itself of some of the stress which is generated from emotions and drives which have not been adequately managed through repression and other mechanisms of defense. Psychic tension becomes partially de-energized by conversion into motor activity. This can only be a partial discharge, since the precipitating causes of anxiety are still operative, and they constantly replenish the quantum of anxiety. Hyperactivity provides relief to a child who may be unsuccessfully repressing feelings of hostility which would prove too disabling if expressed directly. This also applies to libidinal drives which have not been efficiently repressed or sublimated.

The recognition of hyperactivity as a symptomatic form of behavior does not establish its cause. Unless its origins are revealed and treated through psychotherapy hyperactivity will remain, or it will eventually change into other symptoms, perhaps depression.

Hyperactivity can also result from diseases or injuries affecting parts of the nervous system.

To complicate matters even further, there are some children, quite normal in all other respects, who may be described as hypermotile, because of the extraordinary amount of physical motion which they use in pursuing various activities. Hypermotility is largely a metabolic phenomenon, and it is determined by such elements as body weight, hormones, intelligence, and the quality of environmental stimulation. Hypermotility differs from hyperactivity in that it is not accompanied by chronic tension and anxiety in its expression.

Social Withdrawal

Social withdrawal is still another kind of atypical behavior which is manifested by children with much variability, and which must be carefully considered in context with other factors for accurate determination of a problem.

Withdrawal can range from a condition of moderate shyness in the presence of peers to self-protecting isolation, in which circumstance a child never initiates contact with peers or withdraws if others attempt to make contact with him. Yet, even this latter form of social insulation can stem from causes which are quite different and which, therefore, will affect the problems of diagnosis and treatment planning. One insecure child may be utterly fearful of a peer group because of the demands he anticipates the group will make of him, or because he thinks that others will victimize him. With another child, a similar degree of social withdrawal may result from his own potential hostility, which is so massive that he unconsciously keeps apart from others who might inadvertently set it off.

Paucity of Language

Another factor which influences diagnosis and treatment of young children is their limited ability to communicate on verbal levels. Their vocabulary is altogether inadequate for the purpose of expressing emotions and attitudes which are complex and dramatic. Further, troubled children tend to distrust communicating with adults, because they have learned through unhappy experience that the actions of adults often belie the meanings of their words.

While young children are, in a sense, prisoners of language, they are receptive to adults who convincingly demonstrate a desire to help them by using methods of communication which the children themselves find comfortable.* For them, play and other forms of motoric activities are more natural communicative pathways. Subtle complexities of thought and feelings, which would be difficult to describe otherwise, become expressed more readily through a spontaneous "language" consisting of words, gestures, enactments of life situations with dolls and puppets, paintings and drawings, and still other methods. The content of this "language" is no less subject to the influence of unconscious determinants than that which is purely verbal.

PSYCHOLOGICAL INSIGHT, ITS PLACE IN CHILD PSYCHOTHERAPY

Differences Between Children and Adolescents and Adults

The development of insight is a complex psychological phenomenon. It evolves in a patient through the accretion of many, separate and repetitive perceptions of the antecedents of his emotional disorder and its manifestations in his symptoms and behavior, and also, through an awareness of the unique mechanisms of defense which come into being in order to cope with stress. Insight is a consequence of inductive discovery which takes place over an extended period of time.

*Ginott, Haim: Group Psychotherapy with Children. McGraw-Hill, Maidenhead. This excellent book describes a method of therapy which combines interpretation and communication through play. It is particularly suitable for preschool children.

Insight cannot be experienced without catharsis. An intellectual grasp of the psychodynamic elements of an emotional disorder, without a sufficient discharge of the repressed emotions which are etiologically related to the disorder, will produce no significant modifications in either behavior or personality. On the other hand, when, as the result of successful therapy, there is an eventual integration of logically interrelated affective and cognitive elements, a patient acquires a global awareness of the nature of his disorder. This fusion of ideas and emotions, which represents true psychological insight, becomes the motive force which modifies personality.

The foregoing elements of insight formation apply in the psychotherapy of adolescents and adults, varying in degree only with differences in the presenting problems and with idiosyncratic differences between patients.

Most young children, however, are incapable of developing such insight: the elements involved are not in consonance with their intellectual and emotional capabilities. They have not yet reached a level of maturational development which makes it possible for them to experience psychological insight. Insight is an essential outcome for successful treatment of many emotional disorders of adolescence and adulthood, but it has no strict equivalent in the treatment of most children.*

Derivative Insight

That element in group psychotherapy of young children which parallels insight formation in older patients is a derivative form of insight.† Such insight is not ideational; it is actively experienced in the group and is a therapeutic consequence of the dynamic interaction which has taken place between each child and the therapist, and with the other children.‡ The child senses change in himself without knowing, or having to know, the antecedents of his emotional disorder and the therapeutic influences which induced improvement. For the most part, the alterations which take place in a child's behavior and personality as a result of therapy are produced independently of any interpretations which may or may not be given by a therapist, and without purposeful intellectualization on the child's part.

* In the treatment of a psychoneurotic child (a tenuous diagnosis in early latency) some degree of insight is necessary before there can be a remission of symptoms. However, the following pre-conditions are important: the child must possess superior intelligence, so that he can ideate at a level which the analytic procedures require; there must be enough anxiety so that he will be sufficiently motivated to tolerate the demands of analytical investigation.

† S. R. Slavson: Child Psychotherapy. New York, Columbia University Press, p. 192.

‡ In the treatment situation, the quality of transference in young children also differs from that of adolescents and adults. S. R. Slavson has used the term "substitute" relationship, because he feels that the young child is still too closely involved with his parents emotionally and dependently to be able to invest a therapist with the same libidinal cathexis which is attached to the parents, ibid., p. 173.

RESISTANCE AND RESISTIVENESS

A lack of responsiveness on the part of many young children to the analytic forms of psychotherapy is often erroneously attributed to resistance, when it is actually a form of resistiveness—mostly conscious—against clinical procedures which they find threatening. This resistiveness is based on the fact that interpretations given during therapy inevitably impinge too directly on libidinal and hostile feelings which children have toward their parents, and which they dare not express directly.

The roots of children's resistiveness to interpretive procedures in psychotherapy are found in the psychological developments which are prominently involved during the latency period. At that time there is a shifting of a child's libidinal interest to the parent of the same sex, and to a lesser extent, to peers of the same sex. This change, and also, the child's increased capacity for sublimation, both operate to abate anxiety which was generated in the oedipal conflict. The mechanism of repression is very active during this stage of development even with "normal" children. The threatened ego "demands" efficient performance from this most important ego defense. In cases where there are disturbances in psychosexual development, the mechanism of repression is probably even more actively involved in protecting the ego, but often with less success. For these reasons, methodological approaches in psychotherapy with latency children which attempt to uncover drives and emotions which have been repressed, or which are actively *in the process of being repressed*, are vigorously countered by children. They have no other choice when a therapeutic procedure threatens defenses which are actively elaborating to protect the ego.

Young children are emotionally dependent on their parents, even during the very time when parental behavior may be exerting its destructive effects. Because of these dependent feelings, the children need to preserve the integrity of their primary relationships, and they are characteristically resistive to therapeutic processes which, directly or implicitly, tend to expose or denigrate their parents. Troubled children seek understanding; they do not wish to understand their parents, particularly when to do so would weaken the parental images.

Resistance or resistiveness occur infrequently when young children are treated through methods which are experiental, where the outcomes derive primarily from relationship experiences with the therapist and with other children. A group treatment practice such as the therapeutic play group does not engender resistiveness in young children because it does not touch upon the behavior of parents, nor does it elicit direct expressions of children's feelings about parents. Group therapy of this type, in contrast to analytic forms of therapy, does not threaten ego defenses. It substitutes rehabilitative, therapeutic experiences for the original, traumatic experiences. The ego defenses are modified as inner stresses are dissipated or reduced.

A therapeutic program for disturbed children must aim at the deficits which were based in earlier, life experience through a reconstructive experience in the context of the transference relationship. Many defects in ego functioning do yield to "second chance" opportunities through noninterpretive forms of group psychotherapy if the relationship between a child and the therapist becomes psychologically homologous to that which exists between the child and his parents. Young children become emotionally malleable in the therapeutic relationship, and significant changes can be effected in personality without involving them in exploration of the origins of their problems and the unconscious meanings of behavior.

With emotionally disturbed children in early latency, it is possible to effect more dramatic modifications in ego functioning through psychotherapy than would be possible with older children, adolescents and adults. Because psychotherapy with such children is instituted at a time when they are still in a personality determining phase of development, it can significantly influence the course of development. However, with each succeeding year without proper treatment, a young child's potential for change drops significantly because of the rapid expansion and reinforcement of the ego defenses.

TREATMENT PLANNING FOR CHILDREN IN EARLY LATENCY

The fact that children differ from adolescents and adults with respect to their ability to develop insight and in terms of the nature of the transference relationship to the therapist does not preclude the possibility of successful treatment of their emotional disorders. What does become apparent is the need to be mindful of the essential differences in planning treatment for young children.

Determinations of efficient approaches in psychotherapy with young children are of more practical consideration than attempts at critical diagnoses of emotional disorders which, because they have not yet "ripened," defy strict classification. Further, it is unrealistic to attempt to establish critical criteria on the basis of which it would be possible to select the forms of treatment which, in all instances, would be unequivocably suited to the problems of young children. Successful treatment of emotional disorders in young children demands flexibility in the application of treatment methods, a degree of empiricism, and facility in moving from one form of treatment to another if a change becomes indicated.

The measure of clinical efficiency is the evolution of emotional health in a patient. A clinical approach which produces negligible change in children's behavior and personalities is faulty, either in its design, implementation, or both. One which is of a nature to reinforce or extend deviant behavior is certainly contraindicated. An example of the latter is when an unusually permissive treatment method is used with a young child who requires limits and redirection.

RELEVANCE OF THE SEX OF THE THERAPIST IN CHILD PSYCHOTHERAPY

In treating emotional disorders of children, it is fundamental that the clinical approach be such that children readily become able to develop a tolerance for its procedures. This development will be facilitated if the treatment method fosters the rapid growth of transference between a child and his therapist. Further, the method will have rehabilitative potential if it can actuate the reenactment of those situations which, in their original context in the family, were responsible for the formation of emotional problems. This latter factor is uniquely important in treating young children because the families usually continue to exert damaging influence.

An optimal treatment approach for young children might be termed "naturalistic," because it includes elements of immediate, psychological reference to primary forces in the lives of the children.

For Pre-Oedipal Children

There are many implications in the foregoing with respect to treatment planning for young children, one in particular being the sex of the therapist. For example, children up to the age of four years, approximately, who have emotional disturbances of a functional type, are best treated by female therapists through individual therapy, because their disturbances are reactive to faults in experience and to errors in parent management especially involving the mother. A young child's libidinal interest is at first directed primarily toward the mother, who is closely involved with him at various levels: nurturance, protection, play, and early habit training. While it is true that the father also may assume some of these responsibilities, his involvement is minimal as compared to the mother's, and he is perceived by a young child as adjunctive to the mother. Until the onset of the oedipal period, with its attendant emotional conflict, the mother is essentially the primary "agent" for success or failure in child rearing.*

During the Oedipal Period

During the oedipal conflict phase of development, the role of the father in relationship to the child—either boy or girl—becomes aggrandized, and

* In cases where the presenting problem of a child is not severe, and when errors in child management are not the result of neurotic behavior on the part of the parents, maladjustment in the child can often be eliminated through working with the parents exclusively. As they learn to modify their ways of handling the child, he will begin to respond in more acceptable ways.

this rather rapidly when compared to the pace of earlier development. Because of the psychodynamic nature of the oedipal conflict, libidinal cathexis related to the father increases. In view of this new and psychologically formidable influence on child development, in cases where psychotherapy becomes necessary, consideration can be given to the possibility, or advisability, of a male therapist.

However, even during the oedipal phase, should a child's development continue to be impeded by a persistent dependent tie to the mother, the pre-oedipal problem will remain nuclear. In this circumstance, despite the fact that symptoms and behavior related to the oedipal conflict may begin to fuse with earlier elements of potential character disturbance, the therapeutic program would still be best implemented by a female therapist. The choice of therapist continues to be influenced by factors related to the young child's primary relationship needs. In this instance, the child still requires gratification of infantile needs until he has developed greater frustration tolerance and a capacity for sublimation at more effective levels. When this is achieved through therapy, forces inherent in the oedipal conflict become ascendant and the therapeutic program can justifiably include a male therapist.

GROUP THERAPY BECOMES INCREASINGLY IMPORTANT AT SCHOOL AGE

When an emotionally disturbed child reaches the age of five or six, still another type of experience begins to intrude inexorably, placing additional strain on his already limited coping ability. This takes place when he is separated from the family to attend school for the first time, or a nursery if he is younger than five. Regardless of the level of a child's psychosexual and social development at this time, he becomes exposed to new pressures for social adaptation from peers and from adults other than his parents. He discovers that he is expected to perform at levels commensurate with his chronological age, even though this expectation is not in consonance with his emotional and performance capabilities.*

Once children are in regular attendance in school, the use of group therapy as a treatment procedure becomes increasingly important. This is so even in cases where a child's nuclear problem is pre-oedipal. In the latter case several treatment plans could be helpful, but each should include a female therapist.

* The author once discussed this observation with a counselor in an elementary school in an urban setting which was characterized by severe socioeconomic deprivation. In this neighborhood, young children run about the streets unsupervised, after school. The counselor remarked: "And how! The children around here are not concerned about whether a kid is emotionally 'ready'—and he knows it, too. All they want to know is: 'can he catch, throw, and run—like they can'."

PLAY GROUPS CONDUCTED BY A WORKER TEAM; CONCURRENT INDIVIDUAL AND GROUP THERAPY

One method would be to treat the child in a therapeutic play group conducted by a worker team consisting of a man and a woman. The therapeutic process would operate at various levels. Relationship with the female worker would "feed" the child at nurturance levels; the relationship with the male worker would influence those elements of the child's problem which stem from the oedipal conflict. The other children in the play group would help in loosening the libidinal ties to the female worker by acting as buffers between her and the overdependent child, thus interfering with the continuation of the dependency relationship. They would later serve as identification models for the immature child.

A different treatment approach, but one which would still provide the psychological opportunities for meeting the needs of the dependent child, is a concurrent program of individual play therapy with a female therapist and a therapeutic play group conducted by a man. This approach is recommended over the first if the child's dependency needs are severe and if he is not able to share the attention of the female therapist. This dependency need would not be as limiting a factor in the play group because the relationship to the male worker would be less intense and it would have a different quality.

In a case where a young child's emotional difficulties derive from the oedipal conflict as the *primary* generating force, treatment in a play group conducted by a worker team would be helpful. Transference relationships with both workers provide more opportunities for resolving oedipal-based problems. In lieu of this—because worker teams are not always available—a play group with a male worker is preferable to one conducted by a female. This is so because the male person (father or male worker) is more significantly involved than the female (mother or female worker) in the *resolution* of the oedipal conflict.

INTERPRETIVE VERSUS EXPERIENTIAL METHODS OF THERAPY

It has been well established that the antecedents of many functional emotional disorders are found in early life experiences, and that the disorders themselves are not usually fully defined in children of five and six years of age. These facts must be taken into consideration in planning treatment for young children. Failure to consider the ability of young children to accommodate to the demands of specialized clinical procedures inevitably leads to the use of unrealistic criteria and methods in planning and implementing treatment. It also prevents facile accommodation to changing needs once therapy has been instituted.

For example, successful treatment of a psychoneurosis requires intensive, individual psychotherapy, in which analytical procedures play a prominent part. However, a young child with an incipient psychoneurosis may be entirely resistive to such an approach in treatment because, as has been noted, he lacks a readiness for it. Despite the serious implications of psychoneurotic disorders, young children often fail to respond in analytic psychotherapy unless they are motivated to continue out of excessive anxiety or for another unusual reason.* Yet, many young children who will eventually require analytic psychotherapy for the ultimate resolution of serious problems, but who prove to be inaccessible to individual psychotherapy, can be helped appreciably through an activity form of group psychotherapy in which interpretations of behavior are not given. Group therapy of this type can block further deterioration and, by supporting and strengthening the ego, can maintain such children until they are able to respond to more intensive forms of treatment.†

INDICATIONS AND CONTRAINDICATIONS FOR GROUP THERAPY

S. R. Slavson, a pioneer in the field of group psychotherapy, makes the following statement with respect to the place of group psychotherapy in the treatment of emotionally disturbed children:

" . . . Through our work in activity group therapy we were able to establish the value of activity in psychotherapy with children, though it is also implicit in 'play therapy.' In the past, however, this fact has been obscured by interpreting behavior rather than relying upon the corrective effect of the activity itself and the setting . . . . The study of numerous improvements and recoveries through activity group therapy with prepubertal children has shown that action catharsis and regression in behavior, coupled with support of the ego and substitute gratifications, offer appropriate therapy *for the majority of children with personality problems.*"‡ (italics by this author)

---

* Still another variable which influences the responsiveness of young children to individual therapy is the personality of the therapist. The practice of analytic psychotherapy with young children demands an unusual degree of sensitivity and unique skills.

† The fact that many child guidance clinics still use individual forms of psychotherapy exclusively in treating children is not necessarily an indication that group therapy has been evaluated and found wanting. Within the author's experience, it is usually because these clinics lack personnel with special training in group psychotherapy, or they lack adequate facilities for group treatment. For whatever reason, the author firmly believes that clinics which do not include group psychotherapy as part of the total program *lack an essential tool* in the treatment of emotional disorders of children. Parenthetically, this is becoming more evident in the treatment of adolescents and adults.

‡ Slavson, S. R.: Child Psychotherapy. New York, Columbia University Press, 1952, Chap. VI.

It is the last phrase of the foregoing statement which is most significant and which bears reiteration: . . . *"for the majority of children with personality problems."* This is entirely in keeping with this author's experience in treating emotionally disturbed children in early latency in groups. Perhaps the only difference is that with children in early latency, there is an even greater latitude in the types of problems and the number of children who can be helped through the therapeutic play group.

In activity group therapy, which is a noninterpretive form of group therapy used with children in advanced latency, approximately nine years to puberty, certain problem types are contraindicated. These are: children who are characterologically narcissistic; psychopaths (sociopaths); children with severe rivalry problems, psychotic children. These children are contraindicated because they are either totally unresponsive to this form of psychotherapy, or because they persistently obstruct salutary interaction in the group. Psychoneurotic children are not contraindicated for the same reasons, but they can be helped to only a limited extent through activity group therapy.

It does not follow that children in early latency, who may already have begun to manifest signs of the aforementioned emotional disorders, are also contraindicated for an activity form of therapy. Despite the early signals of what could prove to be, in only a few years, severe personality disorders, these younger children do respond in the therapeutic play group. They are still resilient and their potential for change is much greater than that of children who are only several years older. The ego structure of the younger children still lacks concretion, so that it is possible to abort the further elaboration of emotional disorders and, in some cases, to modify both the direction and intensity of incipient pathology.

The efficacy of the play group as a therapeutic method is attributable to the ease with which it becomes a psychological parallel to the primary group—the family. For it is within the actual family that the causes of most emotional disabilities are found, and it is the family which continues to exert damaging influence on young children. Troubled children are beset by the "here and now" quality of their tensions and unhappiness. The play group offers a field of experience in which current unhappiness can be countered by gratifications and the eventual resolution of problems.

Participation in groups rapidly becomes increasingly important to the growing child, who daily comes into more contact with peer groups, in school and elsewhere. The therapeutic play group is a more familiar approximation of the life mode of children, in contrast to individual psychotherapy, which is a much more unique experience.

In the therapeutic play group, children's doubts and fears are lessened through a sense of mutuality with other children. Further, children can mobilize and ventilate feelings in the transference relationships and can benefit from this discharge (catharsis), without need to recognize the unconscious mechanisms involved.

FAILURES IN PLAY GROUP TREATMENT

The number of young children who are contraindicated for treatment in a therapeutic play group is statistically negligible. This has been established on the basis of many years of experience with such groups. In instances where there were failures in treatment, they were traced to the following reasons:

1. An inability on the part of some children to perceive the play group as an organic unit, composed of different individuals with varying needs. In the permissive setting, some of these children became hostile and destructive, and they acted out in a diffuse manner. These reactions proved characteristic of children who were psychotic.

2. Children with more discriminative powers of perception than the foregoing and who had awareness of the group as an entity, but were, nevertheless, unable to restrain their self-satisfying pursuit of gratifications, or to control the impulsive discharge of infantile behavior. Such children are nonpsychotic, but they are extremely immature (narcissistic character structure).

TREATING UNUSUAL PROBLEM TYPES IN THE THERAPEUTIC PLAY GROUP

The Autistic Child

The possibility of success in treating a young, autistic child in a therapeutic play group increases if he is not completely immobilized by withdrawal, and if the pathological, defensive structure can be made permeable, thus increasing the child's response to peripheral stimuli. Given these circumstances, communicative pathways begin to develop between the autistic child and the therapeutic agents—the worker and the group—and interaction becomes a reality for such children, perhaps for the first time.*

Such children are often treated individually, because it is thought that they will either be unresponsive to a group or, perhaps, driven into deeper emotional encapsulation if they become threatened by a group.

If the composition of a therapeutic play group is carefully designed with reference to the pathological child in particular, the group becomes an effective instrument of treatment. In the treatment of such a child the psychological balance of the group is a critical factor. Only one autistic child should be placed in a play group; if others are included it has the effect of reinforcing apathy. The autistic child requires catalytic stimulation from children who are

---

* Several such children who attended therapeutic play groups for *more than three years*, improved markedly. They first became more responsive to stimulation, and later they began to interact actively with the children in the play group.

essentially ego intact, despite their problems, and who will not subject the autistic child to excessive threat or over-stimulation.*

It is essential that a therapeutic play group which is to contain an autistic child have a greater "index of health" built into its design than is usually found in play groups. The acting-out potential of such a play group must be moderate. Under these conditions, the other children will act both as mild stimulators and healthier models for an autistic child.

Psychodynamic Influence of a Play Group on an Autistic Child

The interaction which takes place between the children in this specially composed play group exposes the autistic child to stimulation which is varied, mildly persuasive, and persistent. Quantitatively, a play group provides more stimulation than individual psychotherapy; qualitatively, the stimulation has greater receptivity for the autistic child because it originates with children. The autistic child defends himself more against adults.

As time passes, the interaction between the other children and the worker repetitively demonstrates to the autistic child the essential tolerance and helpfulness of the worker. Perception of the worker as a safe, nonthreatening adult begins to set in.

It is the children in a play group who first penetrate the autistic defense, making the autistic child more aware of his surroundings. In time he begins to react to overtures from them. When he feels secure enough to initiate contact, it is first attempted with children, much later with the worker. In a sense, the children in the play group act as subsidiary therapists in the treatment of an autistic child.

A considerable time must elapse in treatment before the first modifications in the autistic defenses become manifest. In contrast to the original behavior, these changes have dramatic quality, yet, they represent only a preparatory phase in the treatment process. The dissolution of pathology actually begins when the child develops transference to the worker. Prior to treatment, the autistic child is incapable of forming a transference relationship.

In the play group, in the psychodynamic context of the transference to the worker, who is supportive at all times, rehabilitation of ego function becomes possible. The autistic child finally becomes able to express feelings which were

* Many seriously disturbed young children are found in residential treatment in special schools or hospitals. While this is usually determined by what may be considered practical considerations, it is questionable whether such programs are justifiable clinically. In settings where pathology is rampant, as is the case when seriously disturbed children are grouped together, gross patterns of pathology are universal, rather than unique. Because healthy models are absent, the treatment process becomes increasingly difficult. Given circumstances in which pathological children can be treated by placing them in groups with young children whose emotional problems are not pathological, the treatment process becomes more efficacious.

formerly massively blocked, without fear of disastrous consequences to himself or to others. *A minimum of three to four years* of treatment may be necessary for such children. It is also conceivable that individual treatment may be instituted later and used concurrently with play group treatment.

The presence of an autistic child in a play group does not have negative influence on less disturbed children, because their awareness of pathology as such is limited. Moreover, young children possess an unusual tolerance for exceptional behavior in other young children.

Play Groups for Unusually Aggressive Children

Young children who are very aggressive are ordinarily not manageable either in individual or group treatment, because their aggressive acting out forces the therapist to intervene frequently, which blocks therapeutic outcomes. It is possible to treat such children successfully, but a treatment setting must be provided which will allow for much freedom of expression without excessive intervention on the part of the adult. Further, the therapist must have exceptional tolerance for impulsive and aggressive behavior.

Some of these conditions are met in a play group setting, where the physical design and equipment are of a nature to withstand much expressive behavior. However, the factor which usually negates the inclusion of a very aggressive child in a play group is the vulnerability of other children. If they, in concert with each other, are unable to withstand aggression, the worker has no choice but to interfere and, since this will probably be repetitive, the permissive approach becomes negated, and the treatment process becomes blocked for all the children.

Aggression of the type just described, when found in young children of six or seven years of age, is typical of reactive, primary behavior disorders. Acting out by these children is characterized by the following qualities: diffuse aggression, often with a lack of discrimination in the choice of persons against whom the aggression is directed; perseverative aggression in the face of intervention from others; inappropriate guilt and anxiety responses; lying and other forms of manipulation to prevent retaliation and punishment.

Psychodynamic Influence of the Play Group on Very Aggressive Children

A therapeutic play group is potentially an effective treatment technic for such children, but it must have adequate controls for modulating aggression, while retaining the psychodynamic qualities which are necessary for permissive group practice. These elements can be structured in the play group by placing a young, aggressive child with children who are several years older. In most instances, older children can absorb more aggression from a younger child, and, what is more important, they can also impose controls upon him, if necessary. This curtailment of his acting out makes the younger child more circumspect in behavior. He has little choice if he wishes to continue in the group. Meanwhile, the worker is able to maintain the accepting, permissive role which is fundamental in therapeutic play group practice, *particularly in the treatment of a behavior disorder*.

The worker's continuing acceptance of the child despite his aggressiveness, plus the emotional sustenance (love) which the child receives from the worker through massive gratifications of need over an extended period of time, are the modifying elements in treatment. For the child with a behavior disorder, the experience which takes place in the transference relationship with the worker is the basic behavior modifying force. The play group acts as the *modus vivendi*. As time passes, and the child's aggression begins to yield to the therapeutic influence exerted by the transference relationship with the worker, the play group begins to assume a secondary level of persuasion for the aggressive child. Because his behavior is becoming less disruptive, the group inevitably grants him improved status. This social recognition has now become important to him, and he is motivated to preserve and extend it.

There is an interesting contrast between a specially designed play group for an autistic child and one designed for an overaggressive child:

In the play group containing the autistic child, it is the children at first who act as the primary therapeutic influences. They serve an ancillary therapeutic role as mild stimulators and as healthier ego models. While these functions are important therapeutically, they are passive functions, in the sense that they are not consciously pursued by the group, nor are they at first consciously perceived by the autistic child. This differs from a designed group for a child with a primary behavior disorder. In this group the children are physically active in controlling the acting out child; their responses to the overaggressive child are quite conscious and causally determined by the behavior of the overaggressive child. Also, the acting out child is made conscious of the implications of his behavior as far as the other children are concerned.

THERAPEUTIC PLAY GROUPS CONDUCTED BY A WORKER-TEAM

There are problems presented by children in early latency which respond better to a therapeutic play group if it is conducted by a worker-team consisting of a man and a woman. Such a group is particularly effective with the following: children whose emotional disturbances can be attributed to traumatic deprivation caused by the loss or extended separation from one or both parents; or, when the family is intact, children whose problems are caused by parents whose sex-role functions in the family are poorly defined.

The purpose of the worker-team is to provide a healthier psychological approximation of an intact family group.*

In order to fortify the children's perception of a worker-team play group as an intact familial unit, the group should be composed of boys and girls, in equal numbers if possible. Because of the unusual demands such groups place on workers, it is wise to limit the overall number of children to a maximum of six.

Intensification of Interaction in the Team Group

The therapeutic impact of a worker-team on the children in a play group is formidable. The psychodynamic interaction within the group is considerably more complex than that which takes place in a play group with a single worker. Unlike a play group with one worker, in the team group each worker must be concerned not only with his or her own unique psychological role, but also with its complementary relationship to the role of the co-worker. Because of the more penetrating influence of the team group, it is possible to effect changes in types of problems which are resistive to the methods of individual therapy or to a therapeutic play group conducted by an individual worker.

In essence, a co-worker team must be a functional representation of a good professional "marriage." The emotional balance of the co-workers can be sensed by the children in the play group. If it is good, the workers will be related to as an idealized "parent" combination. The effectiveness of the worker-team will be determined in large measure by the suitability of temperament and personality of its components. This allows for the optimal implementation of clinical knowledge and skills.

The intensification of interaction which is characteristic of worker-team groups is due to the intensification of transference at all levels, particularly between the children and the two workers. The enhanced transferences between the children and the workers also affects the relationships between the children with each other. Rivalry behavior between children is a prominent feature of the interaction in a worker-team group.

The children unconsciously fuse their separate perceptions of each worker, and they react to the workers as a significant pair—as psychological correlatives. Yet, both workers, through appropriate management of their symbolic roles of a mother and a father, reinforce the children's awareness of differ-

---

* Much of the author's experience in the use of the therapeutic play group with emotionally disturbed children in school settings has been in communities where there is a high incidence of broken homes and other conditions which expose children to deprivation early in life. Most of these groups were conducted by individual workers—male or female. Worker-teams would have been more effective. Unfortunately, a lack of personnel made it difficult to form teams in most cases.

ences in sexual identity and in sex-role performance. This differs from transference phenomena in individual psychotherapy with children, and even from play groups with one worker, where transference to the one therapist can exist in multiple forms. In such cases, depending on the needs of the moment, the same therapist may be unconsciously invested by a young child with the identity of either parent.

Influence of the Worker-Team on Sexual Identification of Children

Another advantage of having boys and girls in the same play group is that it fosters the evolution of sexual identification, at a time when this is critically important in personality development. Much of the maladjustment in young personalities is caused by parental mismanagement and from faulty psychosexual development which stems from relationships with parents who act as deficient identification models for their children. In cases where children have lost a parent, the deficiency may be fortuitous, but it is nevertheless total, and it can lead to weakened or distorted sexual identification. The team group provides children with much opportunity for patterning identification and behavior in appropriate directions.

The psychological elements involved in identification become more sharply polarized in terms of sex differentiation because of the presence of workers of opposite sexes, each of whom represents an optimal model for identification. The presence of peers of both sexes further reinforces identification by providing additional, suitable sexual models, and also, *contrast models*. Experience with mixed groups of boys and girls has revealed that the children act as strong modifiers upon each other, not only by demonstrating acceptable male and female roles, but also through blocking inappropriate sex-role behavior in each other. Thus, boys, and sometimes girls, will ridicule a boy who expresses an interest in girl's games and activities; girls will, *mutatis mutandis*, do the same.

A mixed group's normalizing pressures for proper sexual identification are even further maximized because of the tendency to form subgroups by sexes. This creates another level of interaction, which proceeds not between individuals as such, but rather between sub-groups of boys and girls. Boys, with some exceptions, usually engage in more aggressive, active behavior when they act as a subgroup, and they will often tease, chase, or generally annoy the girls in a play group; in contrast, most girls enact more passive roles.

Separation of Roles and Functions of the Workers

The two workers must always be alert to the complexities of sexual and role identification, and they must constantly assess their own and each other's functions in the play group. Ergo, the female worker performs such tasks as cleaning, preparing and serving food, washing children, and other functions which are usually attributed to mothers; the male worker, on the other hand, moves furniture, repairs items, and participates in active games.

When acting out behavior by one or more children is such as to indicate a need for limits or redirection, the question arises as to which worker should be responsible for intervention. While it would be unrealistic to formulate selectively the situations which require intervention by one worker as opposed to the other, there are general types of situations which do designate priority of responsibility. For example, a child may begin to smear with paint on paper, table, easel, and even his own person. If a point is reached when this regressive behavior becomes excessive, it devolves upon the female worker to act as the moderator. Generally speaking, when intervention is called for because of excessive regression of anal and urethral types of behavior—such as occurs through the use of paints, sand, and water—and also, when there is extraordinary messing of food, the female worker becomes involved more than the male. On the other hand, when intervention is called for in situations which are prominently aggressive, the male worker usually becomes the respondent, assuming the limiting or deflecting role.*

There are no hard and fast rules to determine each worker's priority as intervener in every instance. Certainly, if a child indicates a preference for one worker in a situation, which, under ordinary circumstances, would involve the other worker, the child's choice should be the determining factor. An example of this might occur when a girl who has been engaged in a "smeary" paint struggle with another child resists the ministrations of the female worker and runs to the male worker, demanding that he clean her up.

In summary, in a mixed play group with a worker-team, the therapeutic influences which promote normal sexual identification are found in:

  the well defined sex identities and roles of the workers
  the interaction between boy and girl
  the interaction between subgroups; male and female.

Manifestations of Libidinal Feelings in the Group

In therapeutic play group practice with children in early latency, there is, generally, more direct expression of a libidinal nature toward workers than is found in similar forms of group treatment with older children. Such libidinal behavior, while it is sometimes verbalized, is more often manifested in the form of physical contact. A child may sit or stand in close proximity to a worker; he may grasp the worker's arm or hand; it is not exceptional for

---

* Regression and aggressive behavior do not automatically indicate that intervention is necessary. The criteria involved in determining when workers should intervene are described in Chapter II.

young children to hug or kiss a worker. Behavior of this type occurs even more frequently in mixed groups with a worker-team because of the unusual degree of transference, and because rivalry behavior between children is sharpened.

A worker-team should permit direct, libidinal expressions of the type described since they are induced by the nature of the therapeutic instrument (psychological family), and further, because it satisfies a felt need in the children. However, the workers must be circumspect in manner to avoid sponsoring excessive libidinal behavior because it can generate severe rivalry. Workers may permit themselves to be kissed, but they should not actively reciprocate. As in all therapeutic play groups, the ultimate demonstration of "love" must derive from long term fulfillment of children's needs. This is a comprehensive experience, and it implies much more than reciprocity in libidinal demonstrativeness.

The Children's Perceptions of the Worker-Team

It is interesting to note how children's perceptions of the worker-team become integrated into their thinking as to how the workers are related and also, how they—the children—expect the workers to behave toward each other. It is not extraordinary for young children to assume that the workers are married to each other. They may question the relationship openly, but seldom do they pursue this line of investigation. The reason for this avoidance applies in all therapeutic play groups, including those conducted by an individual worker: children are not motivated to destroy the symbolic imagery of the workers as significant libidinal objects, something which is so meaningful to them. For reasons of their own, they have need to perceive the workers as if they were, in fact, married. Much later in treatment they will be able to "divorce" them, when the strengthening effects of therapy enable them to cope with reality better.*

Oedipal Conflict Problems as Manifested in the Team Group

A child of five or six years of age is still subject to the influence of the psychological forces inherent in the oedipal conflict. Where there are hindrances to normal development during this critical phase of development, or if there is an actual lacuna in oedipal development caused by the loss of a parent, the consequences may be seriously disabling to emotional health. The effects of such growth disturbing forces may be evidenced early, in the forms of symptoms or as malformation in the structure of personality.

---

* Because of the implications involved, workers should respond to children's questions about their relationship to each other in a simple manner, without elaboration, e.g., to a question: "Are you married?" "No." "Are you friends?" "Yes."

If the oedipal conflict exerts extraordinary impact on a child, anxiety becomes manifested. In instances where this anxiety is pervasive, it is related to the child's inability to make adequate resolution of stressful situations in the oedipal conflict with the defense mechanisms available to him. Anxiety of this type should not be confused with apprehension or transitory fears, which are responses made in situations of an episodic nature.

Anxiety in young children may be seen in different forms: as continuing tension, distractibility, persistent uneasiness; or, it may be more behavioristically demonstrated in the forms of hyperactivity, impulsivity, diffuse aggression, or even self-imposed isolation.

Emotionally disturbed children must, perforce, attempt to cope with the unusual pressures engendered by the oedipal conflict, which, in most instances, has already begun to compromise their coping ability, and which, if conditions remain unchanged, will continue to affect their development and later adjustment.

Children who are exposed to atypical but less severe stress during the period of the oedipal conflict develop less anxiety, but the genesis of their problems will still be found in the quality of their relationships with their parents and the interaction which takes place between them and their parents.

It is not unexpected, then, that much of the interaction which takes place in team play groups between emotionally disturbed young children and the workers will be psychologically attuned to the ongoing oedipal conflicts these children are actively experiencing in their respective families.*

During a period of several years in the therapeutic play group, there takes place a psychodynamic reenactment of the oedipal conflict, one with an ego-strengthening quality. This has the effect of promoting healthier sexual identification, while diluting and countering the debilitating influences of the family. The therapeutic experience inhibits the further elaboration of emotional disorder and alters some of the existing ego damage. These changes are possible because the child's libidinal cathexis, which, prior to treatment was directed mainly toward the real parents, now becomes "shared" by the psychological "parents." The workers act as agents for change; the child's transference relationships with them alter the quality of libidinal cathexis directed toward the real parents.†

This does not mean that the therapeutic play group, as a psychological correlative of the real family, *substitutes* its own experience for the oedipal conflict experience in the family. Rather, by *coinciding with it experientially*,

---

* Exceptions to this are found with highly dependent, narcissistic children, whose emotional disturbances are attributable to pre-oedipal development factors.

† See Slavson, S. R. (Ed.): Analytic Group Psychotherapy. New York, Columbia University Press, 1950, p. 105.

the play group modifies the effects of the disturbing oedipal conflict on the child.

In the case of a child who lacks one parent, and where this condition has been prolonged, the team play group becomes a setting in which elements of the interrupted oedipal development may be experienced and at least partially resolved. The degree of resolution will depend on several factors, each one related to the nature of the child's separation experiences prior to his participation in the play group; his age at the time the loss of the parent occurred; the nature of the compensating behavior of the remaining parent; the possibility of a partial substitution for the missing parent through a relative of the same sex.

When the loss of a parent is sudden and occurs while the oedipal conflict is active, a child may develop acute anxiety. Thie anxiety has two generative components: first, guilt feelings because he may feel responsible for the loss;* secondly, a fear that the remaining parent will also disappear.

A worker-team play group has almost immediate influence on such children; it neutralizes much anxiety by providing the intactness of primary relationship experience at a time when a child is made anxious by subjective guilt and by the fantasied threat of further dissolution in his family.

The Workers as Foci for the Acting out of Oedipal Behavior

As has been described earlier, interaction in play groups proceeds in all directions, encompassing at one time or another all members of a play group, including the worker-team. However, that behavior which is oedipally determined, because it was originally blocked or distorted in the real family, is acted out primarily in relationship to the workers, and it varies in quality and intensity as it is separately manifested toward each worker. Other children may become incorporated into its sphere of operation from time to time, but their involvement is incidental to the interaction between the workers and the child in question.

The primacy of either worker as the libidinal object in the oedipal acting out of a child is determined by the sex of the child concerned. The other worker then becomes an object of rivalry and the focus of the child's challenging, provocative, and aggressive behavior, sometimes expressed overtly, and, at other times, indirectly. A child's expressions of preference and affection for the worker of the opposite sex become gratified on sublimated levels

* Young children can have such anxiety despite conscious awareness on their part that the loss of the parent was the result of death from accident or disease. This sense of guilt is also true in other instances, where separation stems from desertion by a parent; or, in a case of separation determined by a legal action, where the children *continue to see* the separated parent occasionally.

by that worker, as time passes. While this is happening, the other worker, in a consistently benign, helpful role, abets the child's unconscious process of repression and thus prevents the exacerbation of guilt feelings.

The child's ego defenses are "loosened" by the experienced safety in the play group. The behavior of the therapeutic "parents" reduces the inordinate pressures of guilt and anxiety which are attendant to the oedipal conflict. The eventual therapeutic outcome is the development of a healthier super-ego structure and effective sublimations.

The presence of the other children in the play group begins to exert a moderating influence on a child's oedipal conflict reenactment. Because some of the other children have parallel problems and needs, they tend to block the intensity of any one child's oedipal expression, thus aiding the processes of repression and sublimation.

Clinical Programs in Schools, with Particular
Reference to the Therapeutic Play Group

TRADITIONAL EDUCATION; REACTION TO TREATMENT PROGRAMS IN SCHOOLS

Educators may differ in their philosophy, principles, and methods, but in one respect they share a common belief: the primary responsibility of the schools is education. They acknowledge that there are other, non-educational functions carried on in schools which are related to the general welfare of children, but these are considered to be ancillary activities.

No sensible person questions the value of certain supportive services in schools, which, while they seem to have no direct bearing on learning, are nevertheless concerned with the growth and development of children. Examples of such special services are: general health surveillance and medical care provided by nurses and doctors; guidance and counseling to aid normal children with problems related to development and also, to detect exceptional problems. While such services are usually accepted without question, considerable doubt does arise when consideration is given to the use of clinical treatment methods with emotionally disturbed children in normal schools. This is not difficult to understand since treatment programs have traditionally been identified with clinics and private practitioners.

Yet, it is a fact that there has been extensive clinical experience in schools in this country and that many and varied experimental approaches have been used with emotionally disturbed children. Despite this experience no substantive body of knowledge has accrued to guide a clinician who may be interested in implementing a treatment program with children in schools. On the other hand, there are some clinicians who seriously question the advisability of such programs.*

One of the reasons for the lack of comprehensive data on the psychotherapy of children in normal schools is the fact that many experiments were unrealistically implemented, and, as a consequence, proved to be short-lived. In these instances, clinicians merely attempted to transfer the technical

* Krugman, Morris (Ed.): Orthopsychiatry And The School. American Orthopsychiatric Association, 1958; particularly the chapter by Dr. Gerald H. J. Pearson.

procedures of psychotherapy to schools without making allowances for the uniqueness of the setting and attendant problems of an unusual nature. Another error stemmed from a failure to prepare school personnel adequately for the clinical programs, and a corresponding failure to develop methods of continuing, effective communication with them.

It is undeniable that treatment programs within schools must contend with obstructive forces which are not found in clinics. This may not make life easy for the practitioner, but it is one of the realities he must cope with if he is to work in a "foreign country." Since there are compelling reasons which do recommend the school as a *preferred* setting for treating many emotionally disturbed young children, it is mandatory that efficient methods of conducting treatment programs in normal schools be developed.

To speak more directly: I would be among the first to acknowledge the unusual problems associated with clinical practices in schools. For the past seventeen years I have trained and supervised school counselors and clinicians in the use of specialized group treatment methods such as the therapeutic play group within elementary schools. During this time I have had to contend with frustrating situations of many types, which would not have been the case had the play groups been conducted in clinics. However, I am also mindful of the fact that a large number of children improved as a result of treatment, in more than one hundred therapeutic play groups which were conducted in many elementary schools.

QUESTIONS CONCERNING THE APPLICABILITY OF PLAY GROUPS IN SCHOOLS

The doubts held by both educators and clinicians about the feasibility of treatment programs such as the therapeutic play group in elementary schools center about these main questions:

Can emotionally disturbed children assimilate—emotionally and ideationally—disparate kinds of experiences, e.g., a highly permissive play group and a formal class group, both of them concurrent in an environment which is usually conceived as highly organized, authoritative, and sometimes forbidding?

Can educators tolerate and cooperate with a permissive group treatment practice which, in theory and method, appears antithetical to their concept of the school as a setting where obedience and conformance are expected of children? This question is dealt with elsewhere in this volume.*

The answer to the first question becomes meaningful when examined in context with a child's initial reactions when he comes to school, his evolving conceptualization of school, and the integration of these new experiences with his experience prior to entering school.

* Chapter VII.

THE HOME-SCHOOL TRANSITION—TYPICAL AND ATYPICAL RESPONSES

The first major separation of a child from his family takes place when he is registered in school. The nature of his adjustment during the home-school transition and afterwards becomes a reasonable barometer of his future adjustment to group living. For the child, the school is a social miniature; it has the structural and functional aspects and many of the symbols of the larger community. Because of this parallel, the school serves as a "proving ground" in which a child's readiness and capacity for group living receive their first significant test.

School and the community are oriented primarily to groups, and they are governed by rules (laws) which are codified in the interests of the majority. In schools, the behavior of each individual is measured, to a large extent, by his willingness to abide by rules and to work and achieve under them. When the reasonable demands of a group are expressed, an individual is expected to subordinate personal gratification, especially if it threatens the integrity of the group.

The school begins to make each child more conscious of the maturational goals set for him by adults, whether or not he is adequately prepared to meet them. The teacher blends with the school as a symbol of authority. The child learns that the teacher expects him to control immature, impulsive behavior, to learn, and to share with others. School becomes a stepping stone toward the larger social reality which will eventually make even more complex demands. It is the school's psychological similarity to society at large which invests it with enormous potential as an educational force for fostering social maturation in children.

At five years, the approximate age of the beginning school child, immature behavior begins to abate, as the child is becoming responsive to the demands imposed by parents and others. In the normal child, this alteration in behavior is abetted by an increasing tolerance for frustration and an expanding capacity for making effective sublimations. The school now exerts additional pressure for change and social conformance, and it will, hopefully, enhance the child's coping abilities and thus further his development.

Children who are not emotionally ready for the transition from home to school, but who are, nevertheless, inexorably forced into the separation experience by virtue of the fact that they have attained the required chronological age, react atypically. Those children who are still overdependent on their parents come to school with anxiety, sometimes fear. These reactions may be openly displayed or they may be masked, so that a very anxious child may appear passive, acquiescent, and well-behaved. Some children, with less adequate defenses, openly manifest their insecurity by crying and through active resistance against remaining in school. Even more severe reactions may be demonstrated by some children through overt phobic-type behavior, obdurate refusal to separate from parents, or separations accomplished under duress. Finally, there are those children who are separated from their parents under compulsion, but who continue to show their lack of readiness for the transition experience through immature behavior. They resist directions; refuse to participate; reject all rules; have tantrums; fight; make excessive demands for personal attention. Such behavior sometimes yields to the persuasive ministrations of experienced teachers, but more often than not it defies their best efforts. In such a case some schools will discharge the child for at least a year in the hope that he will become mature enough to reenter later.

The home-school transition is a critical event for a child and his parents since both, separately and conjointly, have an important stake in the outcome. As parents prepare a child for school he learns that attendance in school is universal and that he is expected to attend, despite momentary or deeper fears. The child is not unaware, further, that the separation experience which he must undertake is also particularly important to his parents. He is made even more aware of the need to conform when, for the first time, he is actually surrounded by peers in school and as he perceives their reactions. Other children attend school: so must he. When a young child, in the face of these observations and realizations, fails to make the transition, or accomplishes it only at the expense of unusual stress, it becomes a significant defeat, and it is so experienced emotionally and intellectually by the child. The parents are affected similarly, because their child's failure exposes them to a sense of personal failure.

Despite initial and continuing difficulties, many emotionally disturbed children do manage to remain in school, as a result of pressures from several sources: in response to parental anxiety and persuasion; to avoid punishment and deprivations; in response to outside authority (teacher, school); from a real desire to manage the transition successfully, as siblings or friends have done.

Many emotionally disturbed children maintain themselves in school at a price of continuing emotional stress, but the effects are often *less damaging to ego development than a total failure to attend would be*.* Actually, only a small percentage of children prove to be altogether unable to separate from the home at the proper time because of severe personality disorder.

Once children are in regular attendance, it becomes the school's responsibility to detect those who maintain themselves with extraordinary difficulty,

* Parents and schools should be reasonably insistent that a child remain in school, despite tears and tantrums. School attendance represents a fundamental phase in child development, and failure to attend is ego-debilitating.

and to institute therapeutic procedures to help them. In such cases, therapeutic measures are best implemented *within the setting which was, and continues to be, the arena of child maladaptation.* Children are quite pragmatic; they need to experience success in the very place which exposed their failure—the school.

How Children Integrate Their Perceptions of the Permissive Play Group and the Authoritative School

Ideation About the Permissive Group

To return to the question posed earlier: can young children successfully adjust to both the authoritative school and a highly permissive play group experience within the school?

When a child begins to attend a therapeutic play group in a room which has been set aside for this practice within a school, the group is not immediately perceived as unique. While the play group is different from the classroom in many ways, there are elements familiar to the child. The play group includes other children of the same age; the play room may be smaller than a classroom, but it does contain items which are common to the classroom; the worker is perceived as are most adults in school—in the fused image of authority.

Changes in a child's ideation of the special play group occur as a result of perceptions and experiences which are notably different from all of the child's prior school experience. The child discovers the essential permissiveness of the worker and also, that he is free to explore and interact in the play group without directions and without interference, unlike the classroom. This discovery leads to pronounced feelings of ambivalence: the child learns to enjoy the freedom of the play group and its other pleasurable conditions, and yet, he is perplexed because they conflict with his experience in the structured, teacher-supervised class group to which he has already made an accommodation. Exposed to widely disparate types of group adjustment demands, the child becomes confused, at least for awhile.

The therapeutic play group tolerates—even induces—regressive behavior, which, were it to "spill over" from the permissive setting to the classroom, would meet with restrictions. The need to compromise the dissimilar experiences places a strain on a young child's coping ability. Since the play group inevitably becomes a preferred experience, it might be expected that the child would resolve his confusion by behaving in class as he has been permitted to do in the play group. Were this so, the implication would be that the child perceives the class room and the school as extensions of the play room. Experience with many groups has shown that this seldom occurs.

Failure to Tolerate the Permissive Group in School

In instances where children could not satisfactorily compromise the varying demands of authoritative and permissive settings, evaluations revealed that the failures resulted from one or more of the following causes:

A child was placed in a therapeutic play group too soon after entering school. Children should have at least six months in school before being considered for special therapeutic programs. The adjustment strains involved in the home-school transition are trying to normal children, certainly more so to those who are maladjusted. Exposing the latter at the very start of the school career to several groups whose adjustment demands are strikingly dissimilar is unwise. The consequences could range from passive withdrawal to manic behavior.

A child was too immature and behaved impulsively. Such a child lacks resilience and makes no attempt to adjust to the different group experiences. He tries to convert the school into what is for him the "ideal" experience— the play group.

A child whose ego defenses are already rigidly guarding against any breakdown of controls. In such a case, the underlying anxiety about any form of acting out will tolerate no dilution of the defenses which are currently effective. The permissiveness of the play group actually threatens this child. He prefers the structured group, and he refuses to continue in the play group.

A child with a pathological emotional disorder, e.g., schizophrenia.

A child was mentally retarded. Mental retardation of itself is not a contra-indication for treating a child in a therapeutic play group. The extent to which a child's retardation may interfere with his ability to cope with the permissive and the authoritative group experiences can be determined in some instances only through empirical tests in an actual play group.

In the foregoing examples, the use of the therapeutic play group proved to be contraindicated. Other therapeutic procedures were necessary.

The following example describes a child who had to be removed from a play group because the permissive experience in the school proved too disabling and interfered with his class adjustment:

Percy, a six year old boy, was placed in a play group with some reservations as to his suitability for the permissive group. After the play group had met about six times, the worker found it necessary to use limits. Percy was generally impulsive; overdemanding of the worker's time; unresponsive to any of the justified complaints of the other children in the play group. Nevertheless, Percy loved the play group. Whenever he was stimulated, he would sing or hum and move about the play room with his arms stretched over his head, twisting and turning his body as he did so, almost as if he were dancing. Soon an innovation in his behavior occurred: he began to leave the play room every meeting, ostensibly to go to the toilet. This is permitted in play groups, and in the beginning some children leave the room often as one way of testing permissiveness. Usually they return quickly, so as not to miss anything which goes on in the play group. When Percy left the play room, however, he would remain out for as long as eight to ten minutes, an inordinately long time. The worker was becoming concerned about this behavior. An observer was placed in the corridor, outside the play room.

True to pattern, Percy left the play room about ten minutes after the group had assembled. When he opened up the door, he first peered up and down the corridor. The only person in view was the adult observer, who seemed preoccupied with a bulletin board. It is pertinent to note that even the presence of an adult in the corridor (reinforcement of authority) did not in the least affect the spontaneity of the child's behavior.

After Percy left the play room, he stretched both his arms overhead, smiled, sang a melody, ambled in an irregular fashion down the corridor in a direction away from the observer. He would veer sometimes from one wall to another, turning his body in circles as he did so. He stopped at a class room door; opened it without knocking; poked his head in; said something which could not be over-heard; closed the door and continued around the bend of the corridor. The observer, who was following, saw him open several other classroom doors. Once a teacher's voice could be heard, admonishing him. Percy laughingly ran away and continued on his joyful peregrination.

After about five minutes of this activity on the boy's part, the observer deliberately caught up with Percy and accosted him. As far as Percy was concerned, the observer was a stranger. Percy was asked where he was going, but he did not bother to reply. He laughed and started to weave away. The observer blocked his way, and testing the boy further said: "Stop. Tell me where you are going." Percy mumbled: "Bathroom." The observer said: "Hurry then. I'll wait outside and then take you back to your room." Percy seemed to come into focus more sharply in response to this authoritative approach. A few moments later, he sauntered behind the observer who escorted him back to the play room. A few minutes after he was escorted back to the play room Percy again put his head outside the door, but he quickly withdrew it when he spotted the observer in the corridor.

Interpretation: Percy loved the play group; he had every reason to. He used the group and the worker to indulge his narcissism. Not only that: now he began to like the whole school. After all, it was the school which housed the wonderful play room. The reality boundaries between the two—the play group and the school proper—became fluid, and Percy was using his own kind of "magic" to make the school like the play room. The trouble, however, lay in the fact that the boy's already limited ability to maintain himself in the class group was being threatened. For Percy it was more important that he learn to respond better to realistic demands for conformance, than to be permitted to regress. The play group was contraindicated; it was recommended that Percy be removed and placed in individual treatment.

Percy's habit of leaving the play room was not a form of resistance. If he were being threatened by permissiveness, and was resisting in order to protect the adequacy of his ego defenses, his resistance would have been expressed through a *refusal* to attend the play group. To the contrary, he looked forward to each meeting.

The Child's Ability to Integrate Dissimilar Group Experiences

After ten to twelve meetings of a play group, a child can make an effective accommodation to two group experiences which appear to be intrinsically incompatible. This happens without forethought or deliberate planning on the child's part. The therapeutic setting—the play room—is placed in a psychological vacuum, so to speak, as if it were separate from the school. Thereafter, and for an extended period of time, the child "denies" the worker and the play room common identity with the school to keep secure the unique images of the person and the setting which have become so important to him. Initially, the need to do this results from a perceptual disharmony caused by two, disparate group experiences which the child is unable to reduce to a common experiential "denominator." As transference is established the child has an even stronger investment in maintaining the qualitative distinctions between the classroom and the play group. In these ways the play room and the worker become temporally and conceptually differentiated from the authoritative classroom and school.*

The capacity of young children to discriminate between and to respond to the varying demands of contrast environments (play group and classroom), should not be underestimated. While they may have need to keep separate the play room and the classroom, they are not altogether unaware of the distinctions between them. As a matter of fact, the extent to which they are able to distinguish between the separate realities of the classroom and the play room and their capacities to cope with both settings, are significant indices of ego resilience.†

A dramatic example of the quality of separation of the play room from the school is seen in the following material. This group contained four boys; average age, eight years.

For almost two years this play group had been meeting in a small play room because no other space had been available in the school. Despite the limitation of room size, the boys had done well. Much of the aggressive, rivalrous, and dependent behavior which characterized the early meetings had been dissipated. They co-operated more with each other; testing and destructive play had given way to healthy interaction and creative, growth experiences. Group discussions of common problems were more frequent and they were handled efficiently. Prior to this, the boys would argue over the slightest situation. During one group meeting, they

---

* This phenomenon is common in all forms of psychotherapy, and with patients of all ages. For the patient, the therapist and the setting become part of a "different" world. With the dissolution of clinical transference toward the termination of treatment, the patient becomes able to restore the reality contexts of the therapist and the setting. Perhaps the only difference with respect to a child patient is that there is minimal conscious ideation about the exceptional quality of the therapeutic experience.

† Percy, the child described in the last incident, lacked the ability to accommodate.

FIG. 3a

spontaneously conceived and executed a cooperative mural painting to beautify their small play room.*

A new play room became available. It was of good size and well equipped with facilities, tools, and other materials of a type now needed to accommodate the children's expanding interests and skills (Fig. 3a). At one group meeting the worker informed the boys that they were soon to meet in a new play room elsewhere in the school building. They were manifestly threatened by this announcement. When it became apparent that the change was inevitable, the boys reacted almost as a group: One boy said: *"Let's wreck this place so no one else can use it!"* The others concurred. The worker made no attempt to reassure them, nor did she inhibit their behavior. They did no damage to the room. The following week they met in the new play room, but they were constrained in behavior and did not use the new materials. Suddenly one child asked the worker: "Can you get a tent?" She replied that she could not. Then, almost as if the boys had discussed it prior, which they had not done, their thoughts flowed together: "Can you get boards and canvas?" The worker said she would get something they could use. At the next meeting she brought several boards and lengths of heavy burlap cloth. The boys fell to work *as a group*, and they quickly fabricated a tent, into which they then carried a table and chairs (Fig. 3b). When all was completed, they piled in and then invited the worker to join

* Schiffer, M.: A therapeutic play group in a public school. Ment. Hyg., Vol. 41, No. 2, April, 1957.

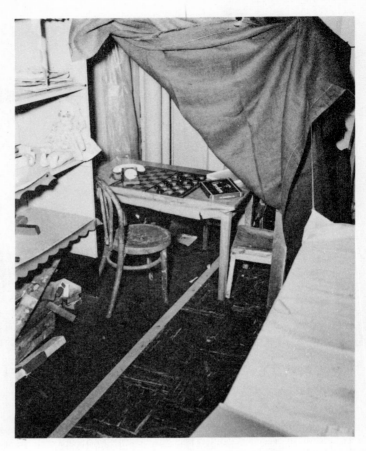

FIG. 3b

them. They had made a room within a room—a symbolic representation of the original play room. During the next few meetings there was much playing, in and out of the tent—the symbol of security—from which they could explore the new meeting room. A measure of their maturation was the fact that they soon gave up the tent and relaxed in the new play room.

THE HALO EFFECT—THE "PART" ALTERS PERCEPTION OF THE "WHOLE"

As a child improves as a result of treatment his perception and ideation of school also undergo modification. This is possible only after an extended period of time in a therapeutic play group—from two to four years, depending on the child and the nature of his problems. Of course, by this time the nature of interaction within the play group as a whole has changed appreciably.

In addition, the play group setting has slowly been restored from its state of psychological separation from the school, and it is now more realistically perceived as part of the school structure.

A reversal process is set into motion, which affects the child's earlier attitudes toward the school. The total school environment has been becoming more tolerable for him. This may be likened to a halo effect which spreads from the play room and alters the aspect of the classroom and the school. The dynamics of this phenomenon are particularly interesting because there have been no intrinsic changes within the school itself, as far as the child is concerned. It is the alteration which has taken place in the child's personality that endows the school with qualities which, for the child, did not exist prior to his treatment in the therapeutic play group.

The child's new perception of the school is accompanied by attitudinal and behavioral changes. As school becomes less onerous to him there is a diminution of earlier feelings of distrust, hostility, and also, in acting out or withdrawal behavior. There are corresponding increases in satisfactory group living and, very often, in the motivation for learning. As the child becomes secure, defensive behavior is less necessary. Defenses either dissolve altogether or they become more efficiently utilized in further service to the ego. As self image improves in the play group, a momentum for continuing success builds up. The ego "wishes" to preserve acquired gains and to extend them even further.

Effects of the Therapeutic Process on Motivation for Learning

A majority of young children who are referred because of emotional problems are also deficient in academic achievement. In the elementary school, learning deficiencies are primarily in the basic subjects—reading and arithmetic. Poor reading ability is particularly disabling because it interferes with learning in all other subject areas. The result is that frustration becomes repetitively compounded by the child's inability to keep pace with his class. If this debilitating pattern of failure in basic skill subjects remains unchanged, failures at all subsequent levels of school life become commonplace, even with children who have good intellectual potential.

Difficulties with reading and arithmetic are attributable to various causes, not all of which are emotional. Regardless of the cause, the disabilities lead to attitudinal and emotional changes which further interfere with learning. Once a child begins to equate school with failure, unhappiness and a loss of motivation set in, often accompanied by resistance against attempts at remediation and a general negativism about school.

The resolution of emotional problems through the therapeutic intervention of the play group is often accompanied by improved achievement in subjects in which children were nominally or grossly deficient. In some cases, this occurs *in the absence of special subject remediation*, and, in other cases, even after intensive remediation has failed.

A successful therapeutic experience which takes place in a school not only alters a child's ideation about school, it also decreases feelings of negativism and resistance against learning. This often leads to successful academic achievement for the first time. Motivation gains momentum, and children who earlier experienced repetitive failures, now begin to demonstrate that which is universal with all young children: intrinsic curiosity and an eagerness to master the tools with which to satisfy the needs to inquire and discover.*

When learning difficulties are caused by psychoses, brain damage, severe visual or other sensory defects, and inhibitions of a psychoneurotic type, other methods of rehabilitation and remediation are necessary.

Changes in motivation and achievement as outgrowths of the therapeutic experience in a play group were seen in several children in a play group which had met for two and one-half years before it was terminated:

Theodore: He had been referred originally because he was unusually quiet. He had no friends; his academic achievement was poor. Theodore had earlier been in a special reading remediation group for a considerable length of time without measurable improvement. This remediation took place prior to his joining the play group. After being in the play group about one year, Theodore was reported by his teacher to have developed sudden interest in his work. There was a decided improvement in his ability to read. This change continued but with marked acceleration. In the sixth grade his teacher described him as being highly motivated—the "star" of her class. She was certain that his success would continue when he went on into junior high school. These changes in Theodore's achievement coincided with improvement in the therapeutic play group.

Walter: He was described as sullen and hostile when referred. Classroom assignments were never completed satisfactorily; Walter seldom brought in homework. Later in the year, his teacher reported that he was interested in

---

* All children have curiosity; this is the energizing force in learning. It starts at first with the infant's growing awareness of the environment which extends beyond the borders of self and parent. His rapidly maturing perceptive ability increases his responsiveness to environmental stimuli. Later, curiosity becomes partially libidinized when the child learns of sexual differences, and again, when the oedipal period of psychosexual development begins. It is either a rationalization of failure or a limited understanding of the psychology of development which leads some educators to the mistaken belief that young children lack intrinsic motivation for learning. This view is held by some who work in schools in neighborhoods which are economically and culturally disadvantaged. In families which are socially, economically, and culturally deprived (and depriving!), the parents' lack of motivation and aspiration damps the natural curiosity of their children, so that they *seem* to be unmotivated when they enter school. It is the responsibility of teachers to restimulate and harness normal curiosity for the purpose of efficient learning.

his work and was doing well. She began to exhibit his papers as examples of superior work. She also commented that his attitude was different: he now was more cheerful. Similar changes were noted in the play group.

Herman: Herman had moved to New York City from a southern state only a short time before he was placed in the play group. The referring teacher said he was extremely quiet, almost fearful of relationships with others. His school work was poor; he was apathetic. The following year his teacher reported that he was participating in class. He actually began to volunteer; something he had never done in the past. Herman also spoke with his classmates; prior to this he had been practically mute. In the play group, Herman had become gregarious; he joined in games and was able to withstand aggressive behavior from some of the other boys.

Matthew: He attended a play group in another elementary school for three years. He was exceedingly difficult to manage in class. Matthew was defiant and sullen. He did no work and had no interest in learning. For a considerable period of time he was markedly defensive, even in the play group. Matthew began to improve when he was in the fifth grade, after almost two years in the play group. When he was promoted to the sixth grade, his interest in learning spurted. Matthew was not the only one who enjoyed the fruits of success. His mother, who had been most uncooperative with the school and seemingly disinterested in her own son, began to respond. She would now visit the school and she was more receptive to some of the suggestions about how to manage her son at home. While these changes were being noted in the classroom, his entire demeanor in the play group had been changing. It had taken about two years for the boy's defensiveness and suspiciousness to dissipate. Eventually he became dependent on the worker, after an extended period of defending against a relationship with her. He made many demands during the time he was dependent. These were consistently gratified by the worker. Matthew later became more secure and independent. He became more participative in the group's activities.

PARENTS' REACTIONS TO SCHOOL-BASED CLINICAL PROGRAMS

The concept of the school as a setting for clinical programs of psychotherapy is relatively foreign to parents' thinking, despite the increased sophistication shown by many of them in matters related to mental health. Their perception of the school has a residual base made up from their own childhood experiences and memories of schools. In later years, innovations in educational practices may have modified their imagery of the school, but not to a marked degree. As far as schools are concerned, parents would still tend to agree with educators that the important function of the school is to help children learn.

Parents may become aware for the first time that a school is interested in their child from other than an educational context when they are invited to the school to confer with a counselor or clinician. While they may not react with equanimity when they are apprised of the school's concern about the child, they can tolerate it because matters related to behavior are generally conceded to be within the purview of schools. It is when their child's behavior is described as exceptional, to a degree that may warrant the need for specialized, clinical help, that parents become more alarmed and defensive. Yet, even at such a time, they are still less threatened by offers of special services within the school than they would be to a suggestion that they seek the necessary help from a family or child guidance agency. This is so because the school is more familiar to parents than a clinic. The specialists within a school—including clinicians—become invested with some of the imagery attached to schools. The skilled interviewer can use this to advantage in reassuring troubled parents and in establishing a base for continuing interviews.

Most parents who adamantly resist becoming involved themselves in treatment, whether it is offered in a school or an outside agency, can still tolerate their child's participation in a therapeutic play group within a school. The idea of a play group for a child is much less threatening, probably because it differs radically from the parents' stereotyped ideas of treatment. Resistive parents may become more accessible later, if their child improves as a result of his participation in a play group. This was so in the following case:

Mike's mother gave grudging consent to her son's participation in a therapeutic play group, in which he was to remain for three and a half years. Under no circumstances would she consider the suggestion that a family agency could help her with myriad problems involving most of her other children and her marital relationship itself. She permitted Mike to attend the play group, but she remained defensive—even belligerent—during several interviews with the school guidance counselor. Her unspoken attitude was plain: "Leave me alone and I'll let you play your 'games' with my son!" Yet, *three years later* she voluntarily requested that the same counselor assist her in getting help for the problems which still beset her. She said that the changes in Mike had pleased her and that she was grateful.

Of course, the attitudes of some parents are sometimes unyielding, and they continue to resist participation in a clinical program, despite improvement in their children. In rarer instances, there are parents who are initially cooperative but who display resistance for the first time *after their children begin to improve*. Still others, who are mildly resistive at first, become increasingly so when the children improve. Reactions of these types are indications of psychoneurotic behavior. Unless such parents can become involved in treatment they will inevitably "defeat" the child's treatment through unconscious and conscious manipulation.

Parents' Perception of School is Modified

When parents do respond to offers of help and they are seen in a school on a continuing basis in advisement, counseling, or treatment, a new dimension is added to their original perception of the school. The school now looms less formidably in their eyes; it borrows some of the qualities of the relationship with the clinician.*

ATTITUDES TOWARDS CLINICAL SERVICES IN SCHOOLS IN DISADVANTAGED NEIGHBORHOODS

Differences in Parents' Attitudes in Deprived Communities

In socially and economically depressed areas of large cities there are unusual circumstances which influence to a considerable degree the manner in which parents will respond to a school's concern about deviant child behavior. In such neighborhoods, the concept of rehabilitative treatment for emotional problems is entirely strange to families which are more concerned with "real" problems: habitation, food, clothing, and dealing with representatives from a welfare department or some other "official" agency.

A developmental or behavior problem of a child which is of a nature to cause consternation in a middle class family might be considered relatively unimportant to a family which has to cope with multiple, immediate pressures of an economic nature. It is a matter of unfortunate fact that parents who live under depressed conditions may become more actively concerned because their child's school maladjustment is making their task of daily living more difficult rather than because of the psychological implications of his behavior. This is often true even after clinicians attempt to make the parents aware of the serious implications of a child problem—as it exists separate from other conditions affecting the family. Such parents are sometimes depicted as being apathetic, or as lacking concern for the child's well being. This is not necessarily correct; in a sense, it is an unfair judgement.

A distraught mother, who is worried about the immediate reality of a husband who has deserted her and the need to provide for her children, may not be readily impressed by the fact that the school considers one of her children a problem because she is enuretic, excessively shy, and friendless. As far as the mother is concerned, she will manage the laundry problem as best she can. On the other hand, her child's recessive behavior *may be accept-*

* The modification of the parents' perception of the school, as a result of a positive experience with a clinician, parallels the "halo effect" with respect to a child in a therapeutic play group. The school does not change; it is essentially static. The global perception of the school—of child and parents—changes by a process of attribution: the school is "better" because a part—the treatment relationship—has become important to the clients.

able to her because it does not aggravate what she considers to be her larger problems.

In another case, parents may be resentful of the school, and also annoyed with their child, because his aggressive acting out behavior has made it necessary for them to take time to visit the school. This may mean a loss of wages because of time off from work, or other inconvenience. Parents who manage their child's acting out in the home with firmness find it difficult to understand why the school cannot do as well. Such parents might even prefer that the school adopt firmer measures to control their child and thus obviate the need for their becoming involved. This attitude, which does not reflect a lack of interest in the child's welfare—as the parents interpret it— does not favor the development of meaningful communication between the parents and a school clinician.

Thus, it is not uncommon that in families in underprivileged, urban neighborhoods, clinical approaches meet with forms of parental resistance* which are determined by a combination of economic, cultural, or ethnic factors and not primarily psychological ones. Such parents may be labeled "uncooperative" when they resist referral to family agencies, or if they terminate after making initial contact.

The agencies are, for the most part, too remote—conceptually and geographically—from the families they were meant to serve.† The result is that many emotionally disturbed children will never have an opportunity to benefit from psychotherapy unless it is "delivered" to them within a setting where they can reasonably be expected to appear daily—the school.‡

Psychological forces entirely unrelated to socioeconomic circumstances may also militate against programs of clinical assistance for children and families in deprived areas. Educationally limited parents may lack sophisti-

---

* Perhaps a more accurate word is inertia.

† In recent years attempts have been made to cope with this real problem through efforts in community psychiatry. Where such specialized services are carried on separate from a comprehensive, medical program geared to the needs of the immediate community, they will undoubtedly fail. Unsophisticated parents can appreciate the need for psychological services only as they are helped to understand that behavioral problems are a meaningful part of total health care.

‡ The author confesses that he has sometimes placed children in therapeutic play groups in schools when it has been impossible to bring a parent in for interview. This has occurred in instances where there was apathy on the part of parents and, in other cases, when outright neglect has kept them from school. It is not unusual in crowded, urban areas that years can pass without some parents ever visiting schools. "Purists" in clinical practice may shudder at the implications of such procedures. This is small comfort to needy children. A considerable number of children have been maintained in therapeutic play groups for years, *without their parents ever being seen.* A more significant fact is that many of these children were helped.

cation about the meanings of psychotherapy, but they are no less subject to the psychological determinants governing thought and behavior than are parents who have been more fortunate in their life experience. Therefore, there are times when they are resistive for reasons which are best described in psychological terms. However, even when resistance has a fundamental, psychological causation it becomes formidably buttressed by a value system which is far different from a middle class one.

Participation of Fathers in Treatment Programs

Mothers are usually the ones who respond to invitations to visit schools in matters affecting their children. This is realistically determined because, in most cases, fathers work during the day. For this and other reasons, fathers are less involved in their children's school experiences, especially during the early years of elementary school. This is true even in situations in which the clinical resource of a school is concerned.

It is interesting to note that in school-based clinical programs it is not unusual for clinicians to initiate and maintain rehabilitative programs for children and families without sustained contact with fathers and sometimes without ever seeing a father. In clinical practice in community agencies, the usual rule is to refuse service unless both parents cooperate.

Responsibility of Clinicians in Schools in Disadvantaged Communities

Experience has shown that school clinicians become influenced by indigenous educational practices—the "mores" of the school. A consequence of this is the dilution of clinical methods through tacit omission of an essential part: participation of both parents. Because a clinical program is carried on in a school it gains no special privilege as far as the basic requirements for efficient clinical performance are concerned.

When a family is not intact due to the absence of the father, clinics within schools and elsewhere have no choice but to work with the family with whatever resources they can command. While this situation is not infrequent in depressed socioeconomic areas, it is still a fact that even in intact families in all neighborhoods fathers tend to remain relatively uninvolved in clinical programs in schools while their wives and children are being seen on a regular basis.

There is another reason which accounts for the nonparticipation of fathers, other than the fact that they work during the school day. In its global context the elementary school is perceived as a maternal symbol. Therefore, it seems only "natural" that mothers should bear the responsibility for maternal affairs. The school increases in its masculine symbolism at secondary levels, and in college it reaches its highest point.

It would become possible to have more fathers participate in treatment programs in schools if the services were offered during evening hours. Some community clinical agencies do this but only to a limited extent. If schools and other agencies hope eventually to provide adequate services for the community, they will have to accommodate to circumstances dictated by reality. This will make mandatory the need to extend the clinical program into the evening on a daily basis. This is not unrealistic: certainly no clinician would question this as it applies to the private practice of psychotherapy.

CONFIDENTIALITY AND CLINICAL PRACTICE IN SCHOOLS

Before a parent can feel free to participate in a treatment program, or even in a supportive, counseling situation wherein information of a personal nature may be confided, he must develop the assurance that the clinician is functioning in his interest and not as an "agent" of the school. Any suspicion to the contrary would certainly obstruct communication and block the further development of the client-practitioner relationship. The parent must feel that his interests are primary. The client has the right of personal privilege, without regard to the setting in which the clinical service is performed. Moreover, a parent's wishes as to whether or not information may be shared with other school personnel must be respected.

This question of confidentiality is most important, and it must be clearly defined for all professional disciplines within a school because it is crucial to the existence of clinical programs. Many problems arise in schools over this question in particular because of the tendency on the part of administrators and teachers to view all school-based personnel as representatives of the school with their primary allegiance to the school. All too often, unfortunately, they look askance at clinicians because of their client-focussed orientation. A failure to develop a professional frame of reference in all school personnel, one in which the needs of the client are acknowledged as paramount, becomes one of the largest obstacles to successful clinical work within schools.

The defensive and suspicious attitudes which teachers and administrators may have about school clinicians are attributable to two factors: an ignorance of psychological principles and practices in psychotherapy; a general insecurity in the teaching role. Those negative attitudes which stem from a lack of understanding of clinical procedures may be ameliorated in time through the development of meaningful communication between the disciplines. Where difficulties arise out of personal insecurity, the clinician must use his special skills to reduce the subjective feelings which threaten teachers.*

---

* Such teachers can feel threatened about what children and parents may be communicating in the privacy of the clinician's office.

PROCEDURAL ELEMENTS OF THERAPEUTIC PLAY GROUP PRACTICE IN ELEMENTARY SCHOOLS

Problem Identification—The Referral Source

Teachers are usually the ones to initiate referrals, either as a result of prior consultations with a clinician or independently. In both cases—particularly the latter—the final responsibility for determining whether the referrals are warranted rests with the clinician. Unless teachers are aided by specialists in child behavior, the referral process will be indiscriminate and much time will be wasted. In the author's experience, when a school-based clinical program does not planfully include in-service seminars in child psychology and sufficient opportunity for individual consultations with teachers, difficulties arise with respect to the identification of children whose problems are severe enough to merit clinical assistance.

Teachers Are Insufficiently Trained in Child Psychology

Much of the difficulty which teachers experience in detecting exceptional behavior in children and in learning to cope with it more effectively is the result of inadequate preparation during the time of teacher training. Teacher training programs on undergraduate and graduate levels are oriented primarily to curriculum and methods of teaching, and they are concerned only incidentally with the study of child development.* Furthermore, very little training, or none at all, is given in the identification of the exceptional child. One result of the failure of the teacher training institutions to concentrate on developmental psychology, so that teachers may know *as much* about the nature of the educational "target"—the child—as they do about curriculum content and teaching methods, is to blunt the teachers' preception of the qualitative differences between personalities. The ability to recognize individuality in all children and exceptionality in emotionally maladjusted children is not fostered.

Some of the faults in traditional teacher training become further compounded later as a result of a continuing stress on educational achievement to the exclusion of other important elements of child development. Supervisors contribute to this by oversensitizing teachers to such matters as competency in teaching methods, the need for measurable educational outcomes, and the need to control the class group. Passive acknowledgement is given to the concept of individual differences, but in actual practice individual children are seen as "different" when they fail to achieve academically or if they do not conform behavioristically.

* There are exceptions, of course. Some schools place heavy emphasis on child development and psychology as they are related to the learning process and to the overall behavior of children.

All too often an exceptional child is identified, not in terms of his uniqueness—which could lead to a better understanding of his needs—but rather, in contrast to the group. Consequently, he is held accountable for failure to be like the group.

Another factor which affects the teachers' accuracy in detecting emotionally disturbed children, is a failure to draw distinctions between forms of child behavior which are episodic and not necessarily conflicted, and those which are *characteristically* exceptional and persistent. Many teachers are unable to—or unwilling to—countenance *any* kind of behavior which may interfere with the smooth progression of the teaching process. Such teachers tend to view the inappropriate behavior of an emotionally disturbed child as a matter of discipline, and they refer such children for summary treatment and not as if they were in need of personal help.

Another complication, one which is less apparent than others, is the failure on the part of teachers to look beyond the manifest content of child behavior for its underlying, less conscious meanings. Again, some of this can be attributed to the limited attention given to the study of child development and behavior during teacher training. There is another reason which accounts even more for this failure to understand child behavior. The search for latent meanings of child behavior makes it inevitable that a teacher examine herself as she affects or is affected by the psychodynamic interaction which takes place between her and a child, and also with the class as a group. Teachers—and other adults—who are able to do this without undue anxiety are the exceptions rather than the rule.

The opportunities for committing technical errors in working with children are numerous because children possess extraordinary potential for inducing countertransference reactions in adults. Teachers, in particular, are vulnerable to this, and it interferes with their objective evaluation of child behavior. The same phenomenon is found in varying degrees in all professional disciplines which are involved primarily with children.

Clinicians Tend To Be Defensive in School Practice

Specialists in counseling and clinical practice have also made unwitting contribution to the difficulties of identifying problem children. Their own needs for professional identification and security in an academic environment which has perhaps grudgingly accepted them tends to make them defensive. This does not promote easy communication with teachers. It can also lead to a mutual defensiveness and persisting separateness between professional disciplines which must be able to work harmoniously. Under such circumstances, teachers begin to feel professionally inadequate when it becomes necessary for them to refer children for "outside" help. Should such attitudes become subtly extended throughout a school, the net effects would be to interfere with the process of early identification of emotionally disturbed children and to delay the implementation of corrective measures.*

It behooves clinical specialists to be conscious of the need to develop better methods of communication with teachers and *to accept responsibility for achieving this*. They should be mindful of the origins of teacher resistiveness and should also avoid involved discussions with teachers of the problems affecting communication. This approach is too didactic, and it tends to promote intellectual confrontations which are not profitable in the long run. It is wiser to become more familiar with the teacher's role and the reality situations within particular classrooms, schools, and neighborhoods.†️ Specialists must also learn the language of the academician. Clinical terminology may facilitate communication in a clinic, but in a school it does not foster communication with teachers.

IMPROVING THE QUALITY OF REFERRALS

Consultations: In Groups and Individually

To refine the process of making referrals, it would be advisable at first to meet with teachers in small groups, because a group generates confidence through a sense of mutual support. Individual conferences may be used later to advantage. Through continuing collaboration, clinicians should broaden teachers' knowledge of child psychology and sensitize them to the signs of emotional disturbance.

The use of assessment forms such as behavior check lists is best avoided because they are mechanistic and relatively unrevealing as qualitative instruments. Much more can be learned through discussions with teachers. School records also become more meaningful when their contents are used as part of conference procedures.

The school's health record card may be a source of important information. If there are entries of an unusual nature they can be discussed with a school nurse or doctor. A history of disease or disability which preceded a child's entry to school may be related to current behavior. This is not uncommon in cases where there have been separations of children from their families early in life because of hospitalization, especially for an extended period of time. A health card may also indicate the presence of a disability which is barely manifest and which may be overlooked altogether by a nonmedical person, e.g., partial deafness, impaired vision, petit mal, and other, minor neurological symptoms.

* Schiffer, M.: Specialization and under-utilization. Ment. Hyg., Vol. 49, No. 1, 1965.

† Only those who have had direct experience in these areas can appreciate the enormous differences in school and classroom management in different sections of large cities.

"Emergency" Referrals

An effective method of reducing the number of "emergency" referrals—which are sometimes made by teachers on the basis of a single episode of acting out behavior by a child—is for the clinician and teacher to survey an entire class in order to identify children who appear to be exceptional in terms of behavior. When it is possible to do this, subjective distortion of the teacher and referrals made from frustration can be kept to a minimum.

Direct Observation

Preliminary detection of troubled children must be followed by other procedures for gathering pertinent information which can be used in determining the need for special services. The referring teacher is still in the most strategic position to provide important observations about a child's behavior and general adjustment in groups. Anecdotal records kept by the teacher are prime sources of information. If a child has been in more than one class it is necessary to consult with all prior teachers. Significant differences in evaluations of the same child by different teachers will probably be due to subjective flaws in the observations of one or more teachers.

The specialist is in a position to obtain information independently, through direct observations of a child in the classroom, during freeplay in a school yard, at lunch time, and at dismissals.

A girl was referred by her first grade teacher, who described her as being very shy. This was confirmed by the kindergarten teacher who knew her from the previous year. However, when the child was observed with her friends, apart from the classroom and the teacher, her behavior was quite different. She was animated; she chattered with children; she was even mildly aggressive. Further exploloration established that she was essentially intact and not in need of help. She had been born in Puerto Rico and came to New York City with her family at the age of four. Her diffidence in school was reactive to a sociocultural environment which was markedly different from that of her home and the community itself.

During the period of initial evaluation, a child should be observed in the specialist's office, either alone or in the company of another child. Through the use of play materials the skilled observer can detect strengths and weaknesses in the child's capacity to adjust to new situations. Direct interviewing procedures, for the purpose of eliciting information about family and attitudes, should be used with discrimination with young children. The process is foreign to them and they feel especially uneasy when requests for personal information are being made by an adult who is relatively strange to them.

Premature Identification

A special precaution is necessary in assessing what is considered to be exceptional behavior in nursery and kindergarten children. Behavior which is a departure from the norm is not always an indication that therapy will be necessary. Children who demonstrate insecurity after entering school, through a variety of behavior patterns, may make better adjustments later, without help. There are persuasive maturational forces within these early age school groups which, under the aegis of a skillful teacher, can be used in the successful resolution of essentially transient problems. While it is advantageous to start therapeutic programs as early as practicable, it is advisable to delay decision for at least six months after a child starts school. Exceptions to this general practice exist when the clinical determinants of emotional disorder are explicitly demonstrated in a child.

At the end of the first semester it should be apparent which children do require help because of continuing disabilities. Their maturational responses to the demands of group life will have been either insufficient or atypical and persistently so. As seen in the group, a child's maladjustment may be categorized in a gross sense as either excessively withdrawn or acting out. On a more personal level, evidences of emotional problems will be observed in symptoms, habit and conduct patterns.

Timing the Parent Interview

Clinicians and teachers, as cooperating professional teams in school, have the necessary skills to discriminate between normal and exceptional behavior in children. They probably have more opportunity to observe how children cope with the varying demands placed upon them by different situations than other adults, perhaps even more so than the average parent.

The cooperation of parents is important, but not primarily to establish the fact that a child has a behavior or personality problem. Therefore, parents should be invited to school for interview only after it has been confirmed that a definitive problem exists.* Premature interviews may subject them to unwarranted anxiety.

Where it has been established in a particular case that a child requires special help it then becomes necessary to involve a parent for the following reasons: to provide information about the child's present and past behavior at home and his developmental history; to describe relationships and other circumstances affecting the family. The parent must also be motivated and supported so that he will continue to cooperate with a treatment program should it become indicated.

SOME SPECIAL FEATURES OF PLAY GROUPS WITHIN SCHOOLS

If emotionally disturbed children are to be helped through psychotherapy, the essential clinical requirements must be met, whether the treatment pro-

---

* This injunction does not apply to general visits made in response to a school's attempts to broaden communication with parents on an individual basis and with the community as a whole.

gram is conducted in a clinic, the office of a private practitioner, or in an elementary school. The elements of psychodynamic interaction are such as to tolerate little compromise if treatment is to be effective. Environmental restrictions which interfere with the proper performance of psychotherapy guarantee failure.

A school-based program of group psychotherapy is afforded no special exemption in terms of the essential requirements. The principles governing the therapeutic play group—which were enunciated in the first chapter—apply in no less measure when the play group is conducted within an elementary school. However, it should be obvious that there are certain circumstances within schools which do influence some of the practical aspects of therapeutic play group practice. Some of these have already been referred to. There are additional modifications of technical procedures which are necessary in school-based programs.

The Play Room in an Elementary School

The play room is best located as remote as possible from classrooms and administrative offices, to offset the possibility of interfering with school activities.* Another reason for locating the play room away from regular school activities is to foster the psychological separation between permissive and non-permissive environments.

The play room should be altered to detract from its school-identified appearance. Blackboards can be covered with burlap or cork board, to which children's paintings may later be attached. If possible, tables and chairs should be different from the types used in classrooms. In any case, table tops can be covered with brightly colored oilcloth or plastic. Closets, walls, and ceiling should be painted in a light pastel shade.

Timing of Group Meetings

Play group meetings should be scheduled to end just before school dismissals—at noon or at the end of the school day. In this way there will be less chance for active behavior to "spill over" to the classroom from the play room. As noted earlier, the question of continuity of behavior from the permissive setting to the school proper has implications with respect to the ability of young children to discriminate between and to adjust to varying stimuli. For instance, when a play group meeting is over and the children leave the play room to return to their respective classrooms, they begin to

---

* The author has made use of such locations as: dressing rooms next to an auditorium stage; a substreet storage room; a large office attached to a gymnasium; a converted locker room.

respond in increasing degree to the "outer" school. The excitement, exhilaration, or the activated behavior, all of which are not unusual in the play room, becomes damped under the influence of the authoritative milieu. The converse is also true; when children coming from classrooms cross the threshold of the play room, restraints and inhibitions which were responsive to the demands of the structured, directed class group are replaced by freedom and relaxation.

The differences in the manner in which children adapt to the two settings become less pronounced during the terminal phases of a play group's history, at which time the children's ideation of the school and the play room as disparate milieus also changes.

The play group worker should consult with the teachers concerned in establishing the best time of the day for play group meetings—morning or afternoon. This is important so that attendance in the play group does not interfere with the teaching program. It is important that children who are acquiring basic language skills such as reading and writing do not miss classroom instruction.*

Movement to and From the Play Room

Young children can be escorted to and from the play room by monitors from upper grade classes. It is best to use the same monitors for any one group. It is interesting how often monitors become aware of the special needs of their charges and learn to handle them with sensitivity, and with an eye to the reality demands of the school.

Perception of the Group Worker in Settings Outside the Play Room

It is important that children in play groups do not become excessively aware of the fact that the worker confers with their teachers, otherwise it would interfere with the development of confidence and trust. Once a play group has been constituted, and after it has begun to meet regularly, the worker should avoid contact with the children outside the play room. Just as the play room becomes psychologically separated from the school for the children, so does the worker. He must avoid being identified with authoritative symbols. The requirement that the worker be perceived as different from all other adults will change, as the children improve through the therapeutic experience and as dilution of the transference takes place. At such a time, there is a purposeful modification of the activities in the play group and the worker's role, to bring both closer to the reality of normal groups.

* This is one example of a point made earlier: the necessity for clinical personnel to familiarize themselves with educational practices.

Meetings Held Outside the Play Room

When a play group has reached a transitional phase, and the worker begins to introduce new experiences to promote maturation and to test reality functioning, the group begins to use other areas of the school. When this takes place, the worker must be prepared to invoke some of the proscriptions against acting out behavior in the "outer" school, if it becomes necessary to do so. This may take the form of mild but realistic limits against excessive noise or running through corridors.

After a group's first experience outside the play room the worker no longer takes the initiative in determining whether subsequent meetings will be held in the play room or elsewhere. One week, one or more children may prefer to stay in the play room to complete a project. Another time, a child may resist leaving the play room because a prior experience "outside" proved frustrating, or because he wishes to exercise control over the group. This leads to conflict situations which the group must resolve because the worker cannot permit them to meet as subgroups, in different places. Such situations lead to arguments, threats, recriminations, and finally, to discussion and compromise.

The play group must also cope with problem situations which originate outside the play room. When outside resources such as a gymnasium or school yard are being used by regular classes, the needs of the play group may be frustrated. These diverse forces, some from within the group and others extrinsic to it but affecting the interaction in the group, give impetus to integrative, maturational development.

The following descriptions are of play groups which were conducted in different schools. They illustrate how therapeutic play group practice in schools is influenced by extraneous factors which, in clinical settings, would not exist:

In one school, the worker complained during a supervision conference that she was having trouble because of an excessive amount of acting out by the boys in her first grade group. She said that they were eager to come to the play room when she picked them up from their classrooms but they were difficult to handle when she returned them later, at which time they continued to behave much as they had been doing in the play room. In the play room she was able to tolerate their behavior.

When she was asked why she did not use older children as monitors, as she had done in the past with other play groups, she said that it was difficult to get them when she needed them. At this point she spontaneously began to speak of an assistant to the principal with whom she was having difficulty because of his rather arbitrary manner with respect to school matters generally. After mentioning this, she needed little assistance in solving the children's (?) problem. She had been protecting the children, and also, her tenuous "professional" relationship with the assistant by attempting to insure the good behavior of the play group children in the school corridors. The play group children were, of course, responding only to errors in the worker's technic. They were reacting to the psychological imbalance caused by her alternate permissive and restrictive roles. They could not be held responsible for the arbitrariness of an administrator.

Two older girls were selected as monitors, each responsible for escorting three children. They were able to manage the boys efficiently.

The second play group was also composed of first grade boys who were being accompanied to and from the play room by competent monitors. However, these monitors complained that on the way back to the classrooms with the children they found it difficult to keep them from running through the halls.

The play group met in a play room which was behind a gymnasium. It was necessary to pass through the gymnasium in coming to the play room and later, when returning to class. It was just too tempting! When the children left the play room, they slid along the marvelously polished floor, then rolled over and over on the gymnasium mats, laughing loudly. When this happened, the monitors generally took off after the children trying to catch them. This became part of the fun, and the children led the monitors a merry chase around and around the gymnasium which, incidentally, was not in use by others. Of course, when finally apprehended, the children were as "high as kites" and disinclined to be quiet in the corridors.

The monitors were instructed to let the children run about the gymnasium after they left the play room. They were to wait patiently at the gymnasium exit door, in view of the children, for at least two or three minutes. After that they were to call to the children but not to chase them if they came tardily. When the children were finally assembled, they were then to be escorted back to class. This was done and there was less trouble in returning the children. It is of interest to add that when the monitors brought the children to the play room at the start of a group meeting, there was no lingering in the gymnasium.

The children in this play group had been responding to several forces: resistance to leaving the play room after the meeting ended; the stimulus of the setting—the gymnasium.

The foregoing descriptions depict situations which occur from time to time in school-based play group practice. These are hindrances which complicate an already complex therapeutic practice. Yet, they are far from insurmountable. The enormous rehabilitative potential of the play group in the school is such that difficulties intrinsic to the setting become comparatively less significant.

6 Analysis of a Therapeutic Play Group in an Elementary School

In selecting a therapeutic play group for analysis from its inception to termination, it was decided to use a record of a school-based play group. As was pointed out earlier, the play group has extraordinary value when used in elementary schools. However, it was also noted that there are factors influencing clinical practices in schools which are quite unique. Therefore, the choice of this group was predicated on two major objectives: to describe and analyze a play group in its entirety—through all its phases of development; to illustrate some of the unusual aspects of play group practice in schools.

It is also of interest that the play group worker in this group was a guidance counselor and not a clinician. While she already had considerable training and experience in guidance counseling in elementary schools, this was her first experience with a therapeutic play group. She had been prepared for it through intensive training, and she was supervised on a regular weekly basis during the life of the play group.

The composition of this play group remained essentially intact for three years, during which time 93 group meetings were held. The only change occurred when one child was removed for reasons which will be explained in the record. This constancy in group composition is relatively rare in schools in urban sections where there is much population movement.*

The elementary school in which the play group met was one with many problems. Recent changes in administration, a heavy staff turn over, a large number of young, inexperienced teachers, and other factors, reinforced the general disquiet within the building. An excessive number of pupil problems overtaxed the guidance services within the school; other services within the community were limited. The neighborhood was on the periphery of the city and was suburban in quality. Most of the residences were one-family type houses, but many were used as multiple family dwellings, to enable the owners to meet the financial pressures of maintenance. The residents, with some exceptions, were part of a large population migration from central urban, slum sections, and they struggled energetically to sustain themselves

* In some of the schools the author has worked in, pupil turnover caused by families moving in and out of a school's geographic area has reached as high as 75 per cent, *in one school year.*

in this new neighborhood of comparative luxury. In many families it was common to find both parents regularly employed; many other families were receiving public assistance.

Family problems were common for reasons other than economic ones. Many families were not intact because of the absence of one parent, usually the father. The incidence of delinquency, narcotic addiction, and alcoholism was not nearly as high as in an urban slum, but it was sufficient to represent a problem in the community.

The five boys who comprised this play group were selected after studying a larger number of referrals. The final selection was made on the basis of their presenting problems and the requirements of a psychologically balanced group. The following are condensed descriptions of the problems when the boys were referred, at which time all were eight years of age, in the third grade.

MITCHELL

The referring teacher reported that Mitchell was "hostile toward authority; he fought with children; was unusually stubborn." He used obscenities freely, even to the assistant principal, who had once forcibly removed him from the classroom. He was restless, and it was difficult for him to concentrate on school work. Mitchell was intelligent, but his motivation and achievement were minimal. Whenever an adult demonstrated interest in him he became uncomfortable. He could not tolerate his teacher's attempts to befriend him; when she manifested her feelings toward him by putting her arm on his shoulder he shrugged her off. His language with peers was replete with threatening remarks such as: "shooting-drowning-put you away!" At other times some of his comments were depressive in context: "I'll take a ride in a boat and drown." Sometimes he was dispirited, unhappy, or felt worthless. Mitchell also behaved in ways which indicated that he had strong guilt feelings. His teacher described how Mitchell once took a ruler and said to her, "Why don't you ever hit me? I'll hit myself with this ruler." He proceeded to do so by tapping himself on the head. At another time he said he wanted to go to "that school which has bad boys," but first he would have to "break a few windows and go to court!"

This was the picture of his behavior at the time he was referred. In first and second grades he had been less aggressive but very sensitive to rejection by peers or adults.

Mitchell was the fifth child in a family of nine children, ranging in age from one to fourteen years. His father was an alcoholic, and he had been separated from the family many times. At the time of Mitchell's referral, he was again out of the home, and his wife stated that she was "fed up" with him and that this last separation was permanent as far as she was concerned. She complained of problems with most of her children, without particularizing. She was overwhelmed and, in frustration, she attributed all of her problems to her husband. She worried that Mitchell might become delinquent like one of his older siblings. Her method of handling the children at home was impulsive and punitive. Mitchell was fearful of her. She had once advised his teacher: "Use your ruler on him!"

Summary: The problem areas were: mixed behavior, vacillating between aggression, open defiance and withdrawal; depression, with feelings of worthlessness and low self-esteem; suspicion and marked ambivalence in feelings toward adults; lack of motivation for learning; incipient delinquency.

Mitchell was accepted for the play group with the following projected goals:

He would have an opportunity for a sustained relationship with an accepting adult, whose support and permissiveness might eventually reduce his suspicion and actual fear of a relationship. If the therapeutic experience was to be successful, the group worker must eventually represent a "safe" libidinal object for Mitchell.

The group would also help him in working through some of his sibling rivalry.

If these aims were realized, in whole or in part, Mitchell might build up motivation for learning because school would no longer be synonomous with frustration and failure.

The group worker was advised to maintain a distance between Mitchell and herself and to avoid making overtures toward him. She was to wait until he initiated such contacts. At all times she must try to meet his requests as they were expressed.

CARL

He was referred by his teacher because of an apparent preference for girls and poor relationships with boys. Carl preferred talking with girls and he liked to touch and fondle them. He teased girls but always avoided the boys. It was the teacher's impression that Carl, if he had any interest in playing with boys, was afraid to attempt it. He was an onlooker during group activities. Carl was unassertive and shy, but in kindergarten and in first grade several episodes of stubbornness, with temper outbursts, had been reported.

The referral material described him as nervous, clumsy, and careless in personal habits. He liked praise and sulked if he was criticized. Carl was attentive during lessons; responsive to directions from the teacher. Once in class during spontaneous play with puppets, Carl chose to be the baby in the "family." He acted his role well, mimicking a baby's voice. In the role play he displayed anger and jealousy of the siblings, and defiance of the father. He also complained about the mother and said: "I hate girls!"

Carl was the second oldest of four boys. He resented his older brother, a year his senior, because he pushed Carl around. While he did not verbalize it, he was patently jealous of his younger siblings. His father criticized his wife's management of the children, accusing her of being too lenient. Both parents were disturbed about Carl's interest in girls and his participation in their activities. Despite their concern it was revealing that they were preparing to give him lessons in music and dancing! Carl and his older brother had to help with household chores, including cooking and cleaning. Carl went shopping with his mother. There were many small evidences that the parents—particularly the mother—were disappointed in the fact that they had not had a daughter.

Summary: The basic problem was that of an eight year old boy with faulty sexual identification. Earlier acting out, aggressive behavior was giving way to a preference for the companionship of girls, at an age when this was psychologically inappropriate.

Evaluation of the referral indicated that a play group could be helpful in the following ways:

The group would provide multiple examples for masculine identification and the other boys could deny and block Carl's need to seek gratifications along feminine lines. *If* Carl's faulty identification was not already characterologically rooted, it was possible that he could be helped to reassert himself in masculine ways. However, should the pressure of the group for masculine identification prove too much for him to sustain, other therapeutic procedures would have to be used.

Carl should also have an opportunity for a relationship with a mother surrogate who had no investment in perpetuating feminine attributes in him. Rather, the group worker would support his efforts for more suitable identification.

The group worker was advised to respond to Carl's requests for attention and assistance selectively. She was to *avoid* helping him any time he became involved in non-masculine activities or games. In other words, she could aggrandize his striving for masculinity, but she was never to support him in inappropriate forms of behavior.

Carl should remain in the play group *at least* three years.

GARY

Gary was an unusually bright boy (I.Q. 157), but his achievement was far below his ability. His kindergarten teacher had described him as "brilliant." Gary fantasied excessively in school; he was often apathetic. When he did home work he applied himself exactingly and slowly and, as a consequence, seldom finished. Occasionally he resisted authority but seldom in an open manner. Instead, he would mutter to himself and act in a sullen way. For the most part Gary responded to his teacher, but children did not like him and they often failed to include him in their games. Sometimes he resented this and complained to his teacher about being rejected. Gary was unable to defend himself appropriately against the aggression of his peers. His own aggression was inappropriately manifested, through dawdling, disinterest, and poor achievement. In a composition assignment about "feelings," he wrote: "I'm never happy." He was interested in prehistoric animals and had a propensity for drawing monstrous creatures; including a little boy who was always calling: "Help!"

Gary had two siblings, a younger sister and an infant brother. His father was regularly employed as a truck driver for a construction firm. It was apparent that Gary was his mother's favorite. She spoke pridefully of his early development and how he had learned to stand at six months of age and walk unaided at eight months. When he was three years old she had already taught him the alphabet, and soon thereafter she taught him to write. It was also apparent that she sought gratification of her own needs through her children, in particular, through Gary.

Her husband resented this and accused her of neglecting him in preference for the children. He was annoyed with her because she conversed with Gary as if he was a "man." At times he became enraged and physically abusive, with the result that his wife and children were fearful. Gary once observed his father assault his mother.

Gary had suffered with severe allergies since early childhood. He had been hospitalized several times and was receiving medication daily. At one time his physical activities had to be limited. Once, at home, he had a sudden and severe asthmatic seizure which required emergency medical treatment. Parenthetically, at no time during the following three years did he manifest such symptoms in the play group, even under stress situations.

Summary: Gary was a very bright, eight year old boy whose academic output was much below his potential. He was defending himself against the neurotic needs of a clinging mother and the fear of an unpredictable, abusive father. He was excessively withdrawn into fantasy, preoccupied with fears of violence, and he had somatic complaints which had emotional etiology.

The play group could help in the following ways:

A long-term relationship with an accepting female worker, who would make no libidinal demands of him, would provide relief from the anxiety stimulating relationship with his mother.

The permissive adult might enable him to develop healthier outlets for suppressed aggression.

Interaction with the other members of the group would interfere with apathy and fantasy and would provide a "field" for his expanding interests and aggression.

The group worker was advised to avoid contact with Gary and to help him only on demand.

Efforts to reduce the resistance of the parents would be continued, with a referral to a family agency as an objective.

These three children—Mitchell, Carl and Gary—will be the focus of interest in the study of this play group. However, in order to enhance understanding of the records, brief descriptions of the remaining two group members are given:

JOHN

His teacher thought John needed help because he had few friends; he stole from other children and was restless. John had a slovenly appearance and looked neglected, although his family was not poor. His mother was not informative during interviews, but she did agree to have her son considered for the play group. As a matter of fact, she thought that an older daughter, who attended the same elementary school, needed help more than John did.

In class and for a long period of time in the play group, John participated in a marginal fashion. At all times, however, he was alertly observant about what took place.

BURT

This boy was aggressive with his peers, sullen and suspicious with adults, and generally unhappy. At times he was very tense, and he would withdraw from all contact with others. He was fearful of his father, who beat him severely for the slightest indication of misbehavior, in school or elsewhere.

RECORDS OF PLAY GROUP MEETINGS AND ANALYSIS

This play group had 93 meetings during a three year period. Because a full reproduction of the records would in itself be larger than this volume, the author has selected content which provides descriptive continuity and at the same time highlights the experiences of three of the children—Mitchell, Carl and Gary. The group will be followed from its beginning to termination, which took place at the end of the first semester in grade six. By terminating the group in mid year, opportunity was provided for follow-up study for one semester. The observations made during the period of follow-up are included at the end of the report.

Before proceeding to the record, a few additional explanations are in order: The children were already familiar with the play room, because they had visited it a few times during the period of group organization. Several references are made to a child named "Peter," who was present only two meetings. He was transferred to another school when his family moved out of the school district area.

Meeting No. 1

Carl and Peter came in first. They went directly to the supply shelves and looked. Peter said, "Where is the bowling game?" Worker said she had taken it out of the room. Carl took a ring-toss game instead and he and Peter began to play with it. Mitchell and Burt came in. Mitchell passed Carl and said, "Hello, Carl," but Carl did not answer. They went to the supply shelves; Mitchell took checkers, and he and Burt sat down at the round table and began to play. They spoke very quietly to each other. Gary and John entered last. John asked the worker if he could paint; she nodded.

Carl and Peter stopped playing ring-toss. Carl put it back on the shelf. He then got drawing paper and crayons. Peter helped him. They went over to the table, divided the crayons and began to draw.

Gary was quiet; he watched John paint awhile. John finished and went over to where Gary was and they began to build with blocks. Someone knocked on the entrance door. Worker did not respond at first but again there was a knocking. Worker lifted the curtain without opening the door, motioned to a youngster on the other side, and then returned to the table. There was still another knock, and a child called out. No one in the play group seemed to notice.

Mitchell and Burt returned the checkers to the shelf and Mitchell joined the block play while Burt watched. Mitchell then brought some blocks over to where Burt was standing and he and Burt began to build. Gary and John were building right next to the shelves and Mitchell had to step over both the blocks and Gary to get blocks for himself. Burt watched, then he, too, got blocks. The children at block play were whispering, and the worker, who sat at a distance, could not hear what they said. Mitchell, Gary and John talked; Burt was silent.

Peter stopped drawing, watched the block play and then began to draw again. Carl voluntarily brought his drawing to worker to show it. Worker nodded. Peter did likewise. Carl asked if he could paint. James' painting was still on the easel and Carl asked worker if he should take it off. Worker did, putting it on top of the radiator vent to dry. Peter took a chair to the middle of the room, sat down and watched the block play.

Burt helped Mitchell arrange the blocks but when Burt put a block a certain way Mitchell changed it. A lively conversation began between John and Gary. Gary began to talk loudly. They were talking about what they should do next. Mitchell, who had a block in his hand, gestured menacingly toward the structure built by Gary and John. They warned him, saying he shouldn't break it.

John decided to include puppets in his block play. Mitchell, Gary, and Burt tried to take them. Burt had the father puppet. He held it awhile, then put it down. Peter tried to get a puppet. He already had one in his hand but Mitchell grabbed it from him. Then Peter took a ball of clay and began to throw it up into the air while the other children glanced at him.

Mitchell knocked over Gary's building with a block. Gary retaliated by throwing down some of his. Mitchell and Gary then began to tussle. Gary jumped on Mitchell, pummeled him a few times and then looked at the worker. Mitchell was smiling. Both boys went back to the blocks. Gary threatened: "You leave this wood alone!" They played for awhile. Mitchell snatched another block and John exclaimed: "He took one!" Mitchell gave it back. John said, "We have one of theirs," and gave Mitchell a block.

Peter watched all this activity. Then he went over to the easel and gave Carl a little advice on painting. After that he watched the block play again, standing with hands in pockets. John got the idea of using dominos with the blocks. Mitchell took some from him. Gary objected to Mitchell's taking them and said, "I'll smack you out." Mitchell taunted: "I'll get something better." He took the ring-toss game and the checkers and used them in his block play. John included the clay in his structure. Burt watched although he occasionally joined Mitchell. Meanwhile John and Gary were still building together. Carl finished his painting, took it off the easel and placed it where worker had put John's painting earlier. Peter took a turn at painting.

Worker set a table with place mats, napkins, saucers, and cups. She poured milk and set out a plate with cookies. She said, "Refreshments are ready." No one responded. Worker said it again, and then she sat at the table. Carl sat. The other children came over, gulped their milk and ran back to play. Gary took a cookie with him. Mitchell came back to get a cookie. He did this three times, while worker was seated at the table. Each time Mitchell walked to the table backwards, reaching for the cookies without looking at worker. Only Carl sat at the table with the worker. He took one cookie, ate it and then took another. Then he got up. There were still a few cookies left. Worker did not notice who took the remainder later—the dish was empty. Burt did not have any cookies; nor did Peter.

Worker began to tidy up the room. John said, "It's time to go," and all the boys joined in putting things away, very hastily. Gary knocked down some blocks in the process, and Peter left his easel for a minute, pushed over some blocks, then returned to the easel to complete his painting. Carl and Peter rushed to the table, took their paintings and went to the door. The worker said, "The monitor will be here soon." John asked if they could come again in the afternoon. Worker replied they would return next week, at the same time. The other boys finished putting things aways and came to door, but the monitor was still not there. They all returned to the play room. John took some clay, as did Carl. Mitchell and Burt began to draw hurriedly. Gary walked over to the window and looked out.

The monitor finally knocked on the door and the children left. Mitchell and Burt went directly to their classroom, which was next door to the play-room.

Analysis: Meeting No. 1

In this first meeting there are many patterns of behavior which are typical of beginning play groups. Even though the setting is different from the class-room, and despite the fact that the worker's permissiveness and her failure to direct activities are unusual, the boys nevertheless react to her as an authori-tative person. Since the worker gave them no directions (which was also the case during preliminary visits to the playroom) they begin to use the materials which are openly displayed. However, they are wary and observant. Some behave in a subdued manner, whispering to each other. To avoid interfering in their activities, the worker spends most of the time seated at some distance from the children. The children, in turn, avoid her, except for Carl, who seeks approval and brings his painting to show her. Mitchell "breaks the ice," and acts out mildly. When he threatens to topple the block structure built by Gary and John, he is warned by them. Mitchell then grabs Peter's puppet. Peter takes a ball of clay and tosses it up and down experimentally. Mitchell finally manages to knock over Gary's blocks and Gary retaliates in the same way. Later he pushes Mitchell around, without hurting him.

In this way, the children explore in the permissive setting and several of them begin to test for limits. Mitchell and Gary (unexpectedly), make several aggressive contacts. The children feel ill at ease when refreshments are served. Not only have they not been directed in their activities, nor limited or reprimanded by the adult when there was some acting out, but they are also being "rewarded!" Note that Burt refuses food altogether. This is essentially distrust of the adult. As a matter of fact, all the children, except Carl, manifest distrust by not sitting with the worker. Her behavior, which to them is quite unusual and unexpected, puts them on guard. Mitchell will not even look at her as he accepts her "gift"—walking backwards!

At the end of the meeting some of the children resist leaving. Again this is a test of the worker.

Meeting No. 2

Gary and John arrived together. They went to the blocks; constructed a sort of fence; sat inside it and continued building. They were very quiet and talked softly to each other. Mitchell and Burt entered the room, and Burt, smiling, walked with Mitchell to the shelves. Burt reached in and got the ring-toss game. Mitchell and he arranged the game so that they used three quarters of the length of the play room. They were laughing as they took turns in throwing the rings.

Peter came in; he went over to the easel and began to paint. Carl stood around for a moment, then walked over to the easel to watch Peter. He was giving him suggestions. After awhile he actually helped Peter paint his picture.

The ring-toss game became noisier. Mitchell and Burt laughed loudly each time they threw a ring. They ran to the post to recover the rings and then back to the place from which they were supposed to throw. Mitchell kept moving the post back, finally using the full length of the play room as a play court. After a few separate throws from this length, both boys threw simultaneously. There was much noisy laughter; both were getting excited and overheated. Burt said, "Whew, I'm going to stop" and with two quoits in his hand he sat down at the round table where Gary and John were now occupied with construction paper. They had put the blocks away.

Mitchell, who remained with the ring-toss game, said, "I'm never going to stop!" Hearing this, Burt got up and returned to the game. He now stood at one end of the room; Mitchell at the other. Mitchell threw the ring to him and he threw it back. Now the rings were being tossed higher and higher. Every once in awhile Gary would look toward the worker, who was seated, making paper place mats in preparation for the snack. After a moment she walked over to Mitchell, who was perspiring, and said, "Did you ever try this game?" Mitchell replied, rather quickly, "I'm going to do ——." Worker did not hear the rest of his remark as Mitchell pointed toward the table where Carl was coloring. Immediately after this the ring-toss game was put away. Mitchell and Burt then got paper and scissors and began to trace the pattern which John had cut out. Peter and Carl came over to look. Mitchell was saying silly things, which made the others laugh. He was laughing too.

Worker began to get ready for snack. John and Gary had left paper and scissors on this table. Worker cleared the table, put mats down, placed napkins, cups and saucers and then brought over the pitcher of milk and a plate of cookies. Burt and Mitchell were sitting at the other table. Worker said, "Snack is ready." Peter immediately came to table and began to drink his milk while standing. Worker said, "Let's all get chairs." She got an additional two chairs and Peter took one and sat down next to her. Carl lifted the pitcher and placed under it a mat he had made. Everyone was seated now except Mitchell who seemed embarrassed and reluctant to join the others at the table. He finally dragged his chair around to a part of the table opposite the worker. When the others began to drink, Mitchell giggled, rubbed his eyes, put his head down. Like last week, he turned away from the worker and began to drink. Everyone else drank quickly, took cookies and left the table to return to their play. Mitchell was now the only one at the table with the worker. Except for some giggling on his part, and by John, who stood nearby, there had been no talking at the table. When Gary left the table he had three crackers in his hand. He looked at the worker when he helped himself to the third one.

Peter took the plastic bag which contained the clay. He started to take some out, then put it back, trying to wipe his hands on the bag. Carl drew a picture which he showed to the worker. Peter went over to the table and began to cut colored construction paper. John and Gary went to blocks and built a fence. They had the baby and the father dolls perched on top of the fence. Gary said, "Let's just use men. We don't want any women." Mitchell began to build on the other side of the room. He took two puppets—a girl and mother; he hit the mother on the head and she fell down. Carl came by picked up the girl and said, "You have the girls." He put it down. Someone said, "Let's have a funeral." Worker is not sure who suggested this: it might have come from Mitchell, John, or Gary. Mitchell took puppets and placed them on the floor with blocks around and over them, but he did not quite cover them.

Worker began to clean up. She picked up some blocks from the other side of the room, put them in the bin and said, "It's time to go." Gary and John put blocks away noisily. At one point Gary deliberately banged two blocks together and looked at the worker. Mitchell helped clean up for awhile. Peter left a piece of his cooky near where he was working. The monitor knocked on the door. Worker opened it and again said, "It's time to go." Carl was the first to leave. Peter did not stay with the monitor but ran off by himself.

Analysis: Meeting No. 2

In this second meeting, one week later, exploration continues, and the children test the setting and the worker more actively. The pace is quicker, and there is increased verbalization. Mitchell and Burt, without conscious planning, evolve a thinly disguised, aggressive experiment with the ring-toss game. Mitchell says, "I'm never going to stop!" His statement purportedly indicates pleasure with the game, but actually it is a challenge to the worker. He does induce some anxiety in her and she reacts to it by setting a limit, prematurely. However, she wisely uses indirect means in attempting to limit his acting out.

Again the boys reveal they are suspicious of the worker by resisting her invitation to have food. Peter stands and eats. Finally the worker again tells them to come to the table. Proximity to the worker heightens tension. There is no conversation, and most of the boys eat quickly and leave, or sit just long enough to take food to eat elsewhere. Mitchell giggles uncomfortably and turns away from the worker as he eats. The boys' behavior at the table gives dramatic meaning to the historic expression: "Beware the Greeks bearing gifts!"

Gary constantly studies the worker to see how she reacts to the behavior of others. At the end of the meeting he dares to test her tolerance openly, by noisily dumping blocks, and then he deliberately bangs several together. Of interest is a comment made by him during the block play, in which he unwittingly reveals the origins of his difficulties. He rejects the female dolls and says to John, "Let's just use men. We don't want any women."

Carl continues making bids for the worker's attention. Again he shows his painting to her and he even makes a place mat, as she had done. Of all the boys in the group, Carl is least anxious in proximity to the worker.

Meeting No. 3—Partial

Mitchell came to the play room before the monitor called for him. Worker said he could stay because the others would be in soon. However, Mitchell said he had to see his teacher again and left the play room. He returned and said his teacher wanted a note. Worker said it would be all right to stay because in a minute the monitor would be at his classroom door to call for him, and then the teacher would know it was time for the play group. Mitchell sat on the floor in the corner, his legs stretched out along the side of the wall. Carl came in and went to the shelves. . . . Carl finished a painting, took it off the easel to put on top of the vent to dry. He picked up a weaving card and wool, took the mother puppet and baby puppet and went over to the round table. He made the mother puppet look at the baby's buttocks. Then the mother hit the baby. After that the mother kissed the baby. Carl then put the puppets away and drew a picture. . . .

Worker placed chairs around the table. Carl helped. Mitchell said he did not want any milk. (It sounded like: "*Your* milk"—directing the remark to the worker.) He continued drawing, sitting with his back to the group. The other boys sat down. Worker looked in Mitchell's direction. Carl said, "Come on." Mitchell insisted, "I don't want any milk or cookies!" The other boys had cookies and drank milk; they got up and returned to play. Carl went over to the table where Mitchell sat and then returned to the table where worker was still seated. He took a cooky, went back to Mitchell and asked him if he wanted it. Burt returned for another cooky, as did John. John later came again and took a handful. Someone said, "Ooo!" Carl took more cookies. Mitchell finally came over and took the last two. . . .

Analysis: Meeting No. 3

During this meeting Mitchell shows a pattern of behavior which is to continue for a long time. On one pretext or another he manages to come to the play room before the others. However, he is not relaxed when alone with the worker. The worker also reported that he has been dropping in to see her during the week, asking to stay. In these ways Mitchell is revealing a need to be the "only" child or, at least, a preferred one. Several times during this meeting, he left the play room and returned. This is another test of the worker; a way of determining whether she will confine him to the play room.

Carl's behavior also falls into a pattern which is to be repeated for a considerable period of time. He functions on the periphery of the group, occasionally initiating brief contact with individual boys. He avoids using materials or games which require active, energetic participation. Instead, he spends his time in painting, weaving, or in revealing play with puppets.

Resistance, or more accurately, the boys' defensiveness against the worker, is revealed in their continuing aloofness at refreshment time. Mitchell shows almost open hostility when he, at first, refuses to drink or to take a cookie. Finally, rivalry is seen for the first time when the boys begin to grab for food.

Meeting No. 4—Partial

. . . Burt put back all the blocks then went over to the easel. Gary's painting was still there. Burt hesitated; he did not know whether he should remove the painting. He made an attempt to put his own paper over it and then looked around as if in doubt. Worker glanced at him. Again he hesitated for a moment, then put his own paper on top of Gary's and began to paint.

Carl and Mitchell went to the shelves. Mitchell told Carl that he knew "just where" Carl lived. Carl said he did not. Mitchell made up a number but Carl said he was wrong. Mitchell teased, saying he had been to Carl's house. Carl insisted that he had not. Carl looked annoyed, but Mitchell continued to tease him. Mitchell picked up a drawing of a rabbit, to use as a pattern. He asked whose it was and John said it was his. Burt went to a table after putting all the blocks away, and he too drew a rabbit. Mitchell now went to the easel and painted, giving some interpretation of the figure he was making. When he finished he took the painting and put it on the little table. As he did so he mumbled something about "she" (worker?).

John and Gary began to argue loudly about what they were drawing. "I'm drawing John," said Gary. "Here's his mother!" John drew also, and made angry references to Gary and his father. Gary then drew a picture of a face with a very long nose. Both boys were now laughing and talking. John was excited. He drew a picture of a boy and said "snot" was coming from his nose.

Mitchell now came to the round table and sat down, watching John and Gary. Carl picked up a cardboard picture frame and said, "What is it? How do you do it?" Burt said he knew how to use it and told Carl what to do.

Carl then got the biggest ball of wool, went over to the round table, sat down and began to work on it. Burt did the same thing.

Worker later set the table and said, "Snack time." Mitchell, Burt, and Carl were already at the table. John sat down at the setting next to the worker. Gary came to the table, put his chair between the worker's and John's then complained that there was nothing there for him to eat. John said, "Here's yours" and pushed the cup of milk from the place setting next to his over to Gary. All of the children drank. Each child, except Gary, took a chocolate marshmallow rabbit, then a second one. Carl took two more and said he was going to save them for later. He put them on his napkin. Burt took another, also to "save." Gary had gone back to the blackboard, saying he was going to draw Mitchell. "He's a shrimp." He said this twice. Mitchell then drew a figure with legs spread apart, added a penis and pointed to it. He whispered to Burt who with Carl still sat at the table. Carl watched, wide-eyed and open mouthed.

John had gotten hold of the rubber puppets. He pushed in the heads. Gary and John punched at each other using the puppets as boxing gloves. Again they pushed in the heads of the puppets. Carl joined them and picked up two female puppets. Mitchell said he wanted one. Carl started to refuse but then gave it to Mitchell, who also punched in the heads. John and Gary began to chase each other around the room, hitting at each other's puppets, making much noise. Soon thereafter the monitor came and worker said it was time to go. The puppets were put back quickly by the boys. Burt and Carl went out carrying their partially finished picture frames.

Analysis: Meeting No. 4

There is an ebb and flow of acting out behavior during early group meetings. This is due to the children's need to test the worker and to "digest" the permissive experience. Such fluctuations are brief and they disappear altogether when the children become reassured that the worker is consistent in her behavior. By remaining peripheral to the group the worker avoids interfering with the children's activities. The boys' behavior is not *directly* influenced by her because she does not initiate or motivate their activities. The behavior of the children is induced by her permissiveness, but it is actuated by their own aggression. If the worker does at times participate more actively, it is determined by the needs of a child or the requirements of a situation. Thus, Burt is left to determine for himself that he can remove Gary's painting. At other times, and for other reasons, the worker may decide to help. She avoided doing so in this instance, as she stated later in a supervision conference, because she feels that Burt is a suspicious, defensive child, and that it is necessary for her to avoid initiating contact with him.

During this meeting, acting out suddenly takes a libidinal turn. Gary and John reveal some anxiety through self-conscious laughter about the long "nose" and "snot." Mitchell later demonstrates his impulsiveness—which was anticipated—by brashly drawing the figure and adding a penis. This is the sharpest test yet of the worker's forbearance, and it represents a critical point in the children's rapidly expanding awareness of the exceptional nature of the play group. Mitchell's addition of a penis to his drawing creates anxiety in the others, which is reflected almost immediately in their heightened mobility and excitement.

Carl, of course, is completely dismayed by Mitchell's astounding aggression. He continues to behave in a now familiar pattern, selecting female puppets with which to play and painting interminable pictures of his house.

Assurance is crystallizing in the group. The boys act out with fewer glances toward the worker to see how she will react. They come to the table more readily for the refreshments, and again they begin to snatch food, some getting less than others.

Meeting No. 5—Partial

Only Carl and Burt were present. The others were absent because of illness. . . . Carl then got the two female puppets and told Burt to get the others. They began punching with them. Worker, who had gone to the round table to get ready for snack time, said mildly, "No punching." Burt said, "All right" and stopped immediately. Carl continued a moment longer, then he also stopped. Burt went over to the easel, began to paint airplanes, and Carl came to watch. He told Burt that he had put the paper on the wrong way but Burt made no response. Carl asked Burt if he had brothers. Burt replied that he had two sisters, nine and twelve. Carl said, "You're the only boy?" Later Burt said to Carl, "You took the girl puppets—you're a girl!"

Burt helped worker clean off the round table. Worker set the table and Carl came over carrying the mother puppet which he put on a chair. Worker and children sat down.

Analysis: Meeting No. 5

The worker limited the aggressive interaction which, incidentally, had been initiated by Carl. This was discussed in supervision conference, and it was determined that the intervention had been inadvisable. There was no real fight; the puppets had been used as boxing gloves, and further, no attempt was made by either boy to hurt the other. They had hit at each other's puppets. While Carl had again chosen female puppets, he had *used them differently*, in a more appropriate masculine activity.

Burt spontaneously touches on Carl's basic personality conflict: "You took the girl puppets. You're a girl!" This awareness of Carl's identification problem is to be repeated in different ways later, by others in the group.

It has been determined, from observations in many play groups, that children sometimes pinpoint the nuclear elements of personality conflicts with direct, incisive observations. A practitioner can learn much by giving heed to the sensitivities of youthful "diagnosticians."

Record and Analysis: Extracts From Meetings Nos. 6 and 9.

During these meetings the children become increasingly relaxed and less defensive, with the result that behavior is even more spontaneous. After repeated testing they are assured that permissiveness is real and consistent. The worker intervenes only to prevent injury or excessive frustration, and the children respond to these occasional limits without feeling rejected, because they are used in their interests. In meeting No. 6 we see an example of such a limit. In this episode the worker demonstrates her tolerance for acting-out which is directed towards her person:

Meeting No. 6—Partial

Mitchell tossed a ring (quoit) backwards over his head, and it zoomed past the worker's nose and landed on the ledge. Burt threw his quoit backwards too. Worker changed her position without a comment. She got up from her seat and stood in front of the large table. She was making tulips for decorations. The boys turned around and began throwing the quoits high up. One brushed against the electric light. As they ran to recover the quoits they laughed excitedly. Mitchell took one of Burt's quoits but Burt pulled it away and they began to wrestle over it. Both boys were out of breath. Burt finally sat down at the round table. Mitchell called him back to play and again there was more of the same running and hurling of quoits. Again Burt sat down. Mitchell called to him to get up. Now they began to wrestle, rolling on the floor. Burt punched Mitchell. Worker said quietly, "No punching." The horseplay continued.

Carl who was cutting colored paper called out twice, "Some one will get hurt," looking at the worker as he said it. At one point the worker walked near where Burt and Mitchell were wrestling, picked up some scrap papers from the floor and put them in the basket. The ring-toss game was also put away. Burt finally went over to the easel and said he was going to paint a house and added that Mitchell was in the house. He made a blob of paint to represent Mitchell, Mitchell drew a strange form on the blackboard and then made it into a face. . . .

Analysis: The materials used in the group, and the setting itself, become incorporated in the acting out. This is further indication of the children's expanding perception of the worker's permissiveness. They also feel free to modify the setting by moving furniture about when the demands of a game or another activity require it. In these ways their perception of the adult broadens and includes the setting, which is an extension of the adult.

The boys are also discovering that the worker is not made anxious by aggression, when it becomes expressed against her through "atttacks" on the setting or, even more directly as when Mitchell "accidentally" threw a quoit close to her. Further, she can accept their need to ventilate aggression against each other from time to time.

Meeting No. 9—Partial

During meeting No. 9, several of the boys used the blackboard in regressive activity. Using letters printed in unusual shapes, but which readily conveyed the erotic intent, John printed an obscene word.

Continuing from the record:

. . . Mitchell joined Bruce and Carl. They were making paper envelopes. Gary and Mitchell were talking and Mitchell said that Gary liked to push. John said, "Gary, you used to be weak, now you're strong." John wrote something on the board, and called it to Gary's attention. He made some explanation of the word. Gary said he knew "another way" of writing the "word" and he started by drawing four lines. He then made up some rhyme for each line, at the same time changing its shape into a letter. The word was obvious to all. John turned around to look at the worker. Then the boys erased the words. They had been using white chalk. John went for the colored chalk. As he passed the boys who were using the stapler he said, "Don't use all the staples. We will need it for next week." "Next year," said Mitchell. . . .

Summary—Meetings 1-10

After ten meetings, attitudes and definitive patterns of behavior have become established. With respect to the three boys on whom the record is focussed, the following changes have been observed:

Mitchell. The element which is most prominent is his marked ambivalence toward the worker. He manifests a need for closer relationship with her, yet he becomes anxious when he approaches her. At such times he reacts with defensive hostility. While he does this in a "kidding" fashion, the hostility is obvious. This was noted in one meeting when he off-handedly told the worker he didn't want *her* milk at refreshment time. On other occasions, he would solicit the worker's help with a piece of work, or ask her to bring special materials. He would then accept the things he requested in a petulant manner. Interpretively, this behavior was essentially that of a child who could not trust love, because during his earlier years it had somehow become consonant with disappointment, fear, and perhaps, danger. It was now obvious that Mitchell would have to be surfeited in the relationship with the accepting (loving) worker over a long period of time. During this time he would figuratively "bite the hand that fed him," until he became assured that she would neither cease to accept him nor would she become angry with him.

For Mitchell, the significant therapeutic interaction in the group would be in relationship to the worker. It was anticipated that he would soon be in sharp rivalry with the other boys, and he was, in fact, becoming very provocative.

Carl. Initially he behaved in a guarded way, very consciously keeping himself at the periphery of group activity. From this position he could more safely protect himself while he assayed the aggressive, threatening potential of the setting, the other boys, and the worker. He began to initiate direct contact with the worker almost from the beginning, probably to gain more security and to seek her approval for "proper" behavior. His interests and deportment were manifestly unmasculine. These were revealed in the content of his drawings, in puppet play, in his manner of speaking, and in his carriage. Carl soon learned that the worker accepted him, but she never encouraged him in his need to seek special approval or in his other characteristic bids for attention. What was more important, he also learned that the worker did not react even when he began to experiment with mild aggression toward others. As a result there followed a rapid proliferation of aggressive behavior, which, while it was mild in contrast to the behavior of others, was something he had not been able to do before.

Carl's expanding aggressiveness is seen in the following sequence:

From Meeting No. 6: John got up. Mitchell jumped on him and had his hands around John's neck. Worker walked near them and Mitchell let go. Both boys were over-heated and John looked almost fearful. Carl and Burt had also been chasing each other and sort of play-hitting. When Burt wanted to stop, Carl started him off again. Carl was laughing. . . .

From Meeting No. 7: They went over to the animal puppets, Burt and Carl each took one and began to poke at each other with them. Mitchell grabbed Carl's puppet but Carl got it back. Carl and Burt then put the puppets away, obtained looms and loops and sat down to work. . . .

Later during the same meeting: Carl tried to take the alligator puppet from John. He tried and tried but failed. John said he had it first. Carl tried again, then got up, put the loom away, went to the easel and painted a picture of a house. . . .

. . . Carl and Gary got chalk and did some drawing on the board. Then they began to chalk each other. Carl laughed loudly while they scuffled and chased each other, yelling. . . .

Some of the boys, when they had need to defend themselves from aggression, would deflect it to the weakest member of the group—Carl. At such times the worker scrupulously avoided defending Carl, in this way exposing him to the critical experience of aggressive interaction with his peers. Consideration was given to the question as to whether Carl's provocation was a form of libidinal teasing, but the worker's further description of it discounted this meaning and gave primacy to the idea that Carl really wanted status in the peer group, independence of action, and freedom from protective adults.

From Meeting No. 7: Worker was putting away some of the materials, Mitchell made a flower and put a face on it, while Burt painted a missile. Carl sat in the worker's big chair. All the children became involved in a game of hitting Carl with puppets. They laughed and shouted. Worker walked closer to listen to what was being said. Carl rushed from the seat, lunged at the others and then got back in the seat again. . . .

From Meeting No. 8: Burt hummed a tune when he finished the hat and looked as if he was going to march around wearing it. John kept talking about his hat. Burt and Gary began to chase each other. They scuffled. Then they joined forces and went after Mitchell, who ran around a bit, away from them. They kept pursuing him but Mitchell said he didn't want to play. Gary persisted. Mitchell, in a louder voice and more forcefully, said, "Gary, I don't want to play; let's get Carl." They then went towards Carl who kept working on his napkin ring. . . .

Carl's experimental attempts with aggression, and most important, the beginnings of a drive for status in the peer group—even at a price which included harassment and punishment from the others—were the prominent elements of his adjustment in the play group up to this point.

Carl must establish himself in the group as an independent member, primarily through his own efforts. The group would eventually accept him as an equal when he behaved in a manner more appropriately identified as masculine. Meanwhile, the worker was not to protect him unless he became confronted by excessive anxiety, fear or frustration.

Gary. Of all the boys in the play group, the alterations which took place in Gary's behavior during the first ten meetings were most prominent. When referred, Gary was described as being excessively withdrawn into phantasy, preoccupied with fears of aggression, sullen, negativistic, and unhappy. During the earliest group meetings Gary functioned in a modulated, controlled way, occupying himself mostly with materials. He did not isolate himself entirely from the boys but his behavior was defensive and self-protective. A preoccupation with violence was seen in his drawings of ferocious, prehistoric creatures. His general unhappiness was revealed in his facial expression. Sometimes he was so introspective that he appeared oblivious to the setting. However, there were other evidences that he was carefully studying the worker's responses to the behavior of the group. There were moments, even during early meetings, when Gary showed a potential for impulsive behavior.

During meetings 6 to 10 there was a rapid acceleration in the momentum of his behavior. His monster drawings were replaced by aggressive hand puppets, which bit, mauled and pummeled. Gary had finally assured himself that the worker permitted aggression and was not made anxious by it. It was not accidental that Gary, the tallest in the group, first began to act aggressively with Mitchell, who was at least a foot and a half shorter than he, and the smallest boy in the play group.

The following sequence shows the change in Gary's behavior:

From Meeting No. 7: Gary and Mitchell took out the Candy-Land game. They sat and played for a short time. When they both got up there was an argument, then a tussle over who should put the game away. Neither one did. Mitchell then asked John if he would play with him. He added that he had just beaten the "champ," referring to Gary.

Burt and Gary began to hit at each other and Carl got involved in this also. Mitchell was now seated at the table, working with loom and loops. The boys chased each other around the table, behind Mitchell. There was laughter and pushing of chairs. Gary sat down on a chair and wanted to be pushed off. Burt tried and failed. Their play increased in intensity, and they began to wrestle. Burt was on the floor with Gary on top of him. At this time worker began to set the table for snack. John said he was tired, sat down at the round table and said he wanted to eat. Worker had not quite finished setting the table but she announced that snack was ready. Mitchell, Carl, and John were seated. Burt and Gary continued to argue over possession of the chairs. They pulled the chairs from each other roughly. Worker walked over, took one chair, put it at the round table in deliberate fashion. Gary had the other chair. He carried it to the table. Burt sat down. Gary said he would "get" Burt. . . .

In this episode there is a rapid transition from "play" to anger. This is becoming characteristic with Gary. Note how the worker timed the serving of food as an indirect form of intervention when she became concerned that Gary was acting too roughly. In this indirect way, a control was established, without reproof or denial. Gary is learning to express his anger more appropriately and without extraordinary guilt or anxiety.

From Meeting No. 8: Gary took the animal puppets, the crow in one hand, the alligator in the other. He then took the wedge figures, putting one in each puppet's mouth. He lunged with them at other children. They continued to work, ignoring him. Gary put the wedgies back on the shelves and walked to the file cabinet, on top of which the worker had placed the pitcher of milk with the plate of crackers. He opened the mouth of the alligator; looked toward the worker, caught her eye and stopped. He put the puppets back and joined the other boys at the round table. He asked where they had gotten the paper. . . .

Gary begins to use Burt more and more in his aggressive acting out. Burt is an angry boy, who aids and gives impetus to Gary's behavior. However, there are times when they tangle directly with each other. In Meeting No. 10, Gary, in one such incident, revealed an intensity of anger which impelled the worker to use a direct limit:

. . . Gary painted for awhile. Somehow he got into an argument with Burt. They squared off and punched at each other. Worker said quietly: "No punching." They continued, seriously. Gary looked quite determined. Worker repeated: "No punching." She touched Gary's arm. They stopped. Gary then took the animal puppets, put wedge figures in their mouths. . . .

Gary has made rapid movement away from introspective, isolative and, at times, inappropriate behavior. After a short initial period of studying the worker's reactions to the acting out behavior of others, particularly Mitchell's, Gary began to make direct tests on his own. He gained support in this by joining forces with others, with Burt in particular. The degree to which Gary had suppressed and displaced aggression before therapy was indicated in the play group by the rapidity with which aggressive "play" changed to direct, impulsive anger.

In a supervision conference, the worker spoke of some anxiety she felt because of Gary's aggressive behavior. This was traced to the fact that Gary, in subtle ways, seemed to challenge and defy her in the manner in which he manifested his aggression. It was decided that Gary must be permitted to act out within limits tolerable to the group, himself, and the worker.

At no time has Gary shown any of the somatic complaints during play group meetings which were described at the time of referral.

There were twleve play group meetings until school let out for summer vacation. Meetings were resumed in the fall, when the children returned. The group was intact; no one had moved away.

Meeting No. 14—Second Meeting After Vacation

The day after the play group's first meeting, the worker met Gary in the hall. With a scowl on his face and in a somewhat angry tone, he asked why he hadn't been called to the play group. Worker told him that she had sent for him and that he had missed it because he was absent. She said he would certainly come next Thursday, when the group was to have its next regular meeting. Gary's teacher reported that he had been very anxious to go to the play group. She added that Gary has been doing homework and was participating in class work. She also reported that Gary was one of the nominees for class president. She was surprised because the qualifications for the position which she had discussed with the class prior to nominations did not apply in the least to Gary! She thought that the youngster who had nominated Gary was probably afraid of him!

Mitchell stepped into the worker's office on Tuesday and asked when he could come in. Worker told him the play group meeting was on Thursday. Thursday morning the worker was writing a note to Mitchell and to his teacher to remind them of the play group when Mitchell entered. The monitors then brought all the other children in except Carl. They said he wasn't in his room and went out again to look for him. Meanwhile, Mitchell went to the blocks and began kicking them out of shelves on to the floor. Burt had a paper airplane which he began sailing as high as he could across the room. Then he ran to pick it up where it fell and hurled it again. John was writing on the board. Burt joined him for a moment, then went back to his airplane. John got the pail of water and a chair and began to wash the board with the sponge. Worker was cutting out leaves and coloring them. She went over to John and turned the chair around to steady it. Carl had gone to shelves for paper and scissors with which he cut out patterns. Mitchell took a sheet of paper and went to the easel. He saw there was paper there already and put his back. He began to paint. He said he was going to leave the play-room as soon as he finished—that his class was in gym—he had to play baseball—the "Yankees were playing." He continued to paint, repeating several times that he was leaving when he finished. Gary played with the blocks. He placed the mother puppet on the top of a raised block in the center. Mitchell finished his painting and left it on the easel. He got more paper, went to the round table and began to make an airplane. John had been hurling his airplane. Gary took two animal puppets, put one on each hand, went over to Mitchell and wanted to spar with him. Mitchell said, "Go away. You always bother me!" Gary went back to block building. Later, Mitchell was cutting paper, and as he went past Gary's block building he threw something at the mother puppet, knocking her over. Gary warned him that he had better not do it again.

Carl went to the easel to paint. He took Mitchell's painting off. Burt and Mitchell were now hurling airplanes. They painted their airplanes, and Gary joined them for a time in this activity. Mitchell picked up his airplane which had fallen beside the table. He said he wanted to open the window behind the table. He called to worker: "Mrs. F-. I want to open the window." The worker took the window-pole. Mitchell said, "Let me do it." She replied, "All right, but let me help you." Worker guided him and together they pulled the upper window down and together replaced the pole. Worker went back to her work, cutting and coloring leaves. Mitchell now hurled his paper airplane near the window and said he wanted to get it out. He threw it up again and again. He and Burt kept adding paint to the airplanes. At one point Mitchell put his airplane down to dry, waited a moment and hurled it. It brushed against Burt's shoe. Everyone looked when Burt complained. Gary growled: "You better not come near *me* with that." Burt looked concerned and tried to wipe the paint off with paper. Worker took a paper towel and wiped it, without comment. Once Burt's airplane fell on top of the shelves and Mitchell climbed up for it. Another time Burt made an airplane for Mitchell and said, "Here, Mitchell." Mitchell, after playing awhile with the airplanes, said he had to go. He left the room, closing the door behind him. A minute later there was a knock at the door. Worker opened it. It was Mitchell. He mumbled something about his class and said he'd rather stay in the playroom.

Gary offered to play checkers with anyone, but the boys ignored him. John went to the easel, painted, and when he was finished took the painting off and carried it toward the worker. She hung it up. Carl asked the worker if he too could make a leaf, and the worker gave him a pattern. Then he asked for a pencil, which worker gave to him. Burt took out the ring-toss game and he and Mitchell used it. They played briefly but then began hurling the quoits up toward the ceiling. Carl joined them and he and Mitchell started to fuss over a quoit. Mitchell punched Carl several times, lightly. Worker, observing this, was about to say, "No punching," when Carl punched back! Worker now walked over and said, "No punching," but they had already stopped. They continued to toss the quoits. They were trying to see how far they could count before each one fell to the floor. They laughed as they played. Gary went to easel and began to paint. He asked the worker for green paint. Worker said she did not have any, adding she would get some for the next meeting.

Burt and Mitchell decided to play checkers just as worker was about to set the round table, which was ordinarily used for refreshments. Mitchell asked if they couldn't play there awhile. Worker set places at the rectangular table instead. The worker finished setting the table and announced that snack was ready. Gary left his painting and the others left the checker game.

Gary announced that he wasn't going to drink his milk. Mitchell sat sideways on his chair, faced away from the worker. They drank milk rather quickly, then they each took one cooky, but soon began to grab for the others. They told Burt, who had two extra cookies wrapped in a napkin, that he was greedy. He said that he hadn't eaten any; he had saved his. They were trying to figure out how many each boy had taken. Gary and Carl remained at the table when the others left. Carl asked for more milk, which the worker poured for him. Gary asked for some also and the worker served him. Gary went back to the easel and the others to the checker game. The worker cleared the table. When Gary finished his painting the worker removed it from the easel and hung it.

Worker began to pick up scattered blocks. John voluntarily came over to help. Gary watched the worker and John. When Gary finished cutting paper he made no attempt to clean up the bits that had fallen on the ledge and floor.

Worker continued cleaning. Gary said that he hoped it wasn't time to leave. All the boys said something about not wanting to leave when the monitors came. Carl started to slide back and forth across the room. Then he went to the easel and painted again. While the monitors waited, he continued to paint. Worker said it was time to go. The boys left.

Analysis: Meeting No. 14

Gary and Mitchell were quite anxious about whether the play group was going to be continued after the summer, although nothing had been told to them to the contrary. The fact that the group experience has become very meaningful to Gary is obvious from the manner in which he reacted when he missed the first meeting after vacation. Mitchell, on the other hand, still shows ambivalence toward the worker, despite his early bids for attention. At refreshment time he turns away from her, as he used to do in earlier meetings of the group. Note that Gary informs the worker that he would not drink milk and later asks for it.

The prominent feature of this meeting is the amount of retesting done by the boys, in order to assure themselves that the worker has not changed. Mitchell kicks blocks off the shelf; Burt and others fly their planes all around the room, even attempting to fly them out the window. At one point they fly the airplanes while they are still wet with paint! John ventures to wash the boards without asking permission, which for him represents aggressive behavior. Mitchell climbs on the tall book shelves to retrieve a plane. Carl is able to defend himself against Mitchell even to the extent of punching!

Any initial doubts the boys may have had after the summer vacation about the continuation of their group and the attitude of the worker are quickly dispelled. The return to the therapeutic experience following a summer hiatus is a process of rediscovery.

Record and Analysis: Extracts from Meetings Nos. 15 to 25.

Meeting No. 15: Mitchell began to make a man from clay. He first rolled it out and then made a flat figure. He then rolled out a small piece, stuck it into the genital area and whispered something to Burt, who laughed aloud. Carl laughed also. John came by, looked at it and said it was "nasty." Gary looked at the worker and then at Mitchell. Mitchell's figure got out of shape and Mitchell remade it. Worker glanced at Mitchell, unsmiling. Carl then made a man out of clay and put it up on the shelf, at the same time asking worker if he could take it home. Worker said, "Yes." Burt looked at an airplane on the shelf. . . . Worker went back to the materials at the table. Carl took a chair and sat on it in front of the shelves. He had the boy puppet and the wedge figures and he pushed them together and apart on the shelf, talking to himself. . . .

Analysis: Mitchell's sex play with the clay is provocative and another test of the worker's tolerance. It stimulated anxiety in some of the other boys. The worker's acceptance of this form of acting out does not imply that she approves of it. Carl makes "a man" and takes it home. Still later, in the same meeting, Carl again selects a masculine object to play with. These are not random choices. Carl has been involved in more aggressive, masculine behavior.

In the following meeting, No. 16, Mitchell and Burt are absent. At refreshment time the others comment about it, and at the same time reveal their rivalry feelings. Their "good" behavior over the sharing of food is also a manifestation of rivalry!

From the Record: The worker began to set the table. She had made six settings, but poured milk only for those who were present. She placed the candy in the center of the table. The boys drank the milk and each one then took one candy, as did the worker. Gary said, "I'm glad Burt isn't here. He would have grabbed them all and put it in his pocket." "Yeah," said John, "he would have," and then demonstrated how Burt would have done it. Carl took two candies, and said he was saving them. Then each boy took another. It seemed as if Gary got the extra two. Gary said, "See how nice this is. We each took one at a time—there was no grabbing!" . . .

Of course, their "good" behavior at refreshments was just temporary. The boys still continued to argue over food. In Meeting No. 17, the following took place: Worker began to set the table and Mitchell voluntarily helped. He carried the Halloween baskets to the table. Worker then began to arrange one at each setting. The other children came over. Mitchell said to worker, "Can I have yours, Mrs. F-?" Worker hesitated and Mitchell said, "I know. I'll give some of the candy in your basket to everyone." He took the chicken corn and distributed it. The marshmallow pumpkin, which was left over, he put in his own basket. Someone said, "Mitchell has two pumpkins." Mitchell said "Mrs. F- gave me hers." Worker again hesitated. The other boys looked at her, somewhat surprised. She said, "I did not give it to you, Mitchell. You took it." Gary said, "He's greedy." Mitchell put the marshmallow pumpkin aside and the worker took it. The boys began to eat. They ate quickly and stood. Only Gary remained at the table with the worker. . . .

. . . Much later in the day, Mitchell visited the play room. He said he was going to take a pack of paper. He went to the side of the filing cabinet and picked out a package of mimeograph paper. Worker said that the paper was for another purpose. He then said he wanted some drawing paper. She gave some to him. . . .

Analysis: Again Mitchell makes special demands. The worker was actually worried about giving Mitchell her basket because of the effect on the others. Mitchell sensed this and spared her the need to make a decision by sharing the contents of her basket with the others. However, when he kept the "prize" item for himself, the worker responded through countertransference, denying that she "gave" it to him. Mitchell seeks reassurance later in the day by soliciting other material objects from her. It would have been better technic for the worker not to have said anything, thus permitting the group to react to Mitchell's statements. They knew that Mitchell had appropriated it.

Also from Meeting No. 17: Gary had a sock filled with chalk. He took a piece of colored chalk from the box, put it into his sock and began to grind it to powder with the leg of a chair. Worker was now seated at the side of the room. She watched him. Burt then took another piece of colored chalk and drew a funny face on the board. Carl came over to watch Gary. Now Gary took the sock and banged it against the floor several times, each time leaving a large chalk mark on the floor. Gary then hit the sock against the black-board, again making blotches of chalk. Carl took a piece of red chalk and drew a circle around one of the marks made by Gary's sock. It looked like a face. Carl then took the mother and daughter puppets, one in each hand. Gary took the crocodile and grabbed at the mother puppet which Carl held. Burt took the crow and grabbed at Carl's other puppet. Carl managed to hang on to both of them, protesting loudly. Gary said, "Where are the wooden ones?" He reached to the shelves and picked some figures up with his animal puppet. Carl held his puppets, covered their faces with red chalk and then put them on the floor. Burt came over and said, "They're killed!" He repeated this three times, excitedly. He then yelled, "They're bleeding!" Carl picked up the mother puppet, pushed it head first into the water, at the same time mimicking in a protesting voice, as if the puppet was talking. Burt came over to the water pail and Carl said to him, "Get the child." He did the same to the girl puppet, immersing her. Burt then brought over the boy puppet. They colored his face red also and dipped him into the water. Carl took paper toweling and wiped the faces; colored them again; dipped them in the water; wiped off their faces once more and laid them on the ledge. Gary came over with the crow puppet and put it into the water. Burt dipped the crocodile in, then took it out. Water spilled all over the floor and Gary played with it for a time. . . .

. . . More water splashed on the floor and the worker went over with a mop and began to dry it. Gary immediately stopped, said there was "a mess," and added that they should clean it up. He called to Burt for help, saying he had made part of the mess. Worker explained, "The floor gets slippery when it's wet." She then got newspaper to dry it more effectively. After that she began to set the table. . . .

. . . Later that day the worker met Carl in the hall, escorted by the assistant principal. He confronted the worker with the fact that Carl had colored chalk, which Carl had said the worker gave him. He added that Carl had marked up other children's clothing. Carl was crying. Worker said nothing; she brought Carl into the room with her. . . .

Analysis: There is much acting out by the boys. It is Halloween and a time for pranks. While they chalk each other up a bit, some of their aggression is expressed against the worker, through the chalk "assaults" on the floor and on the blackboard. A good deal of hostility becomes expressed through puppets. Carl and Burt "kill" various puppets, with Carl showing preference for females in ventilating his hostility! The ebb and flow of hostility and guilt are shown by Carl, when the puppets are "bloodied," "killed," then "saved," through washing and drying. For Carl, in particular, such experiences are exceedingly important because they provide more appropriate pathways for release of hostility and they also increase his feelings of potency. This change in Carl is seen later in the day when he, of all boys, is taken in tow by a school administrator for chalking up other children.

The boys continue to act out for many meetings, with the worker often the indirect target of aggression. On occasions when the acting out behavior threatened to become excessive, the worker used limits deflectively. All during this time, repetitively and consistently, the boys experience the warmth and reassurance of positive acceptance. As transference deepens, the rivalry between the boys increases in severity. Gary begins to show much strength and becomes a dominating force. Burt is also becoming more aggressive. In Burt's family, the relationships of the parents with each other and with the children are deteriorating. Mitchell and Carl are often the objects of Burt's anger.

Meeting No. 35

Gary and John came into the play room. Worker said, "It's good to see you back, John." He made no response. Worker had mailed a note to him during the week, because he had been absent from the last meeting.* Gary said, "He had the chicken pox, like me." John went to the shelves and was looking at the hats and the clay work. Burt entered. Carl, who was behind him, hesitated a moment at the threshold and the worker smiled at him. Then he came in. Worker was cutting out a decoration for the flower pot. John showed a hand trick to the boys. He made believe he cut off the top of his index finger. Carl called the worker's attention to this, in a frightened tone. John did it again while worker watched. Carl said that the trick scared him.

Carl and Burt worked on pot holders, sitting together at the round table. Meanwhile, Gary had taken the plastic bop bag and he was trying to blow it up. Worker went over and gave him a pump. Gary said he couldn't attach the pump and the worker helped him. They both pumped it up and put it back

---

* This is a regular practice when children are absent from a play group meeting.

on the floor. Mitchell took out blocks and began to build. Gary now took the alligator puppet, put the baby in its mouth, crumpled it, and then announced that the alligator was "vomiting it up." Then he began to draw on the board.

John was also playing with puppets. Burt left his pot holder on the table and deliberately knocked over Mitchell's block building. Mitchell got angry but a moment later Burt and he were working together. Carl called out "Can I have your pot holder, Burt?" Burt replied, "No." John had started to dunk the puppets into the pail of water, saying they were going to get a wetting. He dunked them up and down and when he finished he just tossed them carelessly back on the shelf. Then he climbed up on the chalk ledge of the blackboard and walked along it. Burt climbed up on the ledge, too. Meanwhile Gary started to "ride" his chair across the room. Up and back he went, pushing with his feet. He banged against the table and once he fell off the chair! Worker asked him if he was all right. He nodded. Burt also sat on a chair and began to do the same thing. Occasionally they banged their chairs against the bop bag and at other times they banged into each other. Worker quietly suggested to Burt that he avoid the table, and he replied, "O.K." Blocks which were in the middle of the floor were being pushed to the side. Gary got angry with Mitchell who kept putting blocks in the way, and he chased him. Mitchell yelled in protest. Gary did not really hurt him; Mitchell was "acting."

John had begun to make a hat. Mitchell took some blocks and gave them a rather violent shove across the room so that they hit the shelves with a loud bang. Gary objected to this and told Mitchell to stop, but Mitchell continued. Mitchell then observed what John was making and asked John to make a hat for him. John didn't reply. Worker said she'd make one. Gary said he wanted it just like John's. Worker began to make the hat. She asked to look at John's so she could copy it. Carl asked worker to draw a blue circle on a paper, which she did. Burt came over and asked the worker to make one for him. Worker said she would, as soon as she finished the circle for Carl. Mitchell took his hat, made decorations for it, and added a chin-strap. Worker finally cut a circle for Carl and he put a piece of yellow wool on it.

Mitchell said, as he walked near the worker, "Who wants to play a game of checkers?" Worker said, "I do." He said, "All right; this time I'm going to win!" He set out the checker game. Burt and Gary were again sliding up and down the room on chairs, making an awful racket. Worker turned her chair so she could keep her eye on them. Mitchell won the checker game. Worker said, "Congratulations! you are the winner!" extending her hand to shake his, Mitchell offered her his left hand; he was pleased. The other boys heard this and laughed.

Burt asked worker where the other paint brushes were. She said, "They are in the paint jars." He said he wanted to use them as drumsticks as he had done on another occasion. He took two brushes out of the paints, washed and dried them and began to drum on a chair. Carl also got two paint brushes and they played together. Worker announced with a smile that there was going to be a "concert." Mitchell asked the worker if she was going to play another game of checkers with him. Worker said she'd see if there was time—"it might be snack time." She looked at the clock; it was 11:35, too late for another game. She said she had to clear the table for snack. As she passed the shelves she saw the wet puppets which John had thrown back on the shelves earlier. She began to wipe them and also the shelf. The boys had heard her mention the snack, and Gary and John voluntarily began to set the table. Mitchell carried the cooky basket to the table rather ceremoniously. When the worker got to the table with the soda, everything was set and the boys were seated. Mitchell said, "I know what's in there. There are chocolate doughnuts, cookies and an orange! Do you know how I know?" No one replied. Mitchell told Burt to sit near him but Burt refused. Instead he sat next to Carl and the worker. Worker poured the soda and took the napkin off the basket. Everyone grabbed a doughnut. Then each grabbed one vanilla cookie, except Gary and Burt who took two. The others accused them. Gary said challengingly, "So?" and held on to them. Burt put one back. Carl asked them if they had seen the T.V. program last night about dunking doughnuts. Gary knew about it. Gary took the pitcher to help himself to more soda. There was none left. Worker said she'd try to have more next time.

John performed his trick again—"cutting off" his finger. Carl made a face and moved away from him as he did it. Gary explained the trick. Meanwhile, worker peeled an orange. Gary said he didn't want any. The others grabbed the segments when she put them in the basket. Burt was accused of having too many; he said he did not and showed what he held in his hands.

The boys began to stand up. Burt was the last one at the table. He got up finally and the worker started to clear. Meanwhile, Carl and Burt went from one part of the room to another, drumming with the paint brushes, as they had done earlier. Finally, each sat on a chair, with another chair in front and drummed. Carl was in his element, delighted. The boys drummed very well together. Mitchell said he wanted to do it also. He asked the worker for the metal rods which are ordinarily used in making pot holders so that he would have "drumsticks." Then he got a chair to sit on and another to drum on, placing them next to Burt and Carl. They all sat in a straight line. They were drumming and kept trying to start together. Worker hummed "Stars and Stripes" and beat time on a chair. They drummed along, doing very well indeed! Occasionally Mitchell marched out to hit the round table with one stick, like a professional drummer changing instruments. At one point worker paused to examine the chairs. They were being beaten loud and hard! She said, half aloud: "Aren't there any old chairs?" Mitchell had one, but there weren't any others. Worker shrugged and decided to forget about the chairs. She now watched, without participating. Only John did not drum; he was fiddling with the bop bag. He lay on it for awhile, then gradually squeezed all the air out and folded it up. Gary now took his red hat, added some more paper to it and made it look like a drum-major's hat. Worker said, "Look, Gary has a drum-major's hat." Gary marched a bit while the boys continued drumming. They hummed songs.

When the bell rang, Carl exclaimed, "Oh" in disappointment. The boys began to get ready to return to their classes. Carl said he was going to take his hat with him, but Mitchell said he wouldn't because he'd lose it in the play ground. Gary handed his hat to the worker who stored it for him. He and John left. Carl tried on the "professor's" hat that John had made many weeks ago. He put it back. All the hats were now on the shelf. As Mitchell took his jacket, Carl said, "He's got a new jacket." Worker said "Yes—it's very nice, Mitchell." Mitchell made no response, left the play room. Carl wanted to take the paint brushes with him. Burt said, "They have to stay in the play-room," and looked toward worker. Worker said, "Yes." Burt and Carl also left.

Analysis: Meeting No. 35

Much interaction takes place in this meeting. This is characteristic of a play group in its middle phase. Ideation about the meaning of the permissive adult is concretized. There is spontaneity in behavior and affect.

The setting is also used freely. For many meetings the boys have been using the blackboard ledge to walk along while holding on to the top molding. Carl has conquered his fears and has succeeded in doing as the others have done and he is exceedingly proud of the achievement. The activity is quite safe. At no time does the worker permit a child to become endangered. Should she become concerned, as on the occasion when Mitchell climbed the storage shelves—she stands nearby in case she is needed. Note how the worker suppressed her concern about the "drum chairs." Her momentary debate is resolved in favor of the children, not the chairs.

The boys communicate more easily, particularly during refreshment time. There is still much rivalry between them, but there are growing manifest-tions of cooperation, in work and play. Arguing over food, which is a mani-festation of rivalry, remains a problem, but it has become less intense, and a more equitable distribution of the food takes place. It is interesting to see how the boys assume responsibility for setting the table. Their musical attempts are charming and creative. The worker later commented about how happy they were, how satisfying they and she had found the experience. With respect to particular boys, the following episodes are of interest:

Carl is manifestly anxious when John displays his "trick" of severing a finger. This takes place twice and in each instance Carl shows distress. His castration anxiety is apparent, as is Gary's, who sees fit to "explain" the trick on both occasions! It is important to add at this point, that when this play group was near termination, several such incidents were repeated, and Carl no longer showed anxiety.

Gary no longer spends time in drawing complicated pictures of prehistoric creatures and other pictures with horror features. His earlier interest in space, astronomy, and fantastic exploration has not been evidenced for some time. Hostility is expressed directly and more appropriately; there is less need to convert it through phantasy. While Gary has many arguments and aggressive exchanges with the boys, occasionally he still acts out some of his hostility with puppets. Note that the alligator "vomits" back the baby puppet. Anxiety still follows some of his more primitive expressions.

Mitchell's "games" (checkers) with the worker have complex meanings. The worker—and love—are less suspect, but they are still approached with caution. Mitchell would like to be able to "reach" for her directly, but he cannot. He almost makes it. His current pattern is to come close to the worker and "wonder" aloud about "who" will play with him! The worker, of course, understands his gambit and she quickly responds. Note also how she bridges the boy's resistance and makes contact by "shaking hands" with "the winner."

In the next group meeting, No. 36, Mitchell said to the worker, "I know your real name. Irene." Worker smiled and replied, "Yes, that's my first name."

These developments have taken place during the phase of play group evolution in which reexperience with a significant, libidinal object—the worker—is the primary therapeutic force. The children "feed" emotional needs in the transference relationship for a sustained period of time.

Meeting No. 46 was the last one before the summer vacation. For several weeks prior to vacation, the worker has been conferring with teachers and interviewing parents, for the purpose of evaluation. A separate evaluation is done on each boy at the end of each school year, and a final evaluation when a play group is terminated.

From the evaluations:

Mitchell. He is less hostile toward adults in school and is beginning to establish better relationships. Because he originally felt rejected, he had been afraid to trust others. He now "demands" evidences of affection from his teacher and he responds to her limits better. Mitchell's mother could not keep her appointment. In the past, a failure on her part to keep an appointment was generally a sign of resistance, but lately she has been more cooperative because of changes she has seen, and reported, in Mitchell. Later she was able to accept a referral to a family agency for help with other problems involving her family as a whole. Mitchell is to be continued in the play group.

Carl. His teacher described him as being more assertive, bolder. He likes her and has given things to her, but he has also been able to demonstrate anger toward her. At the beginning of the school year he still sought out the girls but now he has found friends among boys. She has noticed that he is more aggressive; on two occasions he threatened an aggressive classmate. His physical carriage has changed; he stands erect and moves more vigorously. He has developed more motivation in learning areas. Despite his mother's concern about Carl's feminine tendencies and interest—expressed in an early interview—she failed to keep her appointment.

Gary. The teacher reported changes in Gary. In communicating with her he has become more verbal, less guarded. His speech is spontaneous and not as deliberate as it used to be. However, he expresses disappointment more readily and sometimes cries when he is overly frustrated. He is responsible in doing his work and he has submitted more special reports than any one else in the class. He completes his homework. Gary is now a member of the school orchestra and he loves it. In general, he is much less removed from his peers; he enjoys activities with them.

This data was particularly interesting because the marital situation in the family was still deteriorating. The father had become more abusive, and Gary had witnessed violent scenes between his parents. Attempts were currently being made to refer the family for help.

Play group meetings were resumed in the fall. New craft materials were added to the general supplies. This was done because the boys had developed increased skills in handicraft work. As a result of growing self-confidence and with a decided diminution in acting out behavior, the boys found more gratification through creative work. One of the new activities was woodwork. The boys were excited with it, and for many meetings woodwork was the activity of greatest interest to them. In addition, active games of advanced types, such as Nok-Hockey, were added. The purpose of such activities is to help sublimate aggression through competitive sports.

As for their relationships with the worker, the boys began to demonstrate more independence. Rivalry between the boys continued to decrease. For a long time the worker had been consistently satisfying needs which stemmed from dependence, without creating new rivalry patterns or aggravating old ones. While she still avoids interfering in their activities she is slowly modifying her role so that it is less permissive. This is done to help the boys develop greater frustration tolerance and to expose them to other reeducative experiences. It is through this process of reeducation that they will eventually make the transition to normal group participation.

When meetings were resumed in the fall, it was immediately apparent that Burt was in trouble. Burt was being battered by the mounting pressures in his family. In the play group this became manifested through increased demands on the worker, and excessive aggression toward the other boys. In class he was reported often for fighting. The boys in the play group were becoming quite annoyed with him.

Record and Analysis: Meetings Nos. 49 to 67

From Meeting No. 49: Then they all went over to the work bench. "Wood!" someone exclaimed. Worker had placed several models of planes on the shelf. Worker said she thought that they would like them. Carl said, "Can I have this one?" Worker said, "Yes." Gary took one, as did John, Mitchell, and Burt. They were arguing as to who would get which one. Carl said, "There's one for everyone." . . .

. . . Mitchell and Carl were arguing over the Nok-Hockey game—about how many points win the game. Mitchell said, "21" and Carl said, "12." Carl told Mitchell he didn't know "anything!" Then Carl counted the red scoring beads on the side of the game board, but some were obviously missing. Worker said, "Let's make the game 12 points; then others will have time to play." Worker added that she would keep score. Worker wrote: "Mitchell—Carl" on the board. Above she wrote "Winners." They began to play. While they played she was cutting plastic twine which Gary had requested. Burt and others asked for some. John wanted an "extra long one," and worker cut it for him. Later he asked for another, and again worker gave it to him. Mitchell and Carl called out the score from time to time and the worker recorded it on the board. Mitchell won. . . .

From Meeting No. 50: Mitchell played Nok-Hockey with Carl, as he had the week before. When Mitchell said he won the game at 12 points, Carl protested. Mitchell said, "Don't you remember?" Carl replied, "O.K." but then started to leave. Mitchell: "You said you'd play again." "O.K." said Carl. They began to play. Once, during the course of this game, Carl yelled, "Mitchell, you're cheating!" Mitchell laughed: "No I'm not." Carl insisted, angrily, "You *are* cheating." Mitchell smiled a little and seemed to give in.

Gary made a sword out of wood. When Carl finished playing with Mitchell, he also made a sword. Gary tried to interest him in a sword fight, but Carl didn't want to. . . . Carl said, "It's quiet around here without Burt." "Yeah," said Gary, "he's always fighting with Carl or Mitchell." Carl said, "That's why I didn't want to come last year." Mitchell boasted, "Oh, I can beat him up." Gary said, "I'll tell him that and he'll beat you up!" Then they talked about other youngsters. They mentioned a boy who could beat no one up.

Carl brought the discussion around to Burt again. He said, "I didn't like to come last year. Burt fights too much." Gary said, "Yeah—he always used to grab the food. He'd say, "Mrs. F. should give it out, but then he'd grab it." Mitchell: "I can't really beat him up." Gary said, "Burt thinks he's cool." Carl: "He's got a sister in the 6th grade; *she* can beat up anyone." There was more talk of who could beat up whom. Gary said, "You mustn't be afraid to fight," in response to Mitchell or Carl, who were saying something to the effect that they would be afraid to get hurt. He added: "John here knows I can beat him up but he fights." "Yes," affirmed John "I always fight." . . .

Analysis: Carl is quite capable now and he tries to hold his own in competition, arguments and discussion. However he is not quite up to a "duel" with Gary. The fraternal manner with which Gary and the others encourage Carl to learn to fight is interesting. The content about Burt is revealing.

From Meeting No. 58: During this meeting, Burt's aggression reached a point where the worker had to intervene directly several times in order to protect Carl. Burt had been chasing Carl, who appealed to the worker for protection. Each time after she had intervened, Burt would again chase Carl, shoving chairs at him and threatening him. Carl said he had to go to the bathroom and did so, obviously to escape Burt. Burt, however, followed him out of the play room and returned with him. Later, when Burt again pushed Carl around, Mitchell tried to intervene but without success. Burt became furious at one point and threatened to throw a piece of wood at Carl. The boys were "fed up" with Burt.

The question of Burt's continuation in the play group had been under consideration for several weeks. It was now evident that the group could not cope with Burt's aggression and that it would not be helpful for the worker to continue to intervene in order to protect Carl and the others.

Prior to the next meeting of the group, Burt was seen alone and in a discussion with the worker he was told that she would see him individually, at a different time. In telling this to him she avoided speaking in detail of his aggressive behavior and its effects. Instead, the worker explained that in helping children she sometimes saw them individually and sometimes in a group, whichever way she thought would be best. Burt took this in stride. As a matter of fact he seemed to prefer the new arrangement.

At the next meeting, when the group inquired about Burt's absence, the worker repeated essentially the same information which she had given Burt. There was no further questioning by the boys, but interestingly enough, for the first time inquiry was made as to the purpose of the play group. Gary asked the worker, "Why did we start to come?" The worker replied "To make you happy." Gary said soberly, "It does make us happy!"

From Meeting No. 60: Despite the critical comments about Burt, which had been expressed by the boys prior to his removal from the group, they showed ambivalent feelings about his absence. During this meeting, and for several meetings thereafter, there is some regression to forms of behavior which were prominent earlier in the group's development.

. . . At refreshment time Gary said, "Look at all this. Burt isn't going to get any!" Worker started to say something, but Mitchell interrupted: "Burt comes—uh—he comes tomorrow. Right, Mrs. F?" looking at the worker. The worker nodded. Mitchell added: "It's better to come by yourself." Worker asked, "Why?" and Mitchell replied, "I don't know. It's just better." Gary denied this: "It is not. You have no one to play with."

From Meeting No. 65: John at one point took the scissors and pointed them at Carl. Carl, with some anxiety, said, "Stop it, John!" . . .

Once more Carl shows anxiety about cuts, wounds, and sharp implements. John senses his anxiety. It was he who, in earlier meetings had made Carl anxious with his "lost finger" trick!

. . . Mitchell banged his leg. He cried out: "Ow, Ow!" and held his leg. He said he had hurt it right over an old wound—the one "with stitches!" Worker said, "Let me see." Mitchell pulled up one trouser leg and showed his "wound" to the worker. She said, "Yes—that can hurt. Shall I put some cold water on it?" "No," said Mitchell. This was unusual behavior for Mitchell. Ordinarily he would never tell anyone what was wrong, and he had always avoided any kind of physical contact. Worker had the feeling that when he yelled, "Ow, Ow," he wasn't hurt but just wanted her attention. During the previous group meeting he had sat next to her for almost half of the time when she read "Wizard of Oz" to the boys. At that time he leaned with his head on his hand and he kept sliding closer to the worker. He would have liked to lean against her.

From Meeting No. 67: Mitchell and Carl came in first. Mitchell said, "Let's take all the paper and not give it back even if they beat us up." Carl agreed. When Gary came in he saw what was going on. "Give us some paper," he demanded. They refused. Gary said, *"We're supposed to be a group—not enemies!"* He said this twice, looking toward the worker and laughing. Later, during snack time, Mitchell asked Carl to sit next to him. They made up a game called "ski-jump" and all played, with Carl as an equal participant. . . .

These incidents depict a growing sense of "groupism." While there is still argumentation and occasional aggression, there are stronger evidences of the boys' growing capacities to suppress personal needs to further the integrity of the group.

From Meeting No. 70: Gary came in before the meeting. He told the worker that he wanted to divide the paper so that Carl and Mitchell couldn't take all of it. He asked the worker to help; he divided it into four equal parts, which he then stapled. At his request, the worker wrote the names on the top sheets and put them on the shelf. Later, Mtichell took all the paper, erased the names and told John that he was not going to get any! John said he didn't care. Gary entered the room, expecting to see the paper as he had left it. He expressed surprise and approached Mitchell, who said that he and Mrs. F. had divided it. Mitchell said, "I have it." Carl had taken half. Then Mitchell thought a moment and said, "All right, I'll give you half, but you have to promise you'll always share with us." Gary said, "Sure, I promise. I wanted to share it." However, Carl said, "I'm not sharing *mine* with John." Gary criticized him: "Mitchell's sharing his paper with me!"

The meeting was very quiet. They were friendly and helpful to each other. Someone noticed Gary's "Mona Lisa" painting. (This was a comical representation he had done the week before.) Worker said, "It is Gary's 'masterpiece'." They laughed, and then they all began to paint "Mona Lisa's family." Gary made a sign: "Mona Lisa's Family," which was to be hung above all the paintings. Each boy had painted a member of the "Family." John's painting turned out to be a "monster!" Carl painted what he said was going to be the "prettiest one" in the family, a boy. While he was painting he said, "I messed it up. It's going to be a girl!" John said, "Mona Lisa's brother has magical powers; he changes from a boy to girl!" Mitchell painted a father with a beard, then a brother. Mitchell, who sat while he painted said, "My pants are ripped." He said it half to himself, but then he repeated it aloud. Worker said, "Mitchell, there are needles and thread in school. Someone can sew it for you." Mitchell said, "What do you think—I'm crazy? Take my pants off *here?*" Worker said, "You can have it sewn at lunch time and wait in the nurse's office." Mitchell had some discussion with the other boys about what to do and then said, "How many think I should take my pants off *here?*" They all raised hands. Mitchell got his coat, wrapped it around himself and took off his pants. Worker had to help him get one leg clear. The others laughed a little but continued painting. Worker took the pants and sewed them. Mitchell said twice, "Will it keep until 3 o'clock?" Worker assured him and said his mother might want to do it over with black thread since she had only white thread. When the worker finished, one of the boys held the coat in front of Mitchell so he could slip into his pants. John had begun to set the table for snack. Carl had asked worker, while she was sewing, to hang up the "Mona Lisa" pictures. She said she had to finish sewing. Gary said he'd do it. He and Carl then hung most of the pictures. Snack time was pleasant and uneventful.

Analysis: This meeting describes the accretion of maturational forces. A kind of "peace" and reasonableness is patent throughout. Humor and good natured spoofing is part of the interaction. Worker communicates at a level different from earlier practice. The boys discuss and settle problems more easily, without rancor.

Mitchell actually permits the worker to sew his trousers after some initial parrying. This incident is very meaningful, when taken in context with his original, massive distrust and defensiveness.

Carl cannot quite draw the "boy" and ends up with a "girl." John unconsciously touches on the crux of Carl's problem with his remark about the special "magic" which converts one sex to another. On several occasions during the life of this play group, John has demonstrated some anxiety about his own sexual identification.*

The healthful tone of the play group meetings continued, with occasional remissions of acting out behavior, but only on a temporary basis. The boys were more resilient and they were able to sustain themselves well. At the end of this school year, 82 group meetings had been held. When the boys returned after the summer, during which time several had gone to camp for the first time, the evaluations were reviewed, and it was decided to terminate the play group at the completion of the first semester. The boys were all in the 6th grade and, if graduated, they would be transferred to junior high schools. By terminating in mid-year the worker would have an opportunity to study their adjustments without the support of the play group.

The group continued to meet regularly until November, at which time the worker became ill and was absent for two months. The boys were very happy to see her on her return, and the meetings were resumed. Much of their conversations had to do with future school experience. They spoke of the "new" schools they were going to and also spoke much of present school experiences, in more positive terms. They were happier in school. With Gary and Mitchell, in particular, there had been marked improvement in academic achievement. Mitchell had also been elected president of his class. The deteriorating situation in Gary's family continued, but Gary was sustaining himself well in school and elsewhere.

It was during Meeting No. 89 that the worker informed the boys of the coming termination of the group.

From the record:

Gary and John came in and began to launch airplanes. The door was open and John said, "Come on in Mitchell." Worker waited and then she walked to the door. Mitchell was not there but Carl was. She asked him to come in and returned to the room. Carl came in, excited and laughing. He announced: "The principal's got Mitchell!" The other boys continued to play with the airplanes. John offered to make one for Carl, but he shook his head and said he did not want one. Carl kept walking to the door, going in and out of the room. Worker suggested that he stay inside the play room. Mitchell finally came. He looked unhappy and sat at the table where the worker and Carl were now seated. . . .

---

* This element of John's problem was not seen when he was originally referred for help, nor was it evidenced for a long time after he started in the play group. Because this group analysis is focussed on other boys, John's behavior has not been followed closely. However, it is important to note that the permissive play group is also a valuable diagnostic tool.

About ten minutes later, the worker said: "We will be ending the play group soon—at the end of the term—because I don't think you need to come anymore. You are so grown up." Carl, pouting, said, "I won't come to school if there's no play group!" Mitchell reacted by leaving the room, apparently to return to his class. Gary said, "I am going to keep coming!" A moment later he added: "I know why Carl and Mitchell did not want to come today. People say you're 'crazy' if you have to come to the guidance counselor, but I don't care. I *know* why *I come*. All the kids in the class want to come. They keep asking me. Peter keeps asking me if he could come." Gary painted as he talked. He continued: "I know why I came here. My father always said bad things about women—and my father and mother argued a lot—and I came here so I won't hate women!"

. . . Worker began to set for snack. At about 11:30 Mitchell returned. Carl stood in the corner and swung the broom up and down saying: "I'm mad, I'm mad." All of them took turns doing this. Then there was a lot of running around. They began to try to hurl paper airplanes out of the open window. (This they had done two years before.) Worker cautioned them and called them to the table. They sat down and ate the refreshments. Soon the bell rang. Mitchell left immediately, and the others followed.

Analysis: The reaction to the worker's announcement of termination is immediate. The boys attempt to deny a reality which they themselves had been discussing during recent meetings, when they spoke of going to new schools. Now they act impulsively, with mild regression. Mitchell leaves the room (the worker) abruptly, but returns later. Carl childishly threatens not to come to school altogether. Gary simply states flatly that *he* will continue to come. The worker does not try to reassure them; she knows that they must work through their own anxieties about the separation. If the estimations of their growth are correct, the boys should be able to manage the termination experience satisfactorily.

Gary also responds to the announcement of the worker at still another level, by associating back to the origin of the play group and the reasons for it. He shows an unusual awareness of one of the elements of his problem.

Gary also demonstrates the validity of the concept that children in therapeutic play groups, without being oriented to its purpose by prior explanations, nevertheless do know that the group experience is a special one, meant to help them.

At the end of this meeting all of the boys express a common anxiety by acting out in ways reminiscent of earlier play group meetings.

The record of Meeting No. 90 is a gratifying documentation of the changes wrought in these children by the therapeutic experience. The boys continue to show resistance to termination, but in a mild, playful way. Their behavior with the accidental "guest" is revealing—as is Gary's response to the second visitor in the room. The record speaks for itself:

Carl and Mitchell came early to the teacher's rest room, looking for the worker. They asked her if she expected them. Worker said, "Of course," and she went to the play room with them. Carl said, "Gary and John aren't here. They are sick." Worker smiled and said, "Are they?" From Carl's manner, she had understood that he was teasing. In awhile Gary appeared. Worker asked about John. Gary said he was still playing in the orchestra. Mitchell and Carl began to play cards. Someone knocked. Gary opened the door and said to a boy, "You can't come in." This boy, Donald, was Gary's classmate. Donald pushed and persisted, and Gary let him in. Worker said to Donald, "You can't stay here now." Gary and Carl said, "Let him stay." Donald looked around. The door opened again and still another boy entered. He said to the worker: "My mother wants to know why you want me to come here every week." Gary laughed and said, twice, "*He* wants to know why he *has* to come here!" He looked at the worker as he said this. Worker walked the visitor to the door. She spoke to him softly and he left.

John finally came; Gary began to play cards with Mitchell and Carl. John wanted to play just with Donald, but Donald did not want to. John then began to work with the clay. Later Donald joined him. The worker remarked, "Donald's the first person you ever let in here." Gary kidded: "That's because he's a 'dot' man." Worker asked what that was, and Gary explained: There were "dots" on his skin. Mitchell said, "Moles." Then each looked to see if he had "dots."

Donald, the visitor, said to the worker, "What do you have to do to get into this club? Do you have to be bad? Are they bad?" Gary, Mitchell and Carl looked at the worker, waiting to see what she would say. Worker said, "They are very good." There were no more questions about this.

Worker walked in and out of the room while preparing the snack. Gary said to Donald, "When that cake gets cut you have to leave." Worker set the table, putting out five settings. Carl looked at the cake and said it was "no good." Worker, surprised, said, "You all liked this before." Carl began to laugh, and worker said, "Oh you're teasing me." Carl, then Mitchell, ran to get the milk. No one had any intention of sharing with Donald. When the table was set, each boy poured his own milk. The worker added chocolate syrup to each cup and then prepared to cut the cake. Carl finally said to Donald, "Come on, Donald, sit down. You can have some cake." Donald remained standing, shy. Gary said, "He's not used to eating in school." They then all invited him to take some cake. Finally he sat. Worker cut the cake. They all had seconds.

At one point Gary stood in the corner, waved the broom up and down and said, "I'm mad—I'm mad!" They all had done this during the last meeting, after worker had announced that the group was going to be terminated.

Donald said he wanted to come again next week. Gary and Carl said, "Let him."

Before the last meeting, No. 92, an interesting incident took place between Mitchell and the worker, in which Mitchell assures *her* of the growth that has taken place. The worker, faced with an emergency situation involving a child who was not in the play group, has to decide what to do with Carl and Mitchell who came to the play room too early.

From the record:

Worker had sent notes to their classes, to inform the boys that the play group meeting would begin a little late and that she would call for them. However, when she went to the play room to get something, Mitchell and Carl were already there. Worker explained that there was an emergency, and that was why she had sent the notes. She had to go downstairs to the office. Mitchell and Carl said they wanted to wait in the play room. Worker was reluctant, and Mitchell said, *"Can't you trust us after three years?"* Worker said, "Yes" and left. During this exchange, Gary and John also appeared. They, too, remained in the play room.

When the worker returned, Mitchell announced that he had to leave early. Worker said, "All right, we'll eat at 11:30 then." Gary wanted to saw wood and was disgruntled because the tools weren't available. Then Gary and John decided to play checkers but they never started. Carl spotted some hard-covered notebooks in the closet. He had seen them before but now he wanted one. Worker said that she always gave him whatever she could but that these notebooks belonged to other children. He could have paper instead. Carl then said he just wanted to see the notebooks and the worker showed them to him. He saw the typewritten stories; read them briefly; seemed satisfied. Carl cut out some paper. John began drawing on the board and Gary joined him. Worker set the table for snack. Mitchell announced: "I'm not going to eat!" Worker said, "I have what you like—chocolate milk." Mitchell did not sit. Carl asked Mitchell if he could have Mitchell's potato chips. Mitchell said, "Yes," so Carl ate his cookies and the potato chips. Apparently finding his magnanimity too difficult to sustain, Mitchell asked Carl for a taste. Then he complained: "All I had was two pieces of potato chips." Mitchell took nothing else. This was strongly reminiscent of Mitchell's earlier behavior in the group, when he did not come to the table or, when he did, would sit with his face averted from the worker.

Soon after the snack, Mitchell left. Gary began to draw on the board and said "John, John." In tone and manner, it was reminiscent of the way Burt used to tease John. At any rate, Gary kept drawing pictures, saying they were John. Carl joined in, enjoyed himself immensely. He also drew a picture and said it was John. He wrote his name above the picture. In retaliation, John made a drawing of Gary. All the boys were laughing rather good naturedly. Before this took place, Gary had been very quiet. Now Gary and John wanted to draw on paper. When they looked for the paper someone said: *"There's nothing here anymore!"* Carl watched them as they continued to draw pictures of each other. The first bell rang, and Carl said he had to go to his class to get dismissed. Gary and John remained at the table for awhile. Then they left.

TERMINAL EVALUATIONS

Gary

Gary, an unusually bright boy, was referred three years ago. He was isolated from his peer group; participated in group activities on a marginal level; was excessively involved in phantasy; never finished his work; did not work to his potential. He suffered from somatic complaints, with asthma as the prominent symptom. The family situation was highly deteriorative.

From the terminal evaluation report:

Physical changes are marked. When referred, his movements were slow, almost to a point of exaggeration. His teacher had said: "He looked in a daze." Now he appears bright and cheerful most of the time. He stands upright and walks briskly. His preoccupation with phantasy, some of which was expressed in drawing monsters and supermen, has stopped. He participates vigorously in games. He is no longer an isolate, but instead he has become a leader in group activities in class. Gary has friends. His aggression is more appropriate and is manifested within reasonable limits. No somatic complaints were ever seen during play group meetings. However, several asthmatic attacks were reported at home. Conditions in the home are relatively unchanged but Gary seems better equipped to cope with them. The worker's attempts to get the family involved in a comprehensive treatment program at a clinic were never successful.

Academic achievement was measured by group tests given mid-year, in the sixth grade:

Reading: 11th grade level

Arithmetic: 6.4   grade level

This was the highest reading score in the entire 6th grade. Arithmetic skills are much improved; at one time his achievement in arithmetic had been below grade level. Gary was recommended for a special progress class in junior high school.

In the transference relationship with the worker Gary was able to counter and dilute some of the destructive influence of his mother, who generated extraordinary anxiety and guilt in the boy through her unconscious, seductive behavior. She was libidinally overinvested in Gary, perhaps because of her husband's angry, often violent behavior toward her. Gary's perception of his angry father reinforced his guilt, increased anxiety, and led to a blocking of his own aggression.

Gary spontaneously touched upon these elements when he remarked: "I know why I came here. My father always said bad things about women—and my father and mother argued a lot—and I came here so *I won't hate women!*"

The observed acting out behavior of the other boys in the play group, and the worker's tolerance, altered Gary's aggression, in both its quality and expression. Originally, aggression had strong libidinal overtones, because of his mother's seductive behavior and the father's angry reactions. The interaction within the play group helped Gary perceive other modalities of aggression; as a consequence he became able to express aggression openly. Gary no longer needed to "discharge" aggression and anxiety through autistic phantasy and drawings of monstrous creatures attacking a little boy—who always cried, "Help!"

Carl

He had been referred originally because he avoided contact with boys and preferred playing with girls. There were obvious qualities of effeminacy in his carriage and behavior. There was no complaint of misbehaviour in class: Carl was attentive and responsive. He was below grade in achievement. When he was upset about something he stammered.

From the terminal evaluation report:

Carl's manner of walk was once described by his teacher as, "like a girl's." This is no longer so, but he does shuffle when he walks. In appearance he is animated and cheerful, with no evidences of moodiness and sulking. He is more outspoken with teachers and peers, and his voice is clear and audible. Originally, he was shy and at times inaudible. There are still moments when he stammers.

Carl was always creative with craft materials, but now he is also interested in sport and games. While he is less skillful than others, he does participate in activities with boys, in class and elsewhere, and he is anxious to be accepted by his peers. At home, he coaches his younger brother in handling himself with boys. Carl is obviously more aggressive, and he has fought with boys when angered.

Academic achievement measured through group tests at mid-year in the 6th grade:

Reading: 4.1

Arithmetic: 4.8

Carl was receiving remedial help at an after-school center.

In the beginning, Carl's preference for girls and their activities and his physical qualities of effeminacy were apparent, but the etiology of his emotional disorder had never been definitively established. While his parents professed concern because of his interest in feminine things, they nevertheless subsidized the boy's deficiencies in various ways: by giving him lessons in music and dancing; permitting him to shop, cook and clean. They were disappointed in not having had a daughter.

In Carl's case, the interaction with the children in the play group was the significant therapeutic modality. The relationship with the worker was also important, but primarily as an *intensifier* of the group's influence. The group surrounded Carl with masculine imagery, through its persistent demonstration of masculine interests and activities. It is also eventually acted to block Carl, by denying him outlets for feminine expression. As his behavior became more masculine, Carl achieved increased status in the group. This gratified him and strengthened his masculine identity.

The worker carefully supported the process of shifting identification by encouraging Carl's explorations in new areas of experience which were therapeutically important. At the same time, she covertly blocked Carl's involvement in activities which were patently unsuitable for promoting masculine identification. Thus, when she praised Carl, or gave other forms of acknowledgement for achievements such as walking the chalk ledge of the blackboard, or for construction work with lumber, she reinforced Carl's feelings of mastery and also his healthy expression of aggression. Carl's early attempts to aggrandize himself by volunteering to help with setting the table, serving food and cleaning were at first tolerated, eventually blocked.

In essence, the children in the group provided Carl with the stimuli which subsequently led to masculine patterning and social group acceptance; the worker, in the transference relationship, represented a parent substitute, who supported and supplemented the healthy alterations in ego functioning. Since she, unlike Carl's parents, had no libidinal needs to satisfy through the boy, Carl was able to respond to her without anxiety.

Mitchell

He was referred as a severely acting out child. Mitchell was hostile and defiant, unusually stubborn, and restless. He could not concentrate on school work. He was intelligent, but he lacked motivation, and, as a result, his achievement was below grade. While he was belligerent and fought with peers, there were other times when he became depressed, dispirited, and beset with feelings of worthlessness. He was inordinately suspicious of and defensive against adults. He was one of many children in a broken family in which delinquent behavior had already been manifested by older siblings.

From the terminal evaluation report:

Mitchell is shorter than average for his age and is still conscious of this. However, he stands upright and he is alert. A great change is evident in his expression. When he was first known to the worker he looked alternately surly and depressed. Now he smiles often and has a mischievous twinkle in his eyes. Where his speech was originally hostile and sometimes profane, it is now relatively free of these qualities. He no longer speaks morbidly; he is self-assured, more independent. He has developed skill in games, and he likes to demonstrate this to others. There has been much improvement in his attitudes and also in his performance in class, with a pronounced increase in motivation for learning. He was nominated as a candidate for school president. His relationship with his mother has also undergone much change. When first interviewed, she spoke very angrily about Mitchell and the "trouble" he was causing her. She was already identifying him with an older sibling who was delinquent. As Mitchell improved in school, and as reports of accomplishment and praise began to replace earlier complaints of misbehavior, her attitude toward him became more accepting. She, herself, became less defensive and more accessible, and accepted referral to a family agency.

Mitchell's status in his class had changed markedly, for the better. His teacher spoke of him with pride and pleasure.

Academic achievement was measured at mid-year, in grade six:

Reading: 6.2

Arithmetic: 6.4

When referred Mitchell was below grade in both subjects.

As a result of many traumatizing experiences in his family, Mitchell was left with little choice: he had to defend himself against relationships with adults. He had "learned" that trust was synonomous with hurt, rejection, and defeat. His father, an alcoholic, was concerned only with his own pressing needs; his mother, overwhelmed with the oppressive weight of managing nine children and defending herself from her husband, gave Mitchell short shrift. In addition, Mitchell's vacillation between acting out and feelings of depression and apathy had serious implications for his future development.

Those elements of his behavior which were the *least* morbid—hostility toward teachers and authority in general, fights with children, use of obscenities—were responsible for most of his crises in school.

The treatment process had to help this boy reduce his own defenses against emotional involvement. Relationship with the play group worker was the primary goal; the group was of secondary importance. The play group had two important functions in the therapeutic process:

to provide Mitchell with insulation from the permissive worker; he could not tolerate proximity. The record described his anxiety when, during early meetings, he was occasionally alone with the worker.* At such times Mitchell would make excuses and leave the play room. (Even as he made excuses with his class teacher to get to the play room before the other children!)

---

* This was why individual therapy was contraindicated.

through his observations of the relationships of the others in the play group with the worker, Mitchell built up a perception of the therapeutic adult; only then could he "dare" to attempt to make contact with her.

Three stages can be detected in Mitchell's behavior in the play group: In the beginning there was hostility, defensiveness, and a warding off of the slightest demonstration of interest by the worker; then followed a stage of ambivalence, with alternate moments of defensiveness against the worker followed by immature demands accompanied by whining; finally, relaxation, sublimation, autonomous functioning were apparent. At this stage he could tolerate "love" and even reciprocate.

Now the play group became important to Mitchell at another level: it took on meaning as a social force, and Mitchell, who was now eager for recognition and status, sought acceptance in the group on a more mature level.

FOLLOW-UP

The boys remained in this school for one full semester following the termination of the play group. The worker saw them intermittently, never on an appointment basis. The gains reported in the terminal evaluations were sustained; they continued to make satisfactory progress.

Carl was transferred to junior high school at the end of the year but retained on record in the 6th grade because of retardation in reading and arithmetic. He was disappointed when he found out about this plan. Months later it was learned that he was given a trial promotion to the seventh grade by the junior high school.

Gary received an award for effort and achievement at the graduation exercises. This was the first special recognition he had received during his entire school career. His mother was so excited about this that she cried.

Mitchell received two awards at the graduation exercises—one for effort and achievement, and a second for citizenship. His mother sought out the worker and thanked her profusely, saying that Mitchell's achievement was the result of the worker's interest and efforts with him. Then she asked for help with a younger child, who was also presenting difficulties in school adjustment. It is important to note that the worker had much difficulty in obtaining her cooperation when she started to see Mitchell.

7 A Seminar in Child Psychology for Teachers

FORMAL EDUCATION INFLUENCES CHILD DEVELOPMENT

Schools are being held accountable in increasing measure for educational outcomes which extend much beyond what was considered acceptable and traditional only a short time ago. A broader concept of education has already had much impact on curricula and teaching methods. Even more important is the growing realization that because the school significantly affects the psychological development of children it must be more actively concerned with problems associated with child growth and emotional development. While schools do not determine the structure of personality and character, they do have a marked effect on the expanding and elaborating capacities of young egos.*

The cumulative effect of meaningful experience in school fosters personality maturation in children and leads to improved social adaptation. Unfortunately this does not always eventuate. If school experience is persistently deficient, or destructive in impact, much of a child's energy becomes used in protection of the ego. In such a case, the need to defend against frustration, anxiety, or fear aborts the child's potential for growth and creativity.

Teachers' Responsibility-Fostering Growth Experiences

The effectiveness of new approaches in the education of normal children and of rehabilitative methods with disturbed children, or, for that matter, the real worth of all outcomes within schools, is inextricably tied to the professional attributes of those who work with children. In the presence of skilled, knowledgeable, and sensitive teachers and administrators, all children benefit, including exceptional ones. In the absence of such qualities in educators, all children are deprived; some become even more disabled.

Successful education of the young is dependent as much on a teacher's knowledge of the psychology of child growth and the interaction which takes place in groups as it is on her grasp of subject content and her teaching skills.

* This has been said before in many ways: at professional conferences, in educational reports and text books and at graduation exercises. Perhaps it has become a form of professional "lip service"—an impotent substitute for that which can be attained only through dedication, inventiveness, and hard work.

Her efficiency is enhanced as she becomes increasingly aware of the manner in which teaching and learning are both influenced by psychodynamic forces within the class group, and as she recognizes the fact that she contributes to the interaction, often unconsciously.

Normal and deviant child behavior are cognate aspects of psychology, and an understanding of either one is dependent on the other. A clinician's need to understand individual and group psychology in working with exceptional children is never questioned, but the concept that related knowledge is necessary for the teacher may be accepted as an afterthought. A teacher spends most of her working time with children in groups, and her proficiency will be influenced by the extent of her knowledge of child behavior and group interaction—just as with a clinician who uses a specialized group process as a therapeutic tool.

Continuing Seminar—Longitudinal Study of One Play Group

An effective method for helping teachers learn more about child behavior is to involve them in a study of the interaction which takes place in a group of exceptional children. The records of a therapeutic play group can be used profitably as the content of a continuing seminar. An advantage of studying a play group is the fact that it is an *in vivo* group, which, circumstances permitting, can be followed from onset to termination. The process of studying a dynamic group as it evolves over a period of years is highly motivating. One of its unique attributes is that it offers an opportunity to use current observations and analysis to anticipate future behavior of children.

In studying a particular play group in detail and in learning to analyze child behavior for its meanings, the teachers discover that some of the phenomena in normal groups are similar to those found in exceptional groups. Thus, while the continuing study of the play group proves to be interesting in itself, a more important outcome for the teachers is a broader understanding of child behavior in the class room. This develops as the seminar participants, in response to their becoming aware of the existence of parallel forces in different groups, eventually feel free to present their own class-group problems for discussion in the seminar.

While a seminar of this type is less structured in content and method than didactic courses of instruction, it nevertheless has definitive goals:

helping teachers to recognize interaction processes as they are manifested in child groups and to probe for the latent meanings of behavior.

enabling each teacher to learn that she is a significant component of a dynamic group and that she is *involved in its interaction.*

to maximize objectivity so that teachers can examine and evaluate their ideas, technics, and affect responses as these are related to their roles as teachers.

to relax teachers so that they can reduce unnecessary controls, to the effect that constructive interaction within their class groups will have greater expressive latitude.

If a seminar maintains the interest of its participants, there are other positive outcomes. Successful communication in the seminar leads to improved communication on other levels. As teachers become more aware of themselves as important members of the professional team, they also become more accessible to the clinical specialists within the school.

Composition of the Seminar Group

A seminar group which has teachers from all grade levels of an elementary school has merit, despite the fact that curriculum, teaching methods, and child behavior vary considerably from kindergarten to upper grades. Teachers of different child-age groups can learn that they have much to contribute to each other's understanding as they study together. They begin to see a child in perspective, as they perceive the relatedness of present and past behavior and, in the case of emotional disturbance, the etiological determinants. Personality and behavior are no longer viewed as unique aspects of a particular grade and age, but rather, as part of a developmental continuum. As a result of this, barriers to communication between teachers of different grade levels begin to disappear.

Participation of Administrators—Values and Hazards

There are no hard and fast rules to determine whether school administrators and supervisors should participate in seminars with teachers. Much depends on the quality of the preexisting professional relationships between supervisors and faculty members. In the seminar, teachers and supervisors may at times find themselves in disagreement with respect to the analysis of child behavior. Both must feel free to react to each other's ideas without anxiety. All points of view are subject to logical evaluation and no member of the seminar may enjoy a special position which spares his ideas from critical study. Unless this is so, or becomes so in time, the seminar group will remain in disequilibrium and the integrity of the process will be jeopardized. However, when teachers and supervisors do learn to communicate in a tension-free atmosphere, with their energies unfettered by concern for status position, there are enormous gains in their professional relationships, extending beyond the learnings of the seminar into the broader functioning of the school itself.

From a practical point of view, it is inadvisable for a supervisor to participate in a seminar until the teachers have had at least five or six meetings to familiarize themselves with the process. Further, it is also advisable for the seminar leader and a supervisor to discuss in advance the implications of his participation.

Starting a Seminar, Frequency of Meetings

An invitation to join a seminar should be presented to the entire faculty of a school as an opportunity for studying individual and group behavior through the medium of the special play group. Participation should be voluntary and the seminar should be an "open" group, in the sense that teachers may join or drop out at any point. At times this creates management problems for the leader. The seminar group develops its own interaction, which is interfered with if there is excessive fluidity in group composition.

The seminar group should meet weekly; a less frequent schedule dilutes continuity and does not sustain interest. There is some advantage in holding the meetings during lunchtime, in a teachers' lounge or a conference room. Informality fosters relaxed discussion.

Preliminary orientation made by the leader of the seminar should include an outline of the goals, a simplified description of play group theory and practice, and a statement that the records of one play group will be used as the vehicle for exploring the meanings of individual and group behavior of children. The presenting problems of the children who are in the play group are then described. Since comprehensive descriptions of each child would be too much for the teachers to retain at first presentation, and because later study will illuminate problem areas more thoroughly, only a minimal description of each child is necessary.

The Beginning Seminar, Selective Use of Content

It would be unwise for the seminar leader in initiating the study process to dwell on the highly permissive nature of play group practice. Permissive group practices are antithetical to traditional classroom procedures and may be threatening to teachers who have become habituated to nonpermissive, highly disciplined group practices. The *laissez faire* aspect of a therapeutic group is entirely novel to them. Judicious use should be made of the records of play group meetings, with sensible deletions of language which might be offensive. Dramatic descriptions of fights between children, destruction of materials, regressive behavior, and other forms of acting out, should be diluted during the early meetings of the seminar. This is not misrepresentation of the record, but rather a sensible introduction of "charged" material to a group which has yet to build up a tolerance for such content.

During early meetings of the seminar it is particularly important to concentrate investigation on the children in the play group and to *avoid dis-*

cussing phenomena in class groups. By focusing on definitive problems within the special group, teachers are able to be more objective than they would otherwise be in dealing with problems in their own groups. Such problems should be held in abeyance until the teachers develop ease in communication and can present them for discussion without anxiety.

Technics of study are more important than the content of discussion during early meetings of the seminar group. Teachers need to become acquainted with the "ground rules" before they can participate in constructive discussion in a relaxed manner. If the leader allows premature and extensive discussion of problems unrelated to the play group, the following impediments to seminar group management may arise:

The continuity of study of play group interaction is interrupted.

The leader's role is blocked; instead of helping the seminar group develop longitudinally, so that teachers participate in an extended learning process,* the group tends to become a problem-solving group. The leader will then be used as a resource person, and the teachers will expect him to provide "practical" solutions for immediate, often complicated problems.

This bears reiteration: in the beginning seminar the leader should limit the discussion to the behavior of children in the play group. Incursions of problems related to other children, in other groups, should be kept to a minimum. This procedure is not intended to block the teachers from presenting realistic problems of pupil and class management. Later in the seminar they will be encouraged to explore child and group problems whether they occur in play groups or classes. However, at such a time the teachers will be, hopefully, more adequately equipped to grapple with these problems objectively.

The "Climate" of the Seminar

The attitudes of the seminar leader establish the operational tone or "climate" of the seminar. This develops as he presents the records of his own work with a play group for the examination of the seminar group. Because this material is presented without a demonstrated need to defend it, the teachers are exposed to a process of healthful objectivity. As they observe, over a period of time, that the leader is not infallible, they in turn become less constrained to venture opinions.

The teachers are encouraged to weigh the elements of observable behavior of children; to suggest probable causation and interrelationships; to reject meanings which are unsubstantiated; even to respect intuitive reactions but to await the trials of time and evidence before acknowledging a "glimmer" as

---

* The author has conducted such seminars for teachers in elementary schools on a weekly basis, and they have continued from one to three years.

factual. An important outcome is the discovery that, in the process of careful reflection, proof of error is a step toward solution. There is nothing wrong in being wrong.

This approach and other demonstrations of objectivity help to dissipate suspicions and defensiveness, and it enables the teachers to communicate with less reserve.

S. R. Slavson has described the concept of a group's primary code. This evolves from interaction experiences which enable a group to become self-regulating and goal-directed. The primary code of the seminar group is the gainful pursuit of knowledge which will improve the teacher-pupil-educational process. The leader must always be concerned with whether the seminar group is moving in this productive direction, and he should be prepared to help whenever there are psychological "snags" which interfere with this development and which the group cannot cope with by itself.

EASING THE PROCESS OF COMMUNICATION

Orgins of Defensiveness

One of the first procedures in establishing effective communication is to reduce an attitude of defensiveness which is common in many teachers. It is acquired during the years of undergraduate and graduate training and also from later experience in actual teaching. This defensiveness stems from teachers' feelings about professional supervision, which is a major element in teacher training and which continues later during teaching. Educational practices in general are much involved with ratings, reports, evaluations, and relationships with persons in supervisory or administrative positions. As a result of such influences, teachers come to look upon supervision as a measuring process which is primarily concerned with determining their professional adequacy.

This sensitivity on the part of teachers is manifested even more with clinicians, toward whom it sometimes verges on open suspicion. Defensive attitudes militate against reflective problem solving, and they must be recognized and handled by the leader as though they were forms of resistance. This is not resistance in the clinical meaning. Defensiveness on the part of teachers in a seminar is not always caused by unconscious, emotionally charged material. It can be quite conscious at times, and it is often determined by past and present experiences under supervision which were sometimes of a threatening nature.

At the beginning of a seminar it would be unwise for a leader to deal with defensive attitudes directly by identifying and exposing them for discussion. More effective is an evolving process which first fosters relaxed communication and eventually dissipates suspiciousness and resistance.

Fostering Objectivity

The leader should direct the group's thinking along logical, problem solving pathways, using a Socratic approach and avoiding clinical terminology. Excessive use of technical language reinforces the differences between professional disciplines; it certainly does not promote efficient communication. Most psychological concepts can be adequately described in nontechnical language.

Another requirement for objectivity in the investigative process, which develops in the group after repeated demonstrations by the leader, is that of delaying judgment. Analysis of child behavior in the play group may produce less than general agreement and may lead to conflicting interpretations. The leader must help the teachers determine whether there is enough data to validate one meaning over another and, if not, to hold tentative impressions in abeyance until the record provides more illuminating and definitive data. This is illustrated in the following content:

A seminar group had been studying the behavior of children in a first grade play group. The record described how Carl, while playing with construction blocks, built a large square structure and then attempted to make a roof over it with other blocks.* He had been involved in this play quietly, without interference from any of the other children.

Several weeks before this episode took place, Carl's father died after suffering a stroke. Shortly before that, his mother had lost an infant in childbirth and had told Carl when she returned home that the baby was "left" at the hospital because he was sick.

The discussion in the seminar became focused on Carl's preoccupation with the blocks. After some tentative comments as to its meaning, it was suggested that Carl was releasing through play some of the unhappiness and anxiety which followed the recent losses in his family. With that in mind, it was probable that his block play was a phantasy enactment of burial. Some teachers questioned this meaning, stating that neither the verbal content in Carl's play nor other forms of content communication supported such an interpretation. No other possible interpretations were volunteered as to the meaning of block play. The discussion was dropped for the time being.

At the following meeting of the seminar group, which took place after the play group had also had one additional meeting, the attention of the teachers was immediately drawn to the dramatic content of Carl's play.†

Carl had once again built almost the identical kind of covered enclosure, but this time he incorporated doll figures in his play. He placed the baby

---

* See page 77. Carl had enacted this dramatic sequence during two consecutive meetings.

† It is this anticipatory factor—awaiting the behavior which is to take place in subsequent meetings of the play group which is being studied—which provides the high degree of motivation for the teachers' seminar.

figure in the enclosure and covered it with blocks. Then he took the mother and father figures, held one in each hand and enacted a fight between them. At one point the mother figure was thrown down and the father figure was raised high overhead. The phantasy play ended when Carl angrily destroyed the block enclosure.

The teachers evaluated this content with spirited interest. No longer was there disagreement as to the meanings of this play. Rather, the discussion had a quality of discovery, as if they had confirmed the promise of objective investigation. The analysis touched upon many elements germane to the bereavement play of the child. Carl's mixed reactions to the two traumatic experiences in his life were explored. Among these were: his limited ability to cope with the experiences of death and separation; the ensuing anxiety; anger with his mother who "left" a baby in the hospital and who had "fights" with his father, who also went away somewhere "in the sky;" the release of anger which took place when he destroyed the entire structure. It was also observed that Carl seemed more relaxed following this play. It was further suggested that such ventilation through play has much value for young children when they are beset with overwhelming experiences which strain their capacities for making efficient adjustment.

While the foregoing discussion was interesting, the more profitable outcome, as far as the teachers were concerned, was yet to come. One of the participants raised the question: What implications were there for teachers who work with young children, since it was not uncommon for them to be faced with this problem when a child experiences the loss of a family member?

The remainder of the meeting was devoted to this question. The leader directed investigation to child development and early experiences related to separation and death. Many ideas and supporting evidences were presented by the teachers from their own experiences with children in normal class groups. Several teachers described specific methods which they had used in dealing with the problem.

The discussion ranged wide, but the group did crystallize important concepts and made suggestions for managing such problems in the classroom. A brief statement of some of the ideas evolved *by the teachers* follows:

For a young child, separation experiences caused by the loss of a parent or a sibling are emotionally traumatic. This includes separations for reasons other than death.

It is confusing to a child when adults say things which deny the reality of death, e.g., "going away for a long time." Children think that "going away" has something to do with "coming back."

Loss of a parent through death is often experienced by a young child as a desertion. The living parent is sometimes held responsible.

Sometimes a child feels guilty after the loss of a parent. He becomes relieved when knowledge is acquired that others have had similar experiences. Comfort is also experienced when other meaningful persons (teacher) share some of the child's feelings of loss.

Ideation which *helps* a bereaved child to cope with a loss efficiently should not be tampered with. This might include a child's own ideas about "heaven," "the sky," "God."

Children begin to learn about the finite quality of life and the continuity of life through observations of events in their expanding environment. This would include: observations of natural phenomena during changes in seasons, particularly the effects on plant life; deaths of insects; deaths of animals, sometimes pets.

Mourning following bereavement is a normal reaction.

In a negative sense, one episode took place during this seminar meeting which illustrates what should not be done in such seminars. A visitor, a clinician, joined the discussion towards its end. He contributed several ideas in psychological depth, about "unconscious death wishes" and their possible relationship to anxiety and guilt. The leader of the seminar carefully blocked discussion after the clinician's presentation of this statement and picked up other content for discussion.

The validity of the statement was not in question; it was *not necessary* for continuity. More important, such an interpretation can induce anxiety in nonclinical participants.

INTERACTION WITHIN THE SEMINAR GROUP

The Unconscious "Participates"

The seminar group possesses no unique immunity which will spare it from the tension situations produced by interaction. There is a build-up of forces within the seminar which influences, for better or worse, the reflective process. The content of child behavior which is being investigated stimulates affective responses in adults, even as they manifestly attempt to remain objective in their thinking. This occurs whenever intellectualization becomes blocked or distorted by transference elements of a transient nature. It is certainly true that the unconscious of seminar members "participates" in the discussion if it becomes resonant to the behavior of children in a play group, or to the interaction which takes place between the members of the seminar group itself. The intrusion of unconscious forces influences the members of the seminar in complicated and subtle ways.

The emotionally laden responses of the participants act as distorters of objectivity, and they must be recognized by the leader as they arise in a seminar group. They should be viewed as possible contaminants of the discussion and learning process. He must be sensitive to interaction processes which affect the equilibrium of the seminar group. Elements which foster disunity and impede reflective investigation must be "sealed off" by the leader, whenever the group cannot do so itself. The manner in which this is accomplished helps maintain the overall tone of the seminar. If hostility between participants becomes manifest and shows no signs of abating, the leader should help suppress it. If hostility is directed toward the leader it is never reflected: the leader's behavior serves as a demonstration "model" for the group.

Intervention—When Indicated

The leader should intervene at a point whenever discussion threatens to become unduly argumentative or frustrating. Unless he does so, forces inimical to objectivity gain excessive momentum. If a seminar participant reacts to the content of discussion overaggressively, intellect may become misused in the defense of untenable ideas, or to "disprove" logical content. An obstructive influence easily becomes magnified if it induces similar responses in other seminar members. Given this condition, the leader must then be concerned with several questions:

Can the group, by itself, tolerate and work through the emotionally charged episode?

Does the content of discussion contribute in any way to the promotion of productive interaction in the seminar? A group which fails to reduce a problem in communication which has been precipitated by one or more emotionally "charged" participants, but which has otherwise been interacting well, will tolerate the leader's attempts to restore its integrity.

During the early meetings of a seminar group, the leader may have to intervene more frequently because the group—or some of its members—lacks resilience and needs support.

In a seminar group which had been meeting for a short time, a teacher raised critical questions as to the wisdom of permitting children in the play group to help themselves to food at refreshment time. This teacher, who was traditional in training and practice, was obviously anxious—less obviously angry—about the fact that the children were described as having grabbed food, and because there had been an unequal distribution. She added that it "would be better" for the play group worker to portion out the food. In this way the children could be helped to develop a sense of "fairness and good manners."

Several other teachers echoed the sentiment of the "question." One teacher attempted to reinforce this viewpoint by pointing out that the play group procedure would create chaos were it to be used in a classroom when cookies and milk were distributed.

It was apparent that a free discussion of permissiveness in play group practice, particularly as it applied to food, would have been premature. On the other hand, the question had been presented, albeit rhetorically, and it could not be dismissed without comment. The leader replied to this effect: It *was* important for children to develop a sense of fairness and respect for the rights of others. However, there were other questions which were implicit in the problem: What are the best experiences for helping young children develop such qualities? How does self-discipline evolve? Should there be differences in management of child behavior by the adult in the exceptional group (play group), as compared to the normal group?

These questions elicited additional responses from the teachers, with some in favor of imposed limits by the adult, both in class and in the play group. Others argued that children had to experience for themselves in order to develop a capacity for self-restraint. Some indicated that they were not sure to what extent the adult should become involved in such situations. Finally, the leader suggested that the question *be tabled for the time being*, to observe how the children in this play group handled the problem of sharing food during future meetings. The seminar group seemed willing to do so.

Because this group had met only a few times, it was not ready for extended discussion of a problem which had many psychodynamic elements. To have permitted continued discussion at this time would have uncovered even stronger affect reactions, and the result might have been the loss of some seminar participants before they had had an opportunity to develop more flexibility and a tolerance for new learnings. Months later this group was able to discuss this problem and others of equal importance with comparative ease.

There is no question that the investigation of human behavior—whether it be of children in a play group or of any other persons—is influenced by unconscious forces which are bedded in the life experiences of the investigators; in this case, the teachers. It is also true that some of the opinions and judgments which teachers volunteer in the seminar will be reflections of personal qualities which may interfere with their accomplishment as teachers in class. Hopefully, the learning process which takes place in a continuing seminar will eventually help them become more aware of their attitudes and motivation and lead to improved performance. However, until the seminar group is sufficiently advanced, and until the teachers feel secure, it is the responsibility of the leader to filter the content of discussion, focusing on that which is timely, nonthreatening, and which serves the aims of the seminar. The seminar leader must constantly assess the emotional and intellectual tolerances of the group.

Aggressive Leadership Inhibits Dynamic Evolution of the Seminar

Aggressive procedures by a seminar leader to "root out" inhibiting attitudes and beliefs may have poor consequences for individual teachers, and they may threaten the continuation of the seminar itself. Inhibiting factors such as resistance—or resistiveness—resentments, argumentativeness, and other emotional attitudes, do not yield to premature and forceful attempts to change them. They can be ameliorated only when the teachers are able and ready to offer them for exploration.

There is little consolation in the fact that the withdrawal of even one teacher from a seminar can be attributed to resistance, anger, or frustration. For the sake of future efficiency the seminar leader should explore each loss of a participant to determine the reason, and also whether he has contributed to it through a tactical error.

A skillful, persuasive leader can lead a seminar group into glib, intellectual discussion of professional attitudes, and the discussion may appear to be a profitable one. However, this is usually an intellectual "exercise," and basic modifications in attitudes will not take place. Real changes are possible only after individuals are secure enough to explore their own motivations and feelings. This takes time and readiness.

It should be borne in mind that one of the primary goals of the seminar is to enable teachers to recognize themselves as dynamic components of their respective class groups, and that within these groups they, too, are subject to interaction forces which determine behavior. They can begin to tolerate this understanding only after they have first spent much time analyzing the interaction within the play group, including analysis of the worker's technics and responses.

Neurotic Determinants in Interaction

The behavior of some teachers is influenced by neurotic forces, and this might become apparent through the opinions they offer in a seminar and in the manner in which they communicate. Despite the best demonstrations of objectivity and affability by the leader and other members of the seminar group, some teachers may still have a *need* to be provocative, to harass and argue. While they may present themselves in the role of "devil's advocate," this is essentially a negative approach—a spurious attempt to objectify the ongoing investigation in the seminar. When it is determined that such behavior is personality-based and is not episodic and transient, the leader must be alert to its impact on the group and the group's defensive reactions.

When a seminar group responds to the context of a hostile participant's remarks, it sometimes tends to "attack the attacker." This may be self-defensive, or in defense of the leader, who may have been the object of hostility. The leader must block retaliation by the group if the instigator becomes unduly threatened. In a sense, the leader denies the group the privilege of excessive counterhostility.

When provocation by any teacher is neurotically determined, the leader must avoid dealing with its motivation and address the attention of the group only to that part of the content which is *intellectual* and which bears on the general discussion. The leader separates ideation from affect and, in so doing, impels the group to do likewise. A teacher who cannot create a "field" for neurotic expression has no choice but to find greener pastures and will eventually withdraw from the seminar. Such individuals do require psychotherapy.

The seminar leader should observe caution whenever a participant presents material which is highly subjective or emotional. It is not unusual to find one or several teacher participants in each seminar group who characteristically tend to act this way. Uncritical probing for the meanings of exaggerated emotional responses by the leader risks touching upon deeper, unconscious factors.

It is the author's experience that obstructive behavior which is neurotically determined does not occur frequently in teachers' seminars. When it is evidenced, it is often possible to keep it *within limits tolerable to the group*. It is only when such behavior has a sadistic component, and the seminar becomes a convenient arena for neurotic gratification, that it becomes impossible to cope with it.

Ethics-Responsibility of the Seminar Leader

In the practice of analytic group psychotherapy, a patient's neurotic behavior becomes "grist" for the interaction in the therapy group, and it is eventually discussed by the patients. The therapist does not usually block the flow of affect from a patient, or its evocations from the group. The teachers' seminar, however, *is not a therapy group*. While the dynamics of a seminar may, at times be parallel to those in a therapy group, *they are not utilized* by the leader in the same manner. The goals of a seminar are different from those of a treatment group.

It would be unethical for a seminar leader to subvert the seminar group by subtle manipulation and attempt to change it into a therapy group. Patients—if they are to be patients—have the privilege of self-declaration. Besides, it does not follow that all emotionally charged communication in a seminar is necessarily neurotic in origin.

THE "TRADITIONALIST" TEACHER IN THE SEMINAR

Teachers differ from each other with respect to training, experience, attitudes, and temperament. A seminar group may contain some who are traditional in the "old school" sense and others who may be more flexible, even permissive, in classroom practice. It would be unwise to assume that the former are intractable and incapable of participating in fruitful discussion. Habit may be a hard taskmaster, but even hard taskmasters often respond to reason.

A problem frequently encountered with teachers is a resistiveness to new learnings, particularly when they have become habituated by traditional educational practices. It is not fair to threaten teachers by arbitrary assaults on imbedded habit patterns. The effect of such methods is to promote insecurity and anger in those who find comfort in the "old ways." Teachers who may be circumscribed in their professional methods and thinking may become accessible to study procedures designed to induce changes in attitudes, if these procedures stimulate interest and are not unduly frustrating. They will continue to participate in a seminar if they feel that their ideas and opinions are received with respect, even if these views conflict with others. Many such teachers will tolerate closer examination of the validity of their ideas after they have been sufficiently exposed to a seminar group which has learned to communicate in a relaxed, constructive manner.

Young teachers who have been trained under the "new" and shining concepts of modern education can demonstrate their own brand of inertia. They can be impatient with ideas contrary to their own, particularly when they are presented by older teachers. This interaction between teachers of different professional "generations" often has the quality of adolescent rebelliousness against authority. Conversely, the reaction of older teachers is sometimes more a defense against the implicit "challenge" of youth than it is a rejection of conflicting professional views.

If it becomes necessary for the leader to question a concept or a practice, it is important that he first make a positive comment on an element which is acceptable logically before questioning other ideas which appear invalid. By "accentuating the positive" and then examining questionable content, the seminar leader may be able to support an insecure participant who has just begun to communicate in the group, soften an iconoclast, increase the tolerance of a traditionalist—and still focus on the validity of ideas.

The following examples from different seminar groups containing "old guard" participants illustrate successful and unsucessful outcomes:

This seminar group was composed of teachers who taught lower grade classes. Some of them had originally referred the first grade children who were in the play group which was being studied. Three of the teachers had taught for many years and were known to be traditionalists and resistive to innovations in educational philosophy and practice. However, they did attend the seminar voluntarily. At the time this episode took place, the seminar group had met about half a dozen times.

One part of a play group record described how two children were playing a game and how one of them was cheating. The other child objected and spoke aloud to the play group worker, calling her attention to the cheating. The play group worker did not respond.

This incident was picked up by one of the three older teachers. With some surprise she questioned the fact that the worker had not responded. Through further questioning she confirmed that the worker was aware that cheating had actually taken place and that she had chosen not to interfere. The teacher's surprise changed to mild indignation when the seminar leader now explained that it was correct technic for the play group worker to accept such behavior without comment; that the process had to be such in order for the children to perceive the reality of the permissive adult.

It became evident to the leader that this explanation did not sit well with the questioner, nor with several other teachers who probably shared her views. Attempts to elicit other responses to this question from other members of the seminar group did not succeed. The teacher who had stated the original question added that it was altogether "wrong" *in any group practice* to "overlook" cheating. She and two other teachers did not return to subsequent meetings of the seminar.

The seminar leader had erred in technic: he had responded inappropriately to the threat to the moralistic standards of the resistive teachers. This could not be tolerated by them because they were not yet receptive to a process of searching for psychological meanings of behavior.

The initial reply of the leader should have been addressed to the moralistic aspect by *acknowledging* that cheating was "wrong," and that teachers *should* respond to it in class when it was called to their attention. Further, this is how teachers *can* reinforce values and social learnings. Then the leader might have been in a better position to add that the *play group was different* because of the exceptional problems of the children, and that differences in technic would become more meaningful as time passed.

It is conceivable that even given such a response from the seminar leader, these teachers might still have refused to compromise the values they believed to be immutable. However, the leader was doomed to fail in this instance because of his actual response to the content.

In another seminar group which had been meeting for many months, the teachers were trying to fathom the underlying meanings of the behavior of one girl in the play group in particular. It was necessary to obtain information about her current adjustment in the classroom. While some of this information was available, it was felt that her teacher, who was not a participant in the seminar, would be in the best position to describe the child's behavior in detail. This suggestion, voiced by the leader in the seminar, evoked an immediate and negative response from several teachers, who stated emphatically that it would be a "waste of time" to invite the teacher. They felt that she was unsympathetic towards children and that she would not tolerate the concept of the play group itself. (The teacher in question had not originally referred the child in the play group. As a matter of fact, she never referred children for clinical or guidance services.)

The seminar leader blocked further discussion. (It is unwise to permit a group to discuss members of the faculty.) It was suggested that the invitation should be extended; that it could not be assumed that the outcome would necessarily be a negative one. The invitation to the teacher was accepted, which in itself came as a surprise to many in the seminar.

As had been predicted, the older teacher was defensive and suspicious. The seminar leader briefly structured the problem by stating some of the questions which had been raised with respect to the child's behavior in the play group, and she also gave a description of play group practice and its goals. She added that it would help if the teacher described the child's present behavior in class.

Guardedly at first, but then in a direct and dogmatic manner, the teacher proceeded to give a completely negative picture of the child. While no one in the seminar group responded verbally to this, the expressions on some faces conveyed an unmistakable message: "We told you so!" The silence was heavy. The leader stated that some of the teacher's "observations" were particularly significant at the moment since they had to do with the child's stealing, and that this was one problem which the seminar group was particularly concerned with trying to understand. Discussion was pointedly limited to this single aspect of behavior. The continuing inquiry, listened to intently by the now silent visitor, dealt only with possible motivations for the child's stealing, without reference to moral values. This must have been too much for her to bear; she interrupted the discussion peremptorily to ask whether the group thought that it was "right" to steal!

The seminar leader responded quickly, preventing a reply from a young teacher, who seemed all too ready to answer aggressively. She stated that it was certainly not "right" to steal and that this was not being questioned by the seminar group, but that they had to understand the basis for the stealing so that the knowledge could be used in helping the child. The visitor seemed nonplussed. Her aggression was not being reflected; her judgment was not being threatened; the person she most suspected—the seminar leader—had not responded defensively to her implicit challenge; even the seminar group of "youngsters" had not argued with her.

The teachers continued the discussion. They concluded that the items stolen by the child represented symbols of "love." They fortified this analysis by emphasizing the extreme deprivation the girl had suffered from early childhood and the constant rivalry with many siblings for her mother's attention.

The visitor listened attentively and seemed less guarded. She made no further contribution at this meeting. However, she attended the next meeting of the seminar voluntarily.

MANIFESTATIONS OF ANXIETY

Anxiety is another reaction which interferes with a participant's objectivity and sometimes with group harmony. Anxiety may be generated in the seminar when a teacher reacts associatively to the content of discussion in terms of her own child, a relative, or through a deeper transference response from historic, repressed experiences of her own childhood. Regardless of its source, when anxiety is detected in a teacher it is the responsibility of the leader to alleviate it. Since it is not the purpose of the seminar to expose and analyze conflictual material from the lives of the seminar participants, it is necessary for the leader to refocus discussion by diverting it whenever its content induces excessive anxiety.

One group of teachers had been discussing rivalry behavior of children in a play group. The discussion elaborated to include similar patterns of rivalry behavior as they are manifested in classrooms. Parallels were being drawn and the meaning of sibling rivalry in relation to the significant adult —parent, teacher, play group worker—was being stressed in a spirited discussion. One teacher, who had not participated up to this point, looked at the leader with some annoyance and said: "I really do not agree that sibling rivalry has to exist. I cannot recall a time when one of *my* children was ever jealous of the others!" Prior to this teacher's remarks, the leader had supplemented the general discussion with information related to the origins of rivalry and its universality. Several teachers now began to reply, challenging the one who had emotionally denied the existence of rivalry in her own children. The leader interjected, reiterating without emphasis that sibling rivalry between children was manifested to some degree whenever there was more than one child in a family. Intelligent parents, planfully or intuitively, handled it so that its effects were minimized, perhaps even to the extent that it sometimes appeared not to exist. The teacher seemed less anxious and did not pursue the subject. Of interest is the fact that the other teachers tolerated the blocking off of discussion. The group probably sensed that it was in the service of a need, and therefore, in the interest of the group itself.

IMPULSIVE PERSONAL DISCLOSURES

There are instances wherein a teacher can, *without forewarning*, present a serious question about a personal problem. When such a disclosure is made, it usually occurs in a seminar group which has been meeting for some time, and after the participants have become fully relaxed. However, even this is not always predictable. It is wise to operate under the assumption that a personal problem can be "touched off" at any time. In either instance, it is inadvisable to permit discussion of the personal problem of a participant at any level. Tactful measures should be taken to move discussion to other topics. The leader will be in a better position to offer more direct help in individual conference.

One seminar group was discussing dependency needs of a child in the play group. It was the consensus of the teachers that when this child became more secure in the play group, he might begin to show signs of independent behavior in class. The play group worker's technic was under discussion when, without prior warning, one teacher spoke of her concern about her own son. She said that he confined himself to the home, had few friends, and lacked "real masculine interests." The animated discussion was abruptly terminated by this pregnant disclosure, and the group became uneasy. The leader acknowledged that this "probably represented a problem." Then he suggested that they discuss it further at the end of the meeting. It was learned subsequently that the "boy" was a young man of twenty. Several clinical resources were suggested.

In this example, the anxiety of the teacher about her own son was induced by discussion of a parallel problem in a young child in the play group. There are other instances where the association between a teacher's emotionally charged reaction and the ongoing discussion is completely hidden, even to the teacher involved. When this occurs, and the latent factors cannot be deduced by the leader, the wisest course of action is to move discussion into other areas as soon as possible.

This seminar had been meeting for a year. The teachers had been studying a play group of first grade children. During this particular meeting they expressed concern about the responses of one young boy, whose mother had left the city for a prolonged visit to another state without taking him with her. She had made inadequate arrangements for his care during her absence. The implications of this separation were being discussed at length because the child had suffered from various forms of deprivation since his birth. Some of the discussion dealt with the motivation of the mother who had always rejected the boy. It was felt that the play group and his relationship with the worker were very important to him, especially at this time.

One of the participants, a young male teacher who had attended the seminar regularly but who had been a marginal participant, took exception to parts of the discussion. He challenged the opinion of a teacher who had stated that continuing rejection of the child by the mother could lead to trauma which might be hard to undo. The young man continued to speak at length, which for him was unusual. As he spoke, he became increasingly emotional and he began to direct much of his criticisms toward the seminar leader. His hostility was only thinly disguised. He "wondered" whether the play group process helped children ":anyway."

The teachers and the leader were taken aback by his remarks and manner, and for a moment or two nothing was said. The leader then responded to some elements of the teacher's remarks without attempting to defend against the implicit challenge. The rest of the group resumed the discussion, but now in a subdued manner.

Discrete inquiries made later revealed the following: The young man had been married a short time, and both he and his wife were regularly employed. They had one child, eleven months old, who was placed in the care of a neighbor while both parents worked.

It was now obvious that much of this teacher's remarks and emotions were set off by the content of discussion: specifically, the desertion of the boy in the play group by his mother. The teacher's hostility toward the seminar leader was possibly a displacement from his wife, or perhaps a reaction to his own guilt feelings. This could not be a subject for exploration.

RIVALRY BETWEEN SEMINAR MEMBERS

When there is rivalry between teachers in a seminar, it is usually motivated by the need to seek approval or special recognition from the leader. Rivalry can also be manifested towards the leader, but this is much less common. Rivalry usually becomes evidenced intellectually, through difference in opinions, but it also has emotional equivalents. These are reflected in the quality and intensity of speech, through gestures, and other forms of body communication.

It would be unwise for the leader to probe for the unconscious antecedents responsible for rivalry behavior in a seminar group, *particularly* if such behavior is idiosyncratic with one or several participants. Behavior which is characterologically ingrained is not easily modified by exploratory procedures. Probing by the leader runs a risk of discharging emotional responses which could overwhelm the individuals concerned, and even threaten the integrity of the group.

In episodes of rivalry, the leader can avoid disputatious communication by focusing the group's attention on the context of discussion. Discussion can be kept within tolerable limits by confining it to the validity or invalidity of ideas. This may not meet the needs of those participants who are rivalrous, but it prevents persistent contamination of the investigative process. If a seminar group is essentially non-neurotic in composition and is tactfully blocked from dealing with problems which may be threatening to some of its members, it is possible to overcome most obstacles to learning without sacrificing the objectives of the seminar process.

Whenever circumstances permit, it would be better for the seminar group itself to examine and evaluate the content of discussion and to make its own judgments in "contest" situations which result from rivalry between some participants. The leader is thus not placed in a position of having to choose between opposing views. Much of the rivalry that is manifested can be dissipated over a period of time if the leader remains impartial and as the teachers experience other gratifications.

THE OVER-DEPENDENT PARTICIPANT

Occasionally one finds a participant who needs constant reassurance and praise and who seeks such satisfactions through what might be termed "overparticipation." Such behavior is highly individualistic, and it reflects great insecurity in the participant and massive dependence on the authority person (seminar leader). Such a participant may persistently seek approval from the leader *without* appearing to be rivalrous. However, this dependent pattern can activate rivalry in another member of the group who is predisposed to such behavior and who is more aggressive. If a pattern of excessive dependence on the leader does not become oppressive, and if it does not cause intensive resonance in other participants, the group will "mirror" the tolerance of the leader for the needful participant.

One seminar group had to "live" with a teacher who was particularly garrulous but never hostile. Her contributions were relatively unimaginative, or reiterations of what had been already mentioned. The leader's procedure was to tolerate her verbosity but to interject so that she did not consume excessive time. The group displayed no resentment.

READINESS FOR SELF-EVALUATION

As was stated earlier, the seminar is concerned with more than the study of child behavior. No less important are the following aims:

   to enable teachers to recognize themselves as important components of their respective class groups.

to foster awareness that they are significantly involved in the group's interaction.

Such outcomes are attainable if teachers develop a capacity for self-observation and role evaluation. When a seminar reaches this level, the teachers are able to discuss how their own behavior, including their emotional responses, affects children in groups, and how they, in turn, are affected by the group.

Until now, emphasis has been placed on the seminar leader's role in preventing emotional reactions from interfering with orderly processes of reflection, in order to keep tension and frustration from building up in the seminar group while it is gaining experience in objective study. The leader is responsible for blocking the discordant, emotional components of communication until the seminar participants are ready to examine such feelings without over-reacting with embarrassment or guilt. However, if teachers are to comprehend their real significance in psychodynamic interaction in class groups, they must inevitably come to grips with some of their feelings and motivations with respect to children. Therefore, when the leader has determined that a seminar group has *developed a tolerance for such exploration*, the pertinent emotional responses of the teachers are no longer filtered out of the discussion.

The seminar group approaches this phase in its own development* after it has had sufficient opportunity to study a play group—in particular, the technics, behavior *and the emotional reactions of the worker*. As the worker continues to present his reports objectively, without attempting to demonstrate infallibility or to justify his behavior, and also, as he describes some of *his own* affective reactions to children in the play group, the teachers are influenced to act similarly. They become free to express feelings about children and to talk about professional practices.

The mobilizing effect of teacher upon teacher is great, and they become mutually supportive as they develop a tolerance for self-analysis. When they begin to perceive how they contribute to the interaction in classrooms, they realize that in probing for meanings their own behavior becomes no less subject to analysis than that of the children.

Alterations in attitudes take considerable time to evolve, and the seminar leader must always have his finger on the "pulse" of the group to prevent premature intensification of the interaction.

In the following episode which took place in a teacher's seminar, the teachers first explore the meaning of the worker's behavior, and then become able to examine some of their own motivation.

---

* Each group, if it is to be psychodynamic—and this includes the seminar group—must evolve experientially: through establishing its primary code (Slavson), through problem solving, and eventually through reaching its goals.

The play group worker was describing an incident involving an eight year old boy. This child had been guarded in his behavior for a long time, distrustful of the worker and unable to express himself aggressively. Lately he had begun to act more spontaneously. In this incident he asked the worker for a woodwork tool which he then used to dig into the top of the work table. The worker reacted to this first by offering him a piece of wood, but the boy continued to dig at the table. She then suggested that it would be "better" to use the piece of wood. The boy did stop using the tool but soon began to run around the play room with another child, in a chasing game. At one point the worker limited this because it became very activated.

The same boy approached her later with a hand puppet, asking for help in using it. The worker showed him where to put his fingers. Then the record indicated: "I playfully squeezed one of his fingers and smiled at him."

One of the teachers asked why she had squeezed his finger. She looked up from the report and said: "It didn't mean anything. I just squeezed his finger a little." The matter was pursued: "But you did enter it in your report. *I wonder whether you were angry with him because he resisted you?*" This was denied, and the reading of the record continued. Several pages later the record described still another incident involving the same child. Here again a negative response to the child was detectable. The worker put down the report, smiled and said: "You know, I guess I *was* angry with him."

Most of the discussion which took place during the rest of the seminar meeting was concerned with teachers' feelings toward children. The group was relaxed; it did not have the quality of a "confessional" experience for the discharge of guilt. There was frank discussion of how feelings betrayed teachers into errors in management of individual children and a class group.

In another seminar a teacher questioned the leader: "How can you like a child like that? I'd get angry!" The leader asked her why she would get angry and she replied: "Why, even in class some children in particular can make me angry. I sometimes find myself raising my voice—and stop in mid-sentence!" There was general laughter. She continued: "There are some children who are hard to like."

The teachers reacted to this with similar remarks. The leader added: "I guess it wouldn't be natural, or possible, for all of us to like all children equally—or adults too for that matter. But I think you touched upon a problem of particular importance to teachers: the need to recognize feelings in response to children, and further, of evaluating them. For instance, you literally stopped your feeling in mid-sentence." (Laughter)

Laughter reduces tension and makes it easier to talk about matters which produce tension. This was the case in the continuing discussion, in which the teachers spoke of their feelings about children.

It does not follow that all participants in a seminar become equally accessible to exploration of their feelings, or that everyone can necessarily tolerate such examination. Resistiveness to new learnings is sometimes attributable to causes deeper than inertia or habit patterns which are too well entrenched. In some cases a defensive attitude is a form of clinical resistance and is rooted in the unconscious. In such instances it would be altogether unwise for the leader to probe defenses which are necessary for the integrity of the ego. This was the situation in the example which follows:

Teachers from kindergarten, first, and second grade classes were the participants in a seminar group which had been meeting for ten months. The six boys who composed the play group which was the subject of study had been referred from the classes of some of these teachers. The play group had been started at the same time as the seminar,* and there were pronounced changes in the behavior of most of the boys. One of them, Arthur, had been referred originally because he had no friends, almost never spoke aloud in class, and appeared frightened, weak, and helpless.

The teacher who had referred this child was herself a gentle, diffident person. She seldom spoke during seminar meetings; when she did, it was in a subdued manner. However, she was apparently interested because she never failed to attend a meeting of the seminar.

During this meeting she spoke more than ever before. What she had to say concerned Arthur's current behavior. She spoke only of his behavior in her class, without attempting to relate it to developments in the play group. She started by wondering whether consideration should be given to the question of dropping Arthur from the play group because he probably "did not need it any more." This, of course, captured the attention of the other teachers, because, until now, no question of termination had been raised with respect to any child in the play group. When questioned by some of the other teachers as to the reasons for her suggestion, she offered the following additional information:

Arthur had been acting out more in class. He not only spoke out but he was also beginning to tease children. He no longer seemed frightened; as a matter of fact he tried to act "tough," like some of the other boys! She assured the teachers that she was "pleased" with these manifestations of aggressive behavior but she was "worried" lest it become excessive. As she spoke a mild defensiveness became evident in her manner.

The other teachers *did not* react to her information in strong opposition. It was as if they sensed *her* anxiety. The group as a whole was fully aware of the changes in Arthur; they had been evidenced in the play group for at least a month.

It was obvious to the leader that this teacher identified with the child she had referred. Arthur's growing aggressiveness threatened the adequacy of her own defenses against repressed aggression. Intellectualization about the healthful changes in the child—which she could verbalize—was of itself insufficient to dissipate her anxiety, which was being touched off by Arthur's acting out.

The teachers discussed some of the elements of Arthur's problem. The leader then commented to this effect: For some reason Arthur had been afraid to behave like most other boys did when he became angry or frustrated. He had "concealed"such feelings because they frightened him. However, in response to his experiences in the play group, he had become less fearful and was now able to express himself; and he enjoyed doing it. However, there was *no danger* of Arthur's becoming unmanageable, and it *was* appropriate for his teacher to respond to some of his teasing with mild disapproval.

Arthur's teacher seemed relieved by the responses of her fellow teachers and the seminar leader. In their own ways, each had "spoken" in assurance to her ego defenses.

---

* It is important that a seminar group follow the development of a play group from its inception.

The author has used various approaches over a period of many years in attempting to broaden teachers' understanding of child behavior. These methods have ranged from conferences on an individual basis to didactic courses and seminars given as part of in-service training and in the graduate division of a college specializing in teacher training. Of all methods, the continuing seminar, as described in this chapter, has unquestionably been the most efficient learning experience. Its motivational strength lies in the dynamic—often dramatic—evolution of a small play group of emotionally maladjusted young children, and the opportunity to study and analyze the group from its inception to termination.

When a teachers' seminar succeeds in fostering the quality of critical objectivity in the examination of child behavior, it opens new horizons to teachers. This inevitably leads to modifications in teachers' attitudes and methods, with the result that they become more effective in influencing children's learning and development.

Index

GEORGE ALLEN & UNWIN LTD

Head office:
40 Museum Street, London, W.C.1
Telephone: 01-405 8577

Sales, Distribution and Accounts Departments
Park Lane, Hemel Hempstead, Herts.
Telephone: 0442 3244

Athens: 7 Stadiou Street, Athens 125
Barbados: Rockley New Road, St. Lawerence 4
Bombay: 103/5 Fort Street, Bombay 1
Calcutta: 285J Bepin Behari Ganguli Street, Calcutta 12
Dacca: Alico Building, 18 Motijheel, Dacca 2
Hornsby, N.S.W.: Cnr. Bridge Road and Jersey Street, 2077
Ibadan: P.O. Box 62
Johannesburg: P.O. Box 23134, Joubert Park
Karachi: Karachi Chambers, McLeod Road, Karachi 2
Lahore: 22 Falettis' Hotel, Egerton Road
Madras: 2/18 Mount Road, Madras 2
Manila: P.O. Box 157, Quezon City, D-502
Mexico: Serapio Rendon 125, Mexico 4, D.F.
Nairobi: P.O. Box 30583
New Delhi: 4/21-22B Asaf Ali Road, New Delhi 1
Ontario, 2330 Midland Avenue, Agincourt
Singapore: 248C-6 Orchard Road, Singapore 9
Tokyo: C.P.O. Box 1728, Tokyo 100-91
Wellington: P.O. Box 1467, Wellington